Honourable Society of Cymmrodorion

The Transactions of the Honourable Society of Cymmrodorion

Honourable Society of Cymmrodorion

The Transactions of the Honourable Society of Cymmrodorion

ISBN/EAN: 9783337194345

Printed in Europe, USA, Canada, Australia, Japan

Cover: Foto ©Suzi / pixelio.de

More available books at **www.hansebooks.com**

THE

TRANSACTIONS

OF

THE HONOURABLE

SOCIETY OF CYMMRODORION.

SESSION 1899–1900.

LONDON:

ISSUED BY THE SOCIETY,

NEW STONE BUILDINGS, 64, CHANCERY LANE.

1901.

Devizes :

Printed by George Simpson.

CONTENTS.

REPORT

OF

THE COUNCIL OF THE

Honourable Society of Cymmrodorion,

For the Year ending November 9th, 1900.

PRESENTED TO THE ANNUAL MEETING HELD AT THE SOCIETY'S
ROOMS, ON THURSDAY, THE 22ND OF NOVEMBER, 1900.

THE Council, in presenting their Annual Report to the
members of the Society, desire, at the outset, to express
their deep sorrow at the heavy loss recently sustained by
them through the death of their President, the Most Hon.
the Marquess of Bute. During the ten years of his Presidency, Lord Bute took a keen personal interest in the
aims and work of the Cymmrodorion. Himself an accomplished and a devoted student of Celtic Literature, he was
ever in close touch with the objects of this Society for the
furtherance of the study of the antiquities, the history,
and the language of Wales. His constant support of
every movement for the intellectual advancement of the
Principality ; his munificent contributions in aid of literary
and historical research ; above all, his active personal work
in this behalf, have won for him the admiration, the
respect, and the affection of all Cymmrodorion. With
the *Transactions*, which will shortly be issued, the Council

b

are happy to be in a position to include an excellent portrait of the late President.

Earlier in the year the Society had to mourn the loss of one of its earliest members, Principal Edwards, of the Theological College, Bala, one who, as a great preacher and a learned divine, as well as an ardent educationalist, has left his mark deep on the life of the Principality.

Again only last month the Society lost a young and distinguished member, who may be said literally to have laid down his life on the altar of patriotic duty. Professor Alfred Hughes, the administrator of the Welsh Hospital in South Africa, deserves well of his country and of this Society, if it were only for the example he gave of a strong and unbending devotion to duty. In other fields he had many claims to recognition on which it is not now necessary to dwell.

South Africa is responsible for another loss, that of one of our Vice-Presidents, the late Lord Kensington, who fell in the war. Our Obituary List further includes the names of Mr. Stephen Williams, Fellow of the Society of Antiquaries, to whom this Society was indebted for interesting papers on the Monasteries of Strata Florida and Cwm-Hir; Mr. Bernard Quaritch, the well-known bibliophile; the Rev. T. Lloyd Phillips, of Beckenham; Mr. Charles Evans Vaughan, the architect of several of our London public buildings; Principal Williams, of the New Veterinary College, Edinburgh; and of Miss Beata Lloyd Francis, a Welsh vocalist of considerable distinction.

The Council are pleased to report an accession of 41 new members to the Society during the past year, but having regard to the losses already referred to, they would impress upon the Society's friends the need for constant efforts to replenish its numbers and to increase its influence.

During the year the following meetings were held in London :—

1899.

November 30.—ANNUAL MEETING OF THE MEMBERS.

ANNUAL DINNER postponed, owing to the War in South Africa.

1900.

February 7.—Paper on " Welsh Cave Legends," by Professor Rhys, LL.D.

March 21.—Paper on " Owen Lawgoch," by Mr. Edward Owen, of Gray's Inn.

April 11.—Paper on " Pennillion & Penillion Singing," by Rev. W. H. Williams (*Watcyn Wyn*), with Musical Illustrations by *Eos Dâr*.

May 9.—Paper on " Wales and the Norman Conquest," by Professor J. E. Lloyd, M.A., University College, Bangor.

July 4.—ANNUAL CONVERSAZIONE, at the Grafton Galleries.

In Liverpool, in connection with the National Eisteddfod of Wales :—

September 17th and 19th, under the presidency of the Right Hon. the Lord Mayor of Liverpool and the Hon. Geo. T. Kenyon, Deputy Chancellor of the University of Wales.—Papers on " The Defects of Technical Education in Wales," by Principal Reichel, University College of North Wales ; Mr. Owen Owen, M.A., Chief Inspector, Central Welsh Board ; and Mr. Lewis J. Roberts, M.A., H. M. Inspector of Schools ; followed by a Discussion, to which Mr. Humphreys Owen, M.P., President of the Welsh Central Board ; Mr. J. Herbert Roberts, M.P. ; Professor J. E. Lloyd, M.A. ; the Rev. John Williams ; Mr. Thomas Williams, J.P. ; the Rev. Griffith Ellis, M.A., and others, contributed.

It may be mentioned in connection with these meetings that the discussion of the needs of Technical Education, and the want of funds, led directly to the munificent offer of £50,000 (subject to certain conditions) which was made known at the Liverpool Eisteddfod by Mr. Alfred L. Jones. The hope is entertained that some means may be found either to meet or to modify the conditions mentioned, so as to make Mr. Jones' offer available for the object in view.

The arrangements for the coming Session include Papers by Mr. W. Goscombe John, A.R.A., on "Art and Handicraft in Wales"; Mr. Thomas Darlington, H. M. Inspector of Schools, on a subject connected with the teaching of the Welsh Language; Professor J. Morris Jones, on "The Art of Welsh Poetry" (Celfyddyd Barddoniaeth Gymreig); Mr. J. W. Willis-Bund, F.S.A., on "Archbishop Peckham and the Conquest of Wales"; and by Mr. Hubert Hall, Director of the Royal Historical Society, on "The Diplomatics of Welsh Records".

The Council have pleasure in announcing that the members of the Society will dine together on the 10th of December, 1900, at the Whitehall Rooms, Hôtel Mètropole, under the Presidency of Dr. Isambard Owen, M.A., Senior Deputy Chancellor of the University of Wales.

During the year the following Publications have been issued to members, viz.:—

1. *The Transactions* for the Session 1898-99, containing the following Papers, in addition to the Report of the Council and the Statement of Receipts and Payments, viz.:—"Early Fortifications in Wales," by the Rev. S. Baring-Gould, M.A.; "Early Social Life in Wales," by Mr. D. Brynmor-Jones, Q.C., M.P.; a preliminary Paper on "Geoffrey of Monmouth," by Professor W. Lewis Jones, M.A.; and "Argraphwyr, Cylioeddwyr, a Llyfrwerthwyr Cymru," by Mr. Isaac Foulkes.

2. *Y Cymmrodor*, Vol. XIII, containing "Vicar Prichard: a Study in Welsh Bibliography," by Mr. John Ballinger; a "Collation of Rees' *Lives of the Cambro-British Saints*, by Professor Kuno Meyer, Ph.D.; "Further Notes on the Court of the Marches," by Mr. D. Lleufer Thomas, with Original Documents; and a "Note on the Jesus College Peithynen", by Professor Rhys.

3. Part i of *A Catalogue of the Manuscripts relating to Wales in the British Museum* (being No. 4 of the Cymmrodorion Record Series), edited by Mr. Edward Owen, of Gray's Inn.

In addition, there are nearly ready for issue :—

The Transactions for the Session 1899-1900, containing Papers by Principal Rhys, LL.D., Mr. Edward Owen, the Rev. W. H. Williams *(Watcyn Wyn)*, and Professor J. E. Lloyd, M.A.

Y Cymmrodor, Vol. XIV, containing an Essay on the Administration of English Law in Wales and the Marches, by Dr. Henry Owen ; a Paper on The Broughtons of Marchwiel, by Mr. Alfred Neobard Palmer ; a Life of St. Cybi, by the Rev. S. Baring-Gould, M.A. ; a Note on Salesbury's Dictionary and the King's License, and a Welsh Love Song of the 16th Century, supplied by Mr. J. H. Davies, M.A. ; the text and translation of an Irish MS. on The Expulsion of the Dessi, with Introductory Notes, by Professor Kuno Meyer ; and "Side Lights on Welsh Jacobitism," by Mr. J. Arthur Price, B.A.

The following are in the Press :—

Part ii of *The Writings of Gildas*, edited by the Rev. Professor Hugh Williams ; and

Part ii of *The Catalogue of MSS. relating to Wales in the British Museum*, compiled by Mr. Edward Owen,

both of which may be expected early in the ensuing year, and the following are in a forward state of preparation :—

The Black Book of St. David's, edited by Mr. J. W. Willis-Bund, F.S.A., and a new edition of

Geoffrey of Monmouth, based on the Bern text, edited by Professor W. Lewis Jones, M.A.

With reference to the last mentioned publications, the Council beg to remind the members that they are issued at the cost of the Cymmrodorion Record Series Fund. Donations to this fund are invited. The Trustees are Sir John Williams, Bart., Sir W. Thomas Lewis, Bart., and Dr. Henry Owen, and particulars can be obtained from the Secretary to the Society.

The following presents received for the Library were duly acknowledged :—

Byegones, presented by Messrs. Woodall, Minshall, & Co.

The Calendar of the University College of North Wales, presented by the Registrar.

A Set of the Nos. of the Magazine entitled *Wales*, presented by Dr. Henry Owen.

Magic Divination and Demonology, by Professor T. Witton Davies, Ph.D. ; and

Ysgrythyrau yr Hen Destament, by the same, presented by the Author.

Under the Society's Rules the term of office of the following Officers expires :—

> THE PRESIDENT,
> > (now vacant through the death of Lord Bute)
> THE VICE-PRESIDENTS,
> THE AUDITORS,

and 10 members retire in accordance with Rule 4, viz. :—

> MR. R. HENRY JENKINS.
> REV. G. HARTWELL JONES.
> REV. H. ELVET LEWIS.
> MR. T. E. MORRIS.
> MR. ALFRED NUTT.
> MR. EDWARD OWEN.
> DR. HENRY OWEN.
> DR. ISAMBARD OWEN.
> PRINCIPAL RHYS.
> DR. FREDERICK T. ROBERTS.

The Statement of Receipts and Payments for the year is appended to this Report.

THE HONOURABLE SOCIETY OF CYMMRODORION.

Statement of Receipts and Payments.

FROM 9TH NOVEMBER, 1899, TO 9TH NOVEMBER, 1900.

Cr.

	£	s.	d.
To Balance in hand, November 9th, 1899	117	14	7
„ Subscriptions received	418	16	10
„ Sale of Publications, &c.	6	14	7
	£543	**6**	**0**

Dr.

	£	s.	d.
By Rent of Offices, Fire, and Lighting	72	7	0
„ Publications : Cost of Printing and Distributing, Viz. :—*Transactions*, 1898-99	46	18	0
Cymmrodor, Vol. XIII.	71	10	5
„ Editorial Expenses	12	10	0
„ General Printing	24	8	9
„ Eisteddfod Section : Expenses	7	10	0
„ Lectures, Meetings, and Conversazione	58	15	0
„ Library Expenses, Books, &c.	1	15	6
„ Stationery, Postage, and General Expenses	37	17	5
„ Secretary's Remuneration	50	0	0
„ Commission on Publications Sold and Subscriptions collected (1899)	14	10	2
Balance in hand	145	3	9
	£543	**6**	**0**

Examined and found correct,

JOHN BURRELL, } *Joint*
ELLIS W. DAVIES, } *Hon. Auditors.*

H. LLOYD ROBERTS, *Treasurer.*
E. VINCENT EVANS, *Secretary.*

THE MOST HON. THE MARQUESS OF BUTE, K.T.

(Born Sept. 12, 1847; died Oct. 9, 1900.)

President of the Hon. Society of Cymmrodorion, 1891–1900.

Photo. Reproduced from "The Sphere." Photograph by Messrs. Russell and Son.

TRANSACTIONS

OF THE

𝕳onouraßle Society of Cymmrodorion.

SESSION 1899-1900.

PROFESSOR RHYS, LL.D., ON WELSH CAVE LEGENDS AND THE STORY OF OWEN LAWGOCH.

AT the meeting of the Honourable Society of Cymmrodorion, held on Wednesday, February 7th, 1900,[1] Professor
Rhys read extracts from his forthcoming book on *Celtic
Folklore*, especially a chapter entitled "Welsh Cave
Legends", in which he called attention to a certain Owen
Lawgoch or "Owen of the Red Hand", who, with his
men, is represented sleeping in a cave in South Wales
until the bell of destiny rings to wake him to sally forth
to conquer. Then Professor Rhys proceeded to mention
certain so-called prophecies about Owen, and he included
in his remarks concerning him the following passages :—

"But who was Owen Lawgoch, if there ever was such a
man ? Such a man there was undoubtedly, for we read in
one of the documents printed in the miscellaneous volume
commonly known as the *Record of Carnarvon*, that at a

[1] Held at 20, Hanover Square. Chairman, Mr. G. Laurence
Gomme, F.S.A.

B

court held at Conway in the forty-fourth year of Edward III, a certain Gruffyd Says was adjudged to forfeit all the lands which he held in Anglesey to the Prince of Wales, who was at that time no other than Edward the Black Prince, for the reason that the said Gruffyd had been an adherent of Owen—*adherens fuisset Owino Lawegogh (or Lawgogh) inimico et proditori predicti domini Principis et de consilio predicti Owyni ad mouendam guerram in Wallia contra predictum dominum Principem.*[1] How long previously it had been attempted to begin a war on behalf of this Owen Lawgoch one cannot say, but it so happens that at this time there was a captain called Yeuwains, Yewains or Yvain de Galles—"Owen of Wales", fighting on the French side against the English in Edward's continental wars. Froissart in his *Chronicles* has a great deal to say of him, for he distinguished himself greatly on various critical occasions. From the historian's narrative one finds that Owen had escaped when a boy to the court of Philip VI of France, who received him with great favour, and had him educated with his own nephews. Froissart's account of him is, that the King of England, Edward III, had slain his father and given his lordship and principality to his own son the Prince of Wales ; and Froissart gives Owen's father's name twice as *Aymon*, which should mean *Edmond*, unless the name intended may have been rather *Einion*. However that may have been, Owen was engaged in the battle of Poictiers in 1356, and when peace was made he went to serve in Lombardy ; but when war between England and France broke out again, he returned to France. He sometimes fought on sea and sometimes on land, but he was always entrusted by the French king, who was now Charles V, with im-

---

[1] *Record of Carnarvon*, p. 133, to which attention was called in the *Report of the Welsh Land Commission*, p. 648.

portant commands. Thus, in 1372, he was placed at the head of a flotilla with 3,000 men, and ordered to operate against the English : he made a descent on the Isle of Guernsey, and while there besieging the castle of Cornet he was charged by the King of France to sail to Spain to invite the King of Castille to send his fleet again to help in the attack on La Rochelle. Whilst staying at Santander the Earl of Pembroke was brought thither, having been taken prisoner in the course of the destruction of the English fleet before La Rochelle. Owen, on seeing the Earl of Pembroke, asks him with bitterness if he is come there to do him homage for his land, of which he had taken possession in Wales. He threatens to avenge himself on him as soon as he can ; and also on the Earl of Hereford and Edward Spencer, for it was by the fathers of those three men, he said, his own father had been betrayed to death. Edward III died in 1377, and the Black Prince had died shortly before. Owen survived them both, and was actively engaged in the siege of Mortagne sur Mer in Poitou, when he was assassinated by one Lamb, who had insinuated himself into his service and confidence, partly by pretending to bring him news about his native land, and telling him that all Wales was longing to have him back to be the lord and master of his country—*et lui fist acroire que toute li terre de Gales le desiroient mout à ravoir à seigneur.* So Owen fell in the year 1378, and was buried at the church of Saint-Léger, while Lamb returned to the English to receive his reward.[1] When

---

[1] In Lord Berners' translation of Froissart's *Chronicles* (London, 1812) Owen is mostly called *Yuan* or *Evan* of Wales, as if anybody could even glance at the romances without finding that Owen ab Urien, for instance, became in French *Ywains* (or *Ivains*) *le fils Urien,* in the nominative, and *Ywain* or *Ivain* in régime. Thomas Johnes, of Hafod, whose translation was published in 1803-6, betrays the same ignorance ; but he had the excuse of being himself a Welshman.

this happened Owen's namesake, Owen Glyndwr, was
nearly thirty years of age. The latter was eventually to
assert with varying fortune on many fields of battle in this
country the claims of the elder Owen ; and the elder Owen,
by virtue of his memory in France, would seem to have
rendered it easy for the younger Owen to enter on friendly
relations with the French court of his day.

"Now as to Yvain de Galles, the Rev. Thomas Price
(*Carnhuanawc*), in his *Hanes Cymru* (*History of Wales*),
p. 737, devotes a couple of pages to Froissart's account
of him, and he points out that Angharad Llwyd in her
Hanes Tylwyth Gwydir (*History of the Gwydir Family*),
had shown him to have been Owen ab Thomas ab Rhodri
ab Gruffyd, a brother of Llewelyn, the last native prince
of Wales. The names, among other things, form a difficulty. Why did Froissart call his father Aymon ? It is
clear that a more searching study of Welsh pedigrees and
other documents, including those at the Record Office, has
to be made before Owen can be satisfactorily placed in
point of succession. For that he was in the right line to
succeed the native princes of Wales is suggested both by
the eagerness with which all Wales was represented as
looking to his return to be the lord of the country, and by
the opening words of Froissart in describing what he had
been robbed of by Edward III, as being both lordship and
principality,—*la Signourie et princeté*. Be that as it may,
there is, it seems to me, little doubt that Yvain de Galles was
no other than the Owen Lawgoch, whose adherent Gruffyd
Says was deprived of his land and property in the latter
part of Edward's reign. In the next place there is hardly
room for doubt, that the Owen Lawgoch here referred to
was the same man whom the *baledwyr*, in their jumble of
prophecies, intended to be Henry the Ninth, that is to say

the Welsh successor to the last Tudor King, Henry VIII, and that he was at the same time the hero of the cave legends of divers parts of the Principality, especially South Wales as already indicated."

OWAIN LAWGOCH—YEUAIN DE GALLES:

SOME FACTS AND SUGGESTIONS.[1]

BY

EDWARD OWEN.

In the lecture upon " Welsh Cave Legends," an extract from which immediately precedes the present contribution, Principal Rhys related several interesting folk stories which are concerned with a personage called Owen or Owain Lawgoch ; and, the connexion between romance and reality then forming part of the learned Principal's theme, he followed the stories with the question : " Who was Owen Lawgoch, if there ever was such a man ?" Dr. Rhys, indeed, proceeded to reply to his own query just so far as was necessary for his immediate purpose. He gave an extract from the *Record of Caernarvon*, which names a certain Owain Lawgoch as having proved a traitor to King Edward

[1] Read before the Honourable Society of Cymmrodorion at 20, Hanover Square, on Wednesday, the 21st of March, 1900 ; Chairman, Principal Rhys, LL.D.

The paper printed above, though following generally the lecture given before the Society, differs considerably from it. It may be well to explain that a correspondence having ensued between Principal Rhys and the author upon the former's references to Owain Lawgoch and Yeuain de Galles in his lecture to the Hon. Society of Cymmrodorion on the 7th February previously, the present writer was reluctantly prevailed upon to follow Principal Rhys's paper, which had dealt with Owain as a hero of folklore, with a paper which should deal with him as a strictly historical personage. The evidence then available for that purpose being limited almost entirely, for Owain, to the entry in the record best known under its printed title of the *Record of Caernarvon* (Record Commissioners, 1838), and, for

the Third; he next quoted the French chronicler Froissart's account of the doings of a knight in the French service, named Yeuain de Galles; he further referred to the identification of Owen Lawgoch with Yeuain de Galles by Miss Angharad Llwyd, in her edition of Sir John Wynne's *History of the Gwydir Family* (1827); and he finally concluded that "there is little doubt that Yvain de Galles was no other than Owen Lawgoch."

Much of the reasoning upon which that conclusion was founded was admittedly conjectural. The conclusion seemed to be the true one, but the facts upon which it was based were too few, and their connexion too slender, to afford perfect satisfaction to the historian. It is our business to clear up some, if not all, of the doubts that existed.

The exact position of research upon the subject has been indicated, and almost exhausted, in the penultimate

Yeuain, to the chronicles of Froissart, it followed that little more could be done in the short period between the dates of the two lectures than to draw together those scattered notices, and to endeavour to connect them by means of a few entries in the calendars of the public records. Indeed, the sadly incomplete paper presented to the Society upon the 21st March can hardly be described as "read", since a good deal of it existed only in the form of rough notes. But it was manifest that the subject contained great possibilities, for there was here a great Welshman whose name and career were almost unknown to his countrymen. Researches have, therefore, been made amongst the public records and other manuscript depositories, with results which have been embodied in the paper printed above. The success would probably have been greater had the writer been able, as he had intended to do before the paper went to print, to visit the record depositories of Paris. But it is hoped that, while Owain must ever continue an attractive figure in Welsh romance, sufficient has been done to restore him to the more solid sphere of the historian.

I have to thank my friend Mr. J. H. Davies, for kindly assistance, consisting as much of fresh material towards the history of Owain as of criticism, constructive as well as destructive, all of which I have been glad to receive, and have endeavoured to profit by.

paragraph; and what may be termed its bibliography is
not extensive. Miss Angharad Llwyd's note is repeated
in Mr. Askew Roberts's edition of the *History of the
Gwydir Family*, together with a supplementary note of the
late Mr. W. W. E. Wynne, of Peniarth, which will be
alluded to later. The story of Yeuain de Galles told
by Froissart is summarised in Price's *Hanes Cymru*, and
later compilations of Welsh history. A few facts respecting Yeuain appeared in a couple of early numbers of the
Archæologia Cambrensis, and one or two stray notes upon
him have been printed in *Bye-gones*. But in no instance
has the identification of Owain Lawgoch with Yeuain
de Galles been carried further than the point at which
it was left by Miss Angharad Llwyd,[1] and not a single
historical student has made a serious effort to throw
light upon one of the most interesting characters in
Welsh history.

The problem before us is two-fold—

    (*a*) Is the Owain Lawgoch of Wales the same
        personage as the Yeuain de Galles of Froissart?

    (*b*) Who was Yeuain de Galles?

It will be convenient to commence our enquiry by
taking the first historic notice of Owain, and to follow it
by Froissart's account of the career and death of Yeuain.
This method will serve not only to mark the alpha and
omega of Owain's recorded career (assuming, for a
moment, his identity with Yeuain), but will also place before

---

[1] All the facts above mentioned are brought together in an interesting manner in a work entitled *Cantref Meirionydd* (Dolgellau, 1890),
written by Mr. Robert Prys Morris, and published after his death.
Mr. Morris makes one step in advance of Miss Angharad Llwyd, inas-
much as he quotes the entry relating to Owain in the *Record of Caernarvon*. That volume was published in 1838, eleven years after the
appearance of Miss Llwyd's edition of the *History of the Gwydir
Family*.

the reader all that has hitherto been known of him in his dual character.

The Record of Caernarvon, at p. 133, has the following :—

"Inter placita corono coram Ricardo do Stafford et sociis suis justiciariis domini et ultimi principis Wallie in North Wallia apud Conewey, anno regni regis Edwardi tercii xliiij. Gruff Says liber-tenens prædicti principis de comitatu Angles' convictus fuit coram præfato justiciario apud Conewey de sedicione super appello de eo quod adherens fuisset Owino Lawegogh [*an alternative MS.* Lawgogh] inimico et proditori prædicti domini principis et de consilio prædicti Owyni ad mouendam guerram in Wallia contra prædictum dominum principem," &c.

This brief official entry informs us that in or about the 44th year of Edward the Third (25th Jan. 1370—24th Jan. 1371) a person called Owain Lawgogh was a traitor and enemy to the king; but who Owain was, in what consisted his treachery, or at what period it was consummated, is not stated. We know that his follower, Gruffydd Sais, was a free tribesman whose hereditary lands lay in the island of Anglesey.

Turning now to Yeuain de Galles. Though, as we shall see later, Froissart is by no means the only French chronicler who refers to Yeuain, he is our principal source of information respecting him.[1] The passages

---

[1] Froissart was born in 1337 and died in 1410, so that he was strictly contemporary with the circumstances of Yeuain's career which he records. He spent several years in England, and was well acquainted with English political life. His *Chronicles* have been edited by Baron Kervyn de Lettenhove (Brussells, 1870, &c., 25 vols.)—a splendid edition, and by M. Siméon Luce (Paris, 1869, &c., in course of publication)—an equally fine edition, with admirable notes. There have been English translations by Lord Berners (*b. circa* 1469, *d.* 1532), first edition in 1523-5, a second in 1812, a third is announced for issue in January 1901 in Nutt's *Tudor Translations*, and by Johnes of Havod in 1803-10 (reprinted in 1891).

The chronicler's spelling of Yeuain's name, as given in the edition of M. Luce is, as a rule, Yewains, but he varies this form with Yevain, Yeuwain, Yeuwains and, at least once, Iewain.

are as follows from the classic translation of Lord Berners.
Having terminated his account of the defeat of the
English fleet before Rochelle in A.D. 1372 with these
words, "Nowe lette us leave a lytell whyle to speke of
them, and lette us speke of Sir Yuan of Wales, howe he
dyde the same season," Froissart continues, in a fresh
chapter (i, 444, edition 1812) :

"This Yuan of Wales was son to a prince of Wales, whom kynge
Edwarde had put to dethe, I ca'nat say for what cause, and so gave
the principalyte to his sone, and made hym prince of Wales ; so this
Yuan came into Fraunce, and complayned to kyng Charles of Fraunce,
of the injuryes that the kynge of Englande had done to hym, as in
slayeng of his father, and takyng away of his herytage ; so the frenche
kyng retayned him, and advaunced him greatly, and made him
governour of certayn men of warr.   And so the same somer the
kyng delyvered him four thousande fightyng men, and sent him to
the see, and toke shippyng at Harflewe, and so sayled forthe
towarde Englande, and so came to the yle of Gernsay, agaynst
Norma'dy, wherof Aymon Rosse, a squyer of honour with the kyng
of Englande, was capitayne; and whan he knewe yᵗ the frenchmen
were aryved in the yle, and yuan of Wales with them, he was
nothynge content, and so made his somons through the yle, the which
is nat great in quantyte : and so he assembled, what of his owne and
of them of the yle, to the nombre of viii hundred, and so came to a
certayne place, and ther fought with ye sayd yuan, where there was
a sore batayle, and endured a long space ; howebeit, finally the
englysshmen were disconfyted and slayne in the same place, mo
than four hu'dred ; and so this Aymon fled away, or els he had ben
deed or taken : so he saved himselfe with moche payne, and entred
into a lytell castell, a two leages thens, called Cornette, the whiche
the same Aymon had well fortifyed before.   Than after this dis-
confytur, the sayd yuan drewe togyder his men, and hadde knowledge
howe that Aymon was entred into the castell of Cornette ; than he
drewe thyder and layd siege therto, and made dyvers assautes, but
the castell was strong, and well purveyed with good artyllary, so that
it was nat easy to be wonne.   Duryng this siege before Cornette, the
adventur fell on the see of the takyng of the erle of Penbroke and
Sir Guyssharde Dangle, and their company, before Rochell (as ye
have herde before), of the whiche tidynges, whan the frenche kyng
herde therof he was right joyouse, and entended therby the rather
to pursue the warre in Poictou : for than he thought that yf the

englysshmen began ones a lytell to declyne, that lightly the cyties
and townes wolde gyve up, and rendre the selfe to him: than the
french kynge determyned that into Poyctou, Xaynton, and Rochel-
loyse, he wolde sende for that season, his constable thyder with
certayne men of armes, and to make hote warr in those countrees,
bothe by lande and by see, sayenge, that the englysshmen ther as
than had no capitayne nor chefe ruler. Than the frenche kynge sent
his letters to the sayd yuan, who lay at sege before the castell of
Cornet, in the yle of Gernsay; of the whiche siege the kyng was well
enformed, and howe the castell by lykelyhod was inpreignable,
therfor the kyng commau'ded hym after the sight of his letters, to
departe and broke up his siege, and to entre into a shyppe, the whiche
the kyng sent hym for the same purpose, and so to sayle into Spayne
to kyng Henry, to gette of hym barkes and galeys, and his admyrall
and men of warre, to come and to lay siege by the see to the towne
of Rochell. Whan the sayd yuan sawe the kynges message and
commau'dement, he obeyed therto, and so brake up the siege, and gave
leave to his company to departe, and delyvered them shyppes to
bring the' to Harflewe, and himselfe entred into a great shyppe and
toke his course towarde Spayne. Thus befell of the siege before
Cornette, in the yle of Gernsay."

"Cap. ccci. *Howe the kyng of Englande was sore displeased of the
takyng of therle of Penbroke:*

"The kyng of England was sore displeased wha' he herde how the
army that he had sent into Poictou was overthrowen by the
spanyerdes on the see, and so wer all suche as loved hym; howbeit
they coude nat ame'de it for that tyme: tha' the sages of the realme
thought surely that the countre of Poictou and of Xaynton, was
likely to be lost, by reason of the sayd myssehappe; and this they
shewed to the kyng and to the duke of Lancastre. So they were
long in counsayle on the mater, and so determyned, as than, that the
erle of Salysbury, with a fyve hundred men of armes shulde go
thyder. But whatsoever cou'sayle or advyse was taken, ther was
nothyng done; for there came other busynesses in hande out of
Bretayne, that letted that journey, wherof the kyng repented him
after, whan he coude nat remedy it. So it was, that the spanyerdes
who had taken the erle of Penbroke [at Rochelle] (as ye have herd
before) they taryed a certayne space on the see, bycause the wynde
was contrary to the'; howbeit, at last they arryved at the porte
saynt Andrewe in Galyce [Gallicia], and so entred into the towne
about noone, and so brought all their prisoners into the Castell, all
bounde in cheanes of yron, acordying to their custome, for other
courtesy they can nat shewe: they are like unto the almaynes.

"The same day yuan of Wales was arryved with his shyppe in the same porte, and so toke lande, and entred into the same house, wher as Domferant of Pyon and Cabosse of Wakadent had brought the erle of Penbroke and his knightes. And so it was shewed yuan, as he was in his chambre, howe the englysshemen were in the same house as prisoners: and this yuan had great desyre to se them, to knowe what they were; and so he went forthe into the hall, and as he went thyder he encountred with the erle of Penbroke, whome he knewe ryght well, yet he had nat often sene him before: tha' he sayd to him, as in reproch, a erle of Pe'broke, are ye come into this countre to do homage to me for suche landes as ye holde in the principalyte of Wales, wherof I am rightfull heyre, the whiche your kynge hath taken fro me by evyl counsayle and advyse. The erle of Penbroke was abasshed, whan he sawe that he was a prisoner, and in a strange lande, and knowyng nat the man that so spake to hym in his language; and so answered shortely, and sayd, What are you that gyve me this langage? I am, quoth he, yuan, sonne to prince Aymon of Wales, whome your kyng of Englande put to dethe wrong-fully, and hath disheryted me: but whan I may, by the helpe of my right dere lorde, the frenche kyng, I shall shape therfore a remedy: and I wyll ye knowe, that if I may fynde you in any place convenyent, that I may fyght with you, I shall do it, and shewe you the right y[t] ye have done to me, and also to the erle of Herforde, and to Edward Spe'ser; for by your fathers, with other counsaylours, my lorde, my father was betrayed, wherof I ought to be displeased, and to amende it whan I maye. Than stepte forthe a knight of the erles, called sir Thomas of saint Aulbyn, and made hast to speke, and sayd, yuan, if ye wyll say and maynteyne that there is any falseheed, or hath ben, in my lorde, or that he oweth or shulde owe any homage to you, or any of his an'cetries, cast downe your gage in that quarell, and ye shall fynde him that shall take it up. Than yuan answered and sayd, ye are a prisoner; I can have none honour to apele you, for ye have nat the rule of yourselfe, for ye are under the rule of them that have taken you, but whan ye be quyte, than I shall speke with you more of the mater, for it shall nat rest thus; and so with tho wordes, certayne knightes of Spaygne came bytwene them, and so departed them asondre. And so w[t]in a while after the sayd iiii spainysshe capite's ledde forthe their prisoners toward the cytie of Burges in Spayn, to yelde them to kyng Henry, who, as than, was there abyding. And whan king Henry knewe of their comyng, and that they aproched nere to the cytie, he sent his eldest sonne, called Johan, who was called, as than, the chylde of Castell, with great nombre of knightes and squyers, to mete with these englysshmen, to do theym honoure; for the king knewe right well what aparteyned to noblenesse : and wha' they were come to him he dyde them moche honour bothe with wordes and dedes. And than anone after, the kyng sent them into dyvers partes of his realme to be kept."

Froissart's story of how Yeuain was directed to lay siege to Mortagne sur Gironde, and of his melancholy end there, is given in the following words :

"And as ye have herde here before yuan of Wales lay at siege before Mortayne in Poitou, [*recte*, Saintogne] in four bastydes of the which towne the lorde of Lestrade was capitayne. The fyrst bastyde where as parte of the siege lay, as at the syde of a rock, before the castell of Geron [Garonne] one the see, the whiche bastyde yuan hym-selfe kept ; the seconde was bytwene the water and the castell, lowe before a posterne, so that none coude entre nor issue therat ; the third bastyde was on the other syde of the castell ; the fourth was in the church of saynt Legar, halfe a leage fro ye castell : by these four bastydes they within Mortayne were sore constrayned, bycause of the lenght of the siege, for it endured a yere and a halfe, so that they within had nothyng to lyve by, nor showe on their fete, nor confort nor socoure apered none to them fro any parte : wherfore they were sore abasshed. This siege thus enduryng before Mortayne, there issued out of the realme of Englande, and out of the marches of Wales, a squier, a Walshman, called James Laube [John Lambe, ed. Johnes], he was but a small ge'tylman, and that well shewed after, for a very ge'tylman wyll never set his mynde on so evyll an entent : some sayde, or he departed out of Englande, he was charged and enfourmed by some knyghtes of Englande, to do the treason that he dyde, for this yuan of Wales was gretly behated in Englande, and in Gascon, bycause of the captall of Beufz [Buch], whome he toke and helped therto before Soubyse, in Poictou ; for after he was taken, the frenchmen wolde nat delyver hym agayne by no meanes, nother for raunsome nor for exchaunge : yet the erle of saynt Poule was offered for him, and golde and sylver, but it wolde nat be taken ; and whan he sawe that, for pure melancholy he dyed in ye temple at Parys, wherof all his frendes had great displeasure. This walsshe squier, James Laube, the same season arryved in Bretayne, and dyd so moche, that he came into Poictou, and ever as he went he named hymselfe to be servaunt to yuan of Wales, for he spake good frenche ; sayeng, howe he was come out of Wales to speke with yuan ; and so he was anone beleved, and was conveyd by them of the countre, to Mortaygne, where the siege was ; than he wente wisely to yuan, and shewed hym in his owne langage how he was co'e out of his countre to se hym, and to do hym servyce : yuan, who thought none yll, lightly beleved him, and gave hym moche thankes for his comynge, and sayd, howe he wolde right gladlye have his servyce ; and than he deman'ded of him tidynges of the countrey of Wales ; and he shewed him trewe tidynges, and untrewe, for he made him beleve howe all the countre of Wales wolde gladlye have hym to be their lorde. These wordes brought this James greatly in love with yuan, for every man naturally desyreth to go into their owne cou'tres, and to here therof, so yt yuan made him his chamberlayne: and this James every day more and more aquaynted him so with this yuan of Wales, that he had nat so moche trust in no man, as he had in him. So moch this yuan loved this James Laube, that it was his distructyon, and the more pytie, for he was a good and valyant man of armes, and was somtyme sonne to a prince of Wales, who kyng Edwarde of Englande caused to lese his heed, the cause why I can nat tell ; and so kyng Edwarde ceased into his handes all the provynce of Wales ; and this yuan in his youthe came into Fraunce, and shewed all his trouble to kyng Philyppe, than beyng fre'che kyng, who kept him styll about him as lo'ng as he lyved, and was as one of the chyldren of his chambre, with his nevewes of Alenson and other: and in lykewise so dyde king Johan, and than he bare first armes, and was at the batell of Poicters ; howbeit, he was nat there taken : it had been better for hym, that he had ben ther slayne : and whan the peace was made bitwene the kynge of Englande, and the frenche kynge, than this yuan wente into Lombardy, and there contynued in warre ; and whan the warre began agayne bytwene Englande and Fraunce, than he returned agayne into Fraunce, and bare himselfe so well yt he was greatly praysed, and wel beloved with the frenche kyng, and with all the lordes.

"Nowe lette us speke of his ende, the whiche I am lothe to do, savynge to shewe truely what fell in that tyme.

"This yuan of Wales hadde an usage beyng before Mortayne at the siege, that gladly in the mornyng whan he was up and redy, he wolde come before the castell, and sytte downe and kembe his heed a good long space, and syt and beholde the castell, and the countrey about, beynge out of doute or feare of any thynge : and lyghtly there went none with him but this James Laube and often tymes he made him redy, and none but he, wherby at last came his endyng day. On a mornyng betymes, wha' the wether was fayre and clere, and the nyght had been so hote that he coulde nat slepe, howebeit, he rose and dyd on him but a syngle jacket and his shyrte, and a mantell or a cloke above, and so went thyder as he was wonte to go, and sate hym downe, and this James Laube, with hym, every man beynge in their lodgynges aslepe, for it was early in the mornyng, and ther was made but lytell watche, for they thought the'selfe sure of the castell; and whan yuan was sette on an olde stocke of wode, he sayd to James, go to my lodgyng and fatche my combe, for I wyll refreshe me here a lytell season; sir, quoth he, it shall be done: and so he wente and came agayne with the combe: and as he was comyng, I trowe the devyll entred into hym, for besyde the combe, he brought with hym a lytell Javelyne of Spayne, with a large heed of stele, and with the same strake this yuan as he sate, clene through out the body, so yt he fell downe starke deed: and whan he hadde done, he left styll the dart in his body, and so went his way, and drewe under covert of the castell, and soo came to the barryers and was let in, for he made signes to enter, and so he was brought before the Soudye of Lestrade; Sir, quoth he, I have delyvered you of one of the greatest enemyes that ye had; of whom is that quod the Sowdie; of yuan of Wales, quoth James; and howe so, quoth the Soudie; thus, quoth James, and so shewed him all the hole mater, as ye have herd before, fro poynt to poynt: and whan the Soudye herde that, he shaked his heed, and behelde him right felly, and said, A, than thou hast murdred him, knowe for trouthe, all thynges consydred, savyng but that this dede is for our profyte, it shoulde cost the thyne heed: but sithe it is done it can nat be undone agayne; howebeit, it is a great domage of that gentylman to be so slayne: we shall have rather blame therby than prayse.

"This was the ende of yuan, or Owen, of Wales, wheder ye wyll, all is one, slayne by great unhap and treason, wherwith they of the hoost whan they knewe it, were ryght sorie and displeased, and so was every man yt herde therof, and specially kyng Charles of Frau'ce, who greatly complayned his dethe; howebeit, he coulde nat amende it: and so this yuan was buryed in the church of saynt Leger, where as he hadde made a bastyde, halfe a leage fro the castell of Mortayne, and all the gentylmen of the hoost were at his buryeng, the whiche was done ryght honourably: howebeit, for all that the siege helde styll before Mortayne, for there were good knyghtes and squiers, bretons, poictevyns, and frenchmen, who had greatter desyre to conquere the castell than they hadde before, and thought never to departe thens tyll they had wonne it, or elles reysed by puyssance, they wolde so fayne have ben revenged of the dethe of yuan of Wales; and so they lay styll without any sawte gevynge, for they knewe well they lacked vitayle within the castell, and none coulde come to them."

Yeuain (Owen) sleeps his last long sleep, from which it requires more than mortal voice to rouse him, in the

ancient church of St. Legere, on the banks of the Gironde.
A well-known Welsh proverb has it that " Y'mhob gwlad
y megir glew "—brave men are bred of every nation—a
truism which has been abundantly demonstrated by the
events of our own day, but it may be doubted whether
Wales has given birth to a braver man or more engaging
character than Owen of Wales. Froissart is not alone
amongst French chroniclers in recording the daring
actions of the Welsh soldier of fortune—for that he really
was ; while the esteem in which he was universally held,
and the fear he unquestionably inspired in the English
rulers, prove both his reckless bravery and his capacity
for war. He is probably the greatest military genius
that Wales has produced.

He is upon several occasions referred to in the metrical
Chronicle of the Life of Bertrand du Guesclin,[1] the celebrated
constable of France. There is also interesting evidence of
the impression he had made upon his adopted country in
the *Chronique de Saint-Denys*, the writer of which, in
describing the arrival thirty years later of the appeal of
Owen Glendower for French assistance, states that Owen
backed up his appeal by recalling the services to the throne
of France of Yeuain de Galles, "to whom he had succeeded
by right of inheritance."[2]

---

[1] *Chronique de Bertrand du Guesclin, par Cuvelier, trouvère du* xiveme
siècle. Edited by E. Charrière in the "Collection de Documents
inédits sur l'Histoire de France ; première série (histoire politique)."

[2] *Chronique du Religieux de Saint-Denys, de 1380 a 1422.* Ed. by M.
L. Bellaguet in the "Collection de Documents inédits sur l'Histoire
de France." The passage, which is of considerable interest, and does
not seem to have been noticed by any of the writers upon Owen
Glendower, is as follows : Capitulum ix.—Ad arma comparanda Parisius
princeps Wallie misit. Inter plures generosos qui regem Anglie ad
regni fastigium ascendisse injustissime abhorrebant, solus princeps
Wallie, Glindour nomine, non modo eidem viribus contradicendo, sed
et contra eum levando calcaneum nunc marte claro nunc obscuro

A word or two as to his assassin. It has been known that Lamb was rewarded by the English government, since an order for the payment to him of 100 francs for the good service he had performed in the death of Owen of Wales is in Rymer. Less known is the following entry upon the Issue Roll of the Exchequer for Michaelmas, 2 Ric. II [ed. F. Devon].

"4 Dec. [1378]. To John Lamb, an esquire from Scotland, because he lately killed Owynn de Gales, a rebel and enemy of the King in France, on his passage to England to explain certain affairs to the Lord the King and his Council. In money paid to his own hands, in discharge of £20 which the Lord the King commanded to be paid him. By writ of privy seal, &c., £20."

Though the assassination of Owen (as we shall henceforth style him) cannot be proved to have been brought about by the English officials in France, clear evidence still exists that they were delighted by the removal of a dreaded enemy, and both the English administrators abroad as well as the king's council at home hastened to reward the murderer and his accomplices.

In the Public Record Office exists a document which discloses the names of Lamb's assistants. There is still extant an account of the disbursements of Richard Rotour, who, in the year 1378, was constable of Bordeaux, the chief seat of the English administration in the south of France at that period *(Public Record Office: Accounts, &c. (Exchequer Q. R.) France, Bundle 180, No. 9)*. Accompanying

Angliam hucusque infestaverat pro posse. Videns tamen opus tam arduum inchoatum sine exterorum auxilio et mercenario conductu se continuare non posse, nec suam tueri auctoritatem ad Francos decrevit recurrere, arma et auxilium poscere, quos super omnes mortales in armis strenuos reputabat. Et quamvis verecundum reputaret quia alias inauditum scuto Francie protegi Walenses petere, ad id tamen audaciam prestitit quod famosus quondam armiger Yvo de Wallia, cui jure consanguinitatis successerat, in servicio regis Francie Karoli nuper deffuncti occubuerat." (p. 164).

C

the main account are authorities to pay and discharges
for payments made, amongst them being the following—

Public Record Office: Accounts, &c. (Exchequer Q.R.), France,
Bundle 180, No. 10.

" Johan sire de Neuille lieutenant daquitaine pour n're t'ssouuerain
Seign'r le Roi de France 't d'engleterre. A n're tresch'r 't bien amee
mess[ieur] Richart con[nesta]ble de Bourdeaux salut. Com'e nous
sumes a plain informez 't avons bien apperceu la grant amour 't
loiaute que Johan Lambe escuier, Cok   ' 't Will'm Scot ses
compaignons ont tondiz porte au Roi n're dit S'r eulx estautz en la
compaignie des f[rau]nceois 't esp[eci]alment pour la g[rau]nt aventure
't p[er]il en q'lles ils ont mys le'rs corps 't vies po'r la mort de Yuain
de Gales t[rad]ido'r 't ennemy du Roi n're dit S'r le quel fasoit
moult de mals 't des[tru]ction² au paiis 't subgiz du Roi n're dit S'r.
Pour la quele mort lesdiz Johan, Cok 't Will'm ont perdu de leurs
cosins 't parentz que sont estez mys a mort pour cause de la mort
dudit Yuain. Et hen regarde aus choses suisditz 't atendu les
g[rau]ndes p[ro]ffit heno'r 't s[er]uice quils pouont faire en cest
p[rese]nt viage deu[er]s Mortaigine au Roi n're dit S'r 't auci ont fait
on temps passe 't esp[er]ons q' feront par le temps avenir aus ditz
Johan Lambe 't ses compaignons auons donne 't ottvoie la som'e de
Cynk centz vint 't doux liu[r]es 't dix souls de la monoye corrant
pour paier pour jaques bassinetz haub[er]geons h[ar]noys de chambres
gantiletz 't plus'rs diu'rs h[ar]noys 't vestures lesq'll' ils oumt achatez
en la ville de Bourdeux po'r eulx arm' 't arraier 't faire le[ur]s
costages 't despens la q'lle som'e vous mandons 't comandons q' li
paiez bailliez 't deliu[er]ez de largent lequel nagaires vous fut tramis
a n're venue denglet[er]re ou des issues de v're office. Incontinent
vous cestes p[rese]ntz appelle le contrerolleur du chastel ou son
lieutenant as paiementz susditz. Derechief³ vous mandons 't comandons q' a Robert Ffissher esquier vous bailliez deliu[er]ez 't paiez des
issues de v're dit office xxv*li* de la dite mon[naie] p'r ses dispenz
allant en acune negocies de n're dit S'r au dit Rob't p' nous chargez
afair' exploit[er] 't deliu[er]er. Enp[re]nant l'res de reconiss[ances]
ou daquitances de ce q' as p'sones sumoniez ane[re]z paie p' mye

---

¹ Blank in the document.

² A hole in the parchment has partially obliterated this word.

³ From this point to the end of the document the parchment looks
as though the original entry had been erased, and the above
expressions substituted.

lesquells aueqz cez noz l'res volons q' des som'es suisd[itz] vous en
aiez dehue alloance en voz accompt. Don' a Bourdeux le prim' iour
de Nouembr lan mil ccclxxviij soubz le seel roial de n're office."

With this document is the formal receipt of John
Lamb, for himself and his companions, of five hundred
and twenty-two livres ten sous, which had been paid to
him upon the foregoing order of John de Neville. This
runs as follows :—

"Sachent touz ceulx que cez l'res verront ou oriont moy Johan
Lambe esquier auoir hen pris 't receu del honn're 't sagehom'e Mons
Richart Roto'r connestable de Bourdeux cynk centz vint 't deux
liures dix soulz de la monoye courrant a moi donnez 't assignez
p[ar] t'shon're 't puissant S'r Mons. de Nouille lieutenant daquitaine
par cause 't reson sicome es l'res patentz du dit S'r de Nouille
au dit connestable d'reetz plus au plein est contenuz de la quelle
som'e surdite Je ana'ndit Johan Lambe sib'n p[a]r 't en nom
de mes compaignons com'e po'r moy mesmes me reconoisse 't confesse
pleinem't estr' paiez 't le dit connest' cut quitz par ces p[resc]utz
l[ett]res de mon p[ro]pre seel enseales. Donne a Bourd. le xxme
jo'r de Septembr' lan mil ccclxxviij."

The accompanying *facsimile* of this document shows a
portion of Lamb's seal (with an enlargement to twice its
actual size) still appendant to it. The device is a chev-
ron between three lambs, a punning cognizance upon the
surname such as was common in those days. It will
be observed that Lamb's receipt for the blood-money,
and recompense for the loss of his intimates and, perhaps,
relatives, who fell victims to the infuriated friends
of Owen, is dated the 20th September, whilst the date of
the order to John de Neville is the 1st November. The
latter document clearly consists, however, of two separate
mandates which have been amalgamated, a copy of the
later being added to the earlier order on the return of
the former into the issuing department at Bordeaux,
and a date inserted which was probably the date upon
which the amounts expended by John de Neville were
brought to charge in the constable's accounts.

The first entry we shall quote from the constable's book (*P. R. O. Accounts, &c. (Exch. Q. R.), France, Bundle 180, No. 9*) is that of the disbursement to Robert Fisher, which had been authorised by John de Neville in the document already presented. It is in the following terms :—

" In denar[iis] solut[is] Roberto Ffissher, scutiffer[o], pro expensis suis emit[tis] versus obsedionem Mauritan[ei] p[er] mandat[um] consil[ii] Reg[is] ad loquend[um] cum Joh'e Lambe scutiffero p[ro] quibusdam negociis statum domini n'ri Regis tam in partibus aquitanie q'am alibi tangent[ibus]. De liberand[o] 't expediend[o] p'ut p[er] garr[antum] hic liberat[um] plenius declaratur, 't p[er] acquiet' ip[s]ius Roberti de rec' hic lib' cu' testimo[n]io [contra] rotul[atoris] xxv*li*."

Fisher's own receipt for the £25, which was paid to him by the constable of Bordeaux towards the expenses of his journey to Mortagne to "confer" with John Lamb, unfortunately does not accompany the other papers.

The entry of the payment of five hundred and twenty-two livres, ten sous, to John Lamb, the receipt of which by Lamb, on the 20th September 1378, has been already given, runs as follows :—

"Et in denar[iis] solut[is] pro expens[is] Johannis Lamb predicti 't duor[um] socior[um] suor[um] in comitiua sua existenciu[m] cum duob[us] vallet[tis] suis videl' p[ro] div[er]s[is] vestime[n]tis armaturis 't al[iis] eisdem nece[ssar]iis empt[is] 't p[ro]vis[is] quando ordinat[is] fuerunt ad eund' in comitiua d'ni locumtenent[is] ad relenac'o'em loc[i] Mauritan[ei] p'dicti p'ut patet¹
p[er] garr[antum] d'ni locumten' p'd'c'i hic lib' 't acquiet' ip[s]ius Joh[an]nis Lamb de rec' hic lib' 't testimon' contrarotul'. v°xxij*li*. xs."

The entries in the constable's volume are regarded by M. Luce as proving that the murder of Owen was premeditated by the English King's Council and deliberately planned by the English officials at Bordeaux, and, taken in conjunction with the preceding documents, it will be

---

¹ Half-a-dozen words have been erased at this point, and others have not been supplied.

admitted that the evidence in favour of such presumption is decidedly strong.

Lamb continued in the English service, and was entrusted with various duties and sums of money which necessitated entries in the public accounts.[1] Nothing, however, is known of his death.

If Froissart's statement that Lamb spoke to Owen in his own language can be taken to refer to Welsh and not to English, and that he was well acquainted with the course of events in Wales, we should be forced to conclude that he was a Welshman, probably born of the marriage of an English settler and a native woman. It cannot be said that the suggestion is inherently improbable, and the French chronicler's knowledge of the circumstances of Owen's death is so satisfactorily proved by the testimony of the public records of France and of England that we could not refuse to credit him upon a point which must have been well known to all who had acquaintance with Owen. The inference deducible from Lamb's designation in the Exchequer roll as "an esquire from Scotland" is strengthened by the fact that one of his companions was named William Scot, which in those days would mean nothing but William the Scotsman. On the other hand, the name of the third murderer in the tragedy, which is given as Cok, may be intended for the common Welsh appellative coch=red, or ruddy, although it seems to represent rather the Christian- than the surname.

The circumstances of Owen's death bring into strong relief the cruelty and duplicity of the age, and the shallowness of the chivalric spirit which was supposed to ennoble every knightly enterprise; and contrast strongly with the many deeds of courage and devotion to which

---

[1] See *Public Record Office : Accounts, &c. (Exchequer Q. R.), Army &c., Bundle 38, No. 12.*

the chroniclers bear testimony. It was the age of the Black Prince and Sir John Chandos, of Owen of Wales and Du Guesclin. It was also the age of John Lamb.

So much for Owen of Wales. Of Owain Lawgoch, the only historical record of him under that cognomen—the entry in the *Record of Caernarvon*—has already been given. The evidence for their common identity must now be presented.

It will be remembered that the conviction of Griffith Sais as an adherent of Owain Lawgoch, a traitor and enemy of the English king and prince, occurred in the year 1370. Owen of Wales was murdered before the walls of Mortagne sur Gironde in the autumn of 1378.

On the patent roll of the 1st Richard II (22 June, 1377 —21 June, 1378) under date the 1st February, 1378, is the following entry, as abstracted in the first volume of the *Calendar of Patent Rolls, Richard II.*

"Inspeximus and confirmation of letters patent dated 29th Dec., 47 Edward III, being a grant to Mary, wife of William Hervy, of lands in Budefeld, co. Gloucester, forfeited by Owin de Retheryk."

Consequent upon this grant, we have the following day, the 2nd February, 1378, the issue of another order to the following effect:—

"Revocation of the appointment of John de Wotton to the custody of the lands and tenements late of Owin ap Thomas ap Rither[ik] in Budefeld, co. Gloucester, which were forfeited by the said Owin's adherence to the French, and which the late king granted rent free to Mary, wife of William Hervy."

It is clear that the Owin de Retheryk of the first entry is the Owin ap Thomas ap Rither[ik] of the second, but, save that the latter is described as an adherent of the French, nothing beyond the name Owen serves to connect him with Owen of Wales, and the above entries in the printed *Calendar* have, up to the present, provoked no comment from any Welsh historical student.

However, the second volume of the *Calendar of Patent Rolls, Richard II*, contains the following abstract of an entry which is dated the 5th March, 1383—

"Inspeximus and confirmation in favour of Blethin ap Ynian, a Welshman, of letters patent (in French) of the king's uncle Thomas, earl of Buckingham, lately the King's lieutenant in France, dated Vannes, 27 February, 1380, being a pardon to him in the presence of lords Latymer, Bourchier and Morle, and Sir Hugh de Hastynges, for all treasons and other crimes committed by him in the company of Owen (*Ewayn*) Retherrik who called himself (*qui se disoit*) prince of Wales, or with the French."[1]

---

[1] The above abstract somewhat fails to bring out the full force of the entire entry, which therefore is here given at length : —" Rex omnibus ad quos etc., salutem. Inspeximus has patentes carissimi avunculi nostri Thome comitis Bukyngham nuper locum tenens nostri in partibus Ffrancis factas Blethino ap Ynian Wallensi, in hec verba : Thomas fitz au Roy counte de Bukyngham lieutenant de mon tresexcellent et tresredoute seigneur le Roy de Ffrance et d'Engleterre a toutz ceux qi ces lettres verront ou orront, Saluz. Come Blethin ap Ynian Galeis eit demeure en la compaignie de Owayn Retherrik qui se disoit prince de Galis liquel estoit traitour envers nostre dit S'r et avec luy enherdant et demoerant, Et auxi depuis la mort du dit Owayn Retherrik residuelement oue [au] les Francois encontre nostre dit S'r le Roy et ses liges come traitour faux et desnaturel, liquel Blethin ap Ynian nans ait supplie de grace et de mercie et de retourner de son mal oppynion envers nostre S'r avantdites, Et nous ent auoir a sa humiltee consideracion en la presence du S. de Latymer conestable de nostre host, le S. de Bourchier, le S. de Morle, Mons. Hugh de Hastynges et pluseurs autres, et de l'autorite que nous avons de nostre seigneur le Roy ly avons places en nostre grace ly [le] pardonant toutes maners des tresons homicides laiciues roberies rebellions et toutes autres malefices queconque qieles il ad fait envers nostre dit S'r depuis le temps qil estoit premierement en la compaignie du dit Owayn Retherrik et au les diz Ffrancois tanque a la fesance de cestes. En tesmoignance de quele chose a cestes nos lettres patentes a nous mis nostre seel. Doun a Vannes le xxvij jour de Ffevrier l'an mil ccc iiij^{xx}. Nos autem litteras predictas et omnia contenta in eisdem ratahabentes et grata ea pro nobis et heredibus nostris acceptamus approbamus et tenore presentium confirmamus. In cujus etc. T. R. apud Westmonasterium quinto die Martii. Pro dimidio marca solutis in hanaperio."— (*Rot. Pat.*, 6 Ric. II, *p.* 2, *m.* 8).

There could be very little doubt that the Ewayn of the patent of 5 March, 1383, was the same person as he of the patents of February, 1378, and this was rendered certain by examination of the roll of the 47th Edward III, the calendaring of which has not yet been reached, where the entry is as follows:—

" Edward by the grace of God king of England and France &c. Know ye that we have granted to our beloved Mary, wife of William Herny, those lands and tenements in the vill of Budefeld in the county of Gloucester formerly belonging to Owin de Retheryk, which lands and tenements are in our hands, as it is said, as forfeited to us by reason of the adherence of the said Owin to our enemies of France. Dated the 29th December (47 Ed. III.)"

Recollection being next had of the statement of Froissart respecting the pretensions of Owen of Wales, it seemed fairly probable that a forward step had been taken in the identification of the latter. Further, there was the fact that an Owen, called Lawgoch, was described in the year 1370 as a traitor to the English king, and there was the existence of a more or less vague tradition, which represented this person as having met with a violent death far away from his native land: all these converging circumstances pointed to the conclusion, which might be provisionally accepted as a working hypothesis, that Owain Lawgoch and Owen of Wales both met in Owen ap Retherick, or Owen ap Thomas ap Retherick.

The next point in the enquiry, therefore, is, Who was this Owen?[1]

---

[1] It may be mentioned that the reply now presented to this question differs from that given at the reading of the paper on the 21st of March. On that occasion the writer set forth the claims of three Welsh princely houses to the lineage of Owen, and arrived at the conclusion that he was a descendant of a line of Morganwg chieftains. The ascription of Owen to South Wales was strongly combatted at the lecture by Mr. J. H. Davies, M.A., who argued ably in favour of his descent from the Welsh princes of Gwynedd. Mr. Davies

The first writer who appears to have fixed the place of
Owen in one of the princely lines of Wales—that of
Gwynedd—was Miss Angharad Llwyd, the author of *The
History of Mona.* To her edition of Sir John Wynn's
History of the Gwydir Family is appended, in illustration of
the descents mentioned therein, a pedigree of the princes
of Gwynedd starting with Gruffudd ab Cynan, from which
the following extract is sufficient for our present purpose :—

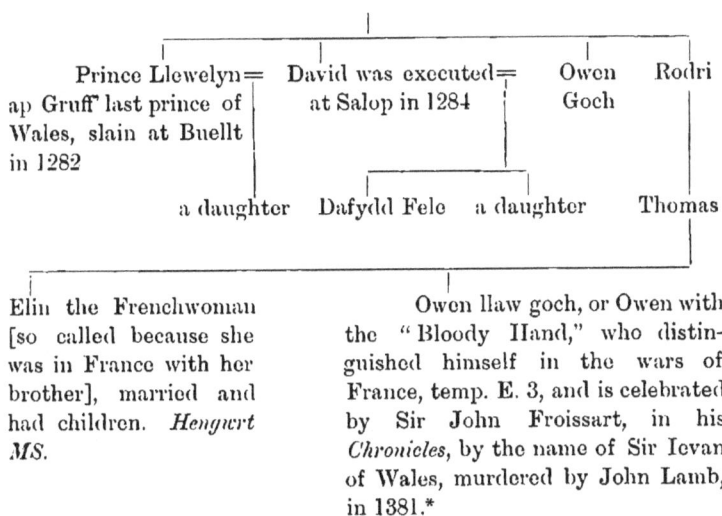

Prince Llewelyn=	David was executed=	Owen	Rodri
ap Gruff last prince of	at Salop in 1284	Goch	
Wales, slain at Buellt			
in 1282			

| a daughter | Dafydd Fele | a daughter | Thomas |

Elin the Frenchwoman	Owen llaw goch, or Owen with
[so called because she	the "Bloody Hand," who distin-
was in France with her	guished himself in the wars of
brother], married and	France, temp. E. 3, and is celebrated
had children. *Hengwrt*	by Sir John Froissart, in his
MS.	*Chronicles,* by the name of Sir Ievan
	of Wales, murdered by John Lamb,
	in 1381.*

* [Note by Miss Llwyd.] "This interesting anecdote identifying
Sir Ievan of Wales (whose chivalrous exploits occupy so large a
portion of Froissart's *Chronicles*), with the son of Tomas ab Rodri, was
discovered in one of the *Hengwrt MSS.* belonging to Gryffydd ap
Howel Vaughan, Esq., of Rûg, whose kind indulgence in permitting
the Editor a perusal of this valuable volume is most gratefully
acknowledged."

quoted certain entries upon the public records with which the writer
was acquainted, but the full import of which he had been unable to
gather. He has now but to say that further research has convinced
him that upon the question of Owen's parentage Mr. Davies was
right and he himself was wrong. In the period that has elapsed
since the lecture, Mr. Davies and himself have been in constant friendly communication, and whatever value this paper may
possess as an original contribution to Welsh history is due as much

Had Miss Angharad Llwyd followed up the clue
afforded her by the Hengwrt volume with a few researches
into the public records, evidence would probably have
been forthcoming which would have greatly strengthened
what, it must be admitted, was altogether insufficient
proof. The Rev. Thomas Price (*Carnuhanawc*) gives Owen
a paragraph at the close of his *Hanes Cymru*, and refers
to Miss Llwyd's identification in terms that betray his
own scepticism. Later historical writers have been influenced by Mr. Price's attitude, and those who have
written since 1878 have been confirmed by the following
note by the late Mr. W. W. E. Wynne, of Peniarth,
appended to a reproduction of Miss Angharad Llwyd's
pedigree in a reprint of Sir John Wynn's *History of the
Gwydir Family*, issued from an Oswestry press in that
year. Mr. Wynne makes the following remarks upon
Miss Llwyd's note, quoted above:

"I strongly suspect that the following is the passage to which Miss
Angharad Llwyd refers. It is in *Hengwrt MS.* 351,[1] the only one she is
likely to have had access to, as being at Rhûg in Col. Vaughan's time.
It is on page 865, and is a copy of a large MS. in the autograph of
Robert Vaughan, the antiquary, *Hengwrt MS.* 96.

"'On Loawgoch alas yn Ffrainc gan Joⁿ Lam ei was drwy frad yn ei

---

to Mr. Davies's labours as to those of the actual writer. It is his
friend's unrivalled knowledge of the Welsh poetry of the 15-17th
centuries that has enriched this paper with the extracts from practically unknown bards. These possess the double interest of showing
Owen on the point of assuming those characteristics of romance
which Professor Rhys has dealt with, whilst still retaining a few of
the elements of a popular leader of men.

[1] *Hengwrt* 351 has been unnecessarily renumbered *Peniarth* 119
(Hist. MSS. Com.: *Report on MSS. in the Welsh Language*, vol. i, part ii,
p.730). It would appear from Mr. Gwenogvryn Evans's *Report* that the
last numbered page in the volume is 742. *Hengwrt* 350 (now *Peniarth*
120) accords more closely with Mr. Wynne's description of the volume
containing the above passage, but this, according to Mr. Evans, has no
more than 607 numbered pages.

wely pan oed yn arfaethy dyfod i oresgyn talaith Cymru. J. B. 30. O. S. P.

"'Elen Ffrances am ei bod yn Ffranie gydai brawd ac yn medry Ffrangeg=   ap Ior ap Ednyved Vychan. p. Llyfr Mr. Edd. Herbert o Drefaldwyn.'

"It would appear from a letter in the *Archæologia Cambrensis*, No. xxi, third series, page 62, quoting an original record in the Imperial Library of France, that the names of Sir Jevan of Wales were 'Ivain agruffin,' doubtless Jevan ap Griffith.'"

A few of the French documents referred to by Mr. Wynne as appearing in *Archæologia Cambrensis*, 3rd Series, vi, 62, are printed *in extenso* at the end of Augustin Thierry's *Histoire de la conquête de L'Angleterre par les Normands*, and will be dealt with later. Meanwhile, it is sufficient to say that the writer of the letter in *Arch. Camb.* does not state that the names of Sir Jevan of Wales were Ivain agruffin, though such an inference might easily be drawn from a cursory perusal. As a matter of fact, the document bearing the seal and signature of Owen (or Jevan) ap Griffith, is of the year 1389, eleven years after the death of the redoubtable captain who, beyond all others, was known to the French as Owen of Wales.[1]

---

[1] The error of the late Mr. Wynne, as might have been expected, has coloured the views of every subsequent writer who has touched upon Owen's career. Thus, a contributor to that invaluable collection, *Bye-Gones*, for 14 Aug. 1895, after quoting from the *Fœdera* the order for the payment to John Lamb, enquires, "Has Evan of Wales ever been identified with any known Welsh character?" The reply on the 23 Oct. is as follows:—"There does not seem to be much hope of identifying Evan of Wales. See a long note on the subject in *Bye-Gones* for April 10, 1889 [consisting merely of extracts from Froissart]. If Froissart himself, as I gather from this note, says he cannot identify Evan with any known character in the old Welsh books, I am afraid the moderns have not much chance of success." The subject is again ventilated in the same publication for the 15th April 1896, when the ascription of Miss Angharad Llwyd, and the note of Mr. Wynne thereupon, as quoted above, are trotted forth. Though the

It will have been observed that the various entries upon the patent rolls describe Owen as the son of Retherick, which in modern English would be Roderick, representing the Anglicised form of the Welsh Rhodri. Rhodri was in Latin made into Rothericus or Rethericus. One entry gives his lineage as " the son of Thomas the son of Retherick," and, as we shall see, there need be no hesitation in accepting this version as the correct one. It seems useless to speculate upon the authority for Froissart's Prince Aymon. It is clearly an error, the cause of which defies explanation.

Now, the Rhodri to whom this pedigree ascends, will be shown to be none other than Rhodri ap Gruffudd, brother to Llewelyn ap Gruffudd, frequently styled the last prince of Wales, and to David ap Gruffudd, who was put to death in 1283. This is in accordance with the pedigree already presented by Miss Angharad Llwyd. Rhodri is a much more shadowy character in history than are his brothers Llewelyn and David, but it is probable that the outlines of his career would have been less obscure had some of our writers upon historical subjects condescended to a little work upon the vast mass of unprinted records, instead of

---

writer was sufficiently acute to note that the document signed " Ivain agruffin " was of the year 1389, and that, therefore, that individual could not have been identical with Owen of Wales, who was murdered in 1378, he nevertheless asserts that "there is abundant evidence to prove that ' Yvain agruffin', as he signed himself, was identical with ' Evan de Galles'". He continues: "It appears to be more likely that, as stated in Harleian MS. 2288, fo. 147, 'Sir Jevan of Wales' is identical with Sir Jevan ap Griffith, illegitimate son of Sir Griffith Llwyd, of Tregarnedd, in Anglesey", thus making confusion worse confounded. The latest hash of Froissart's narrative is also perhaps the most ridiculous—an article in *Wales*, for May 1897, considerably embellishing the already sufficiently romantic career of Owen, whom the writer terms, "the son of Prince Edmund of Wales."

remaining content with picturesque modernisings of well-known chronicles. The able writer of the Welsh historical biographies in the *Dictionary of National Biography*, makes but incidental reference to him when treating of his better known brothers. It is, however, necessary for our inquiry that we should endeavour to penetrate the darkness that surrounds Rhodri's career, and research has disclosed the following particulars concerning him.

Rhodri was little more than a child when, in the year 1241, he accompanied his elder brother David to the English court, to remain there as a hostage for the good behaviour of his countrymen. How long he continued in England is unknown, but it is probable that he did not return to Wales for many years. He does not seem to have got on well with his brother Llewelyn, perhaps because of the English proclivities which he could not fail to have imbibed. At any rate, in the year 1277 he was forced to flee to England for protection, and his injuries constituted one of the subjects of negotiation between the king of England and Llewelyn in the latter part of that year (*Fœdera*, Rolls ed., i, 545). Doubtless foreseeing that his presence in Wales would be a constant source of irritation, Edward determined upon settling Rhodri upon an English estate, a course that was also followed in the case of his brother David.[1] From this time forward Rhodri does not seem to have taken any part in affairs in Wales.

The earliest date at which his name has been met with in the public records, after his removal to England, is

---

[1] It does not appear that Rhodri was made a baron, or was ever summoned to Parliament. David certainly became an English baron when he accepted his English estates, and it was in that capacity that he was treated as a traitor. In the writs issued for his trial the king expressly states that he had been inter majores nostri palacii collocantes (*Rot. Wall.*, 11 Ed. I, *m. 2 dorse* ; 28 June 1283).

1278, when an arrangement which had been concluded
between him and his brother, Llewelyn, came before
the English king. The entry upon the close roll of
6 Ed. I (*m. 4d.*) is thus abstracted in the recently issued
Calendar of Close Rolls, 1272-1279 :—

"Whereas Roderic son of Griffin and brother of Llewelyn son of
Griffin, prince of Wales, on Saturday after the Nativity of St. Mary,
6 Edward, and also on Sunday following, the king being then at
Rothelan, came there into the king's court and demanded against the
said prince his brother his purparty of all the lands that belonged to
David his uncle in North Wales and elsewhere throughout the principality of Wales, which lands the prince then held, and the prince
came before the king in his court and said that he was not bound to
answer to Roderic herein, and he proffered by the hands of the
abbot of Aberconwy a deed under the seal of Roderic and others of
the parts of Wales in these words (here follows copy of grant and
release by Roderic son of Griffin to Llewelyn, prince of Wales, his
brother, and the heirs of his body of all his right in the lands and
possessions in (*apud*) North Wales or elsewhere in the principality of
Wales, for 1000 marks that the prince paid to him beforehand to
acquit the marriage of Emonina, daughter of John le Botillier, with
promise not to disturb Llewelyn contrary to this grant, which is
sealed for greater security with the seals of the bishops of Bangor and
of St. Asaph, the abbots of Aberconwey, Basingwerk, and Bully, with
the addition of the seals of the archdeacons of Bangor and St. Asaph.
Witnesses : Tuder son of Etnyvet, steward of Wales, Annian son of
Kaeradauk, David son of Ennyaun, Rhys son of Griffin, Kenewric
son of Goronow, Master William and David, clerks of the prince.
Dated and done at Kaerinarvon, 2 id. April, 1272). Which deed
Roderic, then in court, acknowledged that he had made, but he said
that he had received nothing of the said 1000 marks, and Llewelyn
asserted that he had paid Roderic 50 marks thereof. At last, after
many arguments between the parties in the said court, it was agreed
in the king's presence in his court at Rothelan, on the said Sunday,
that Roderic quit-claimed to Llewelyn and the heirs of his body all his
right in the lands aforesaid, and Llewelyn acknowledged in the king's
court that he owed to Roderic 950 marks, to be levied, in default of
payment, from his lands and chattels in the principality of Wales by
the sheriffs and bailiffs whom the king shall cause to be sent thither
for this purpose. For greater security David son of Griffin, brother
of the said prince and of Roderic, made acknowledgment in the same
way, and granted that the money shall be levied of his lands and

chattels in England and elsewhere by the bailiffs and sheriffs of the king.

"*Memorandum*, that this acknowledgment is enrolled on the roll of Wales on the dorse of the roll of the same year.

"*Memorandum*, that the aforesaid deed of quitclaim was delivered on the same day to the prince's clerk, to be delivered to the prince, by Roderic's consent."

The grant and quitclaim recited in the above document will be found in *P.R.O : Chapter House, Liber A*, f. 361 (left-hand side of page). There were several John le Botelers, but I am unable to distinguish the member of the family who is here in question, nor have I been more fortunate in discovering anything further respecting the lady Emonina.[1] The agreement between Rhodri and Llewelyn is a little difficult to understand, but its purport seems to be that, in addition to the transfer of the right of granting the lady Emonina de Boteler in marriage, Rhodri relinquished to Llewelyn all his rights in the lands and possessions to which he was entitled, or which he claimed. The settlement of 1278 was practically guaranteed by the king, and it was no doubt in virtue of this agreement that Rhodri, in 1292, obtained an annuity of £40 per annum from the English treasury.

A hitherto unnoticed pedigree in the British Museum *Harleian* 1157 (a volume of Shropshire genealogies compiled at the beginning of the 17th century, but

---

[1] An unaccountable misreading of the document occurs in the above abstract, where the agreement between Rhodri and Llewelyn is said to have been sealed with the seal of (amongst others) the abbot of Bully. This stands for Enlly, or Enlli (as is the spelling in *Liber A*). Not only has the identification of the above extraordinary place been unattempted in the index to the volume, but it has been omitted altogether therefrom ; nor is it recorded under the forms of Bardsey or Enlli. Where is the sense of issuing official calendars to the public records which must necessarily include a large number of entries that contain Welsh place and personal names, without having those entries examined by a Welsh scholar ?

containing a few descents from Welsh princely families)
gave the following clue to his new *locale* :—

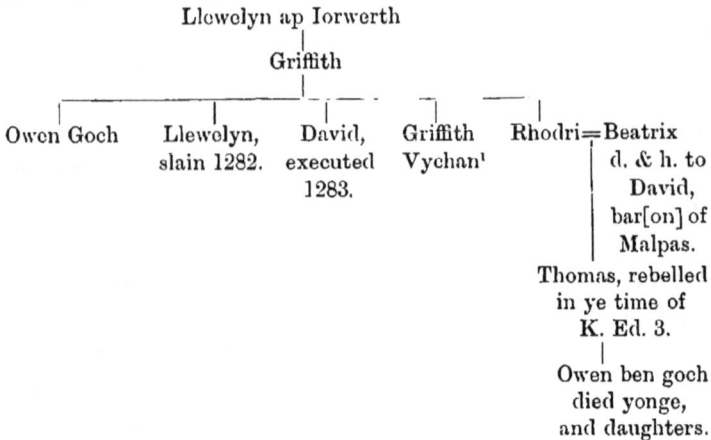

```
                         Llewelyn ap Iorwerth
                                  |
                              Griffith
                                  |
   _____|_____
   |              |              |           |          |
Owen Goch    Llewelyn,       David,       Griffith   Rhodri═Beatrix
             slain 1282.     executed     Vychan¹       |   d. & h. to
                             1283.                      |     David,
                                                        |    bar[on] of
                                                        |    Malpas.
                                                  Thomas, rebelled
                                                  in ye time of
                                                  K. Ed. 3.
                                                        |
                                                  Owen ben goch
                                                  died yonge,
                                                  and daughters.
```

Upon reference to Ormerod's *History of Cheshire* (ed.
Helsby, 1882) under "Malpas" (vol. ii, 598), a pedigree
of the barons of Malpas was found, from which these
descents are extracted :—

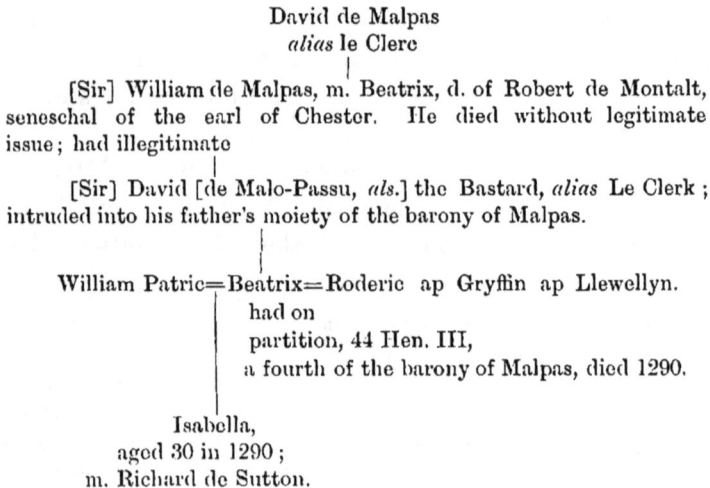

```
                    David de Malpas
                     alias le Clerc
                          |
```

[Sir] William de Malpas, m. Beatrix, d. of Robert de Montalt,
seneschal of the earl of Chester. He died without legitimate
issue; had illegitimate

[Sir] David [de Malo-Passu, *als.*] the Bastard, *alias* Le Clerk ;
intruded into his father's moiety of the barony of Malpas.

```
William Patric═Beatrix═Roderic ap Gryffin ap Llewellyn.
               | had on
               | partition, 44 Hen. III,
               | a fourth of the barony of Malpas, died 1290.
               |
           Isabella,
        aged 30 in 1290 ;
        m. Richard de Sutton.
```

---

¹ Griffith Vychan is unknown to Welsh historians as a brother to
Llewelyn and David. There is, however, some evidence for his

The "abstracts of evidences" upon which this pedigree is founded,[1] and which accompany it, show Rhcdri to have been married to Beatrix de Malpas so early as the 9th Edward I (1281), when they both confirm a grant to the abbey of St. Werburgh. From this date onwards, his name is occasionally met with in the palatinate documents. The following are instances :—

17 Ed. I (1289). Inquisition post mortem upon the death of John de St. Pierre. That the said John held *(inter alia)* of Urian de St. Pierre and Rotheric, son of Griffin and Beatrice his wife, one moiety of Wynercote [Wynercote] in demesne, and another moiety of Richard de Sutton and Isabel his wife, in demesne. (Chester Plea Rolls, 16, 17 Ed. I, *m.* 8*d.*)

---

inclusion in the family of Gruffudd ap Llewelyn ap Iorwerth. In an unpublished list of those who did homage to Edward, prince of Wales, in 1301, which I have discovered only quite recently, is the name of Griffith ap Griffith d'Anglesey. and it is difficult to find another of that name amongst the "gwyr mawr Mon" elsewhere than in the princely line of Aberffraw.

[1] It may be well to put upon record another descent from David de Malpas the elder, which was alighted upon during the course of these researches. In a suit of Isabella, daughter of Philip de Egerton, *et alii*, against John, son of John de Sutton, in the king's bench in Hilary term of 13 Ric. II (*m.* 141), the following pedigree is set forth :—

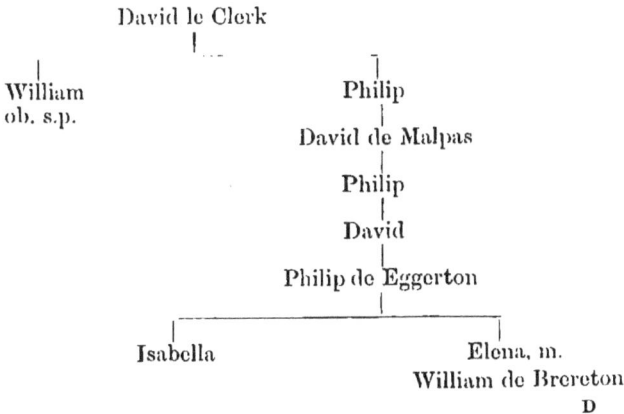

```
                          David le Clerk
                              |
              ┌───────────────┴───────┐
              |                        |
          William                    Philip
          ob. s.p.                     |
                              David de Malpas
                                       |
                                    Philip
                                       |
                                    David
                                       |
                             Philip de Eggerton
                                       |
                     ┌─────────────────┴────────────┐
                     |                               |
                 Isabella                        Elena, m.
                                              William de Brereton
```

D

17 Ed. I (1289). Matilda, wife of Hugh de Pulford, against Robert Parson, of Coddington. Dower of 2 messuages, &c., part of the land being in the several custodies of Roger de Monte Alto, Peter de Ar-derne, Rotheric son of Griffin, and Beatrice, his wife, and Randal de Thornton. (*Ib.*, m. 9.)

In 1290 Beatrix died, apparently leaving no issue by Rhodri. Her possessions[1] passed to her daughter Isabel, who was married to Richard de Sutton, and thence to John de Sutton. He seems to have parted with them pretty freely, a considerable portion falling into the hands of the rising family of Egerton, and another large share going to the founder of the de Cherletons of Powys.[2] Rhodri was, no doubt, tenant by the courtesy of some, but it does not appear what part, of his wife's estate.

[1] These are given in the Calendar of Inq. post mortem as comprising Shokelach castr', Tholyhate passag' in Tilestone vocat' Yhevill, Dokyn-ton maner', Bradlegh maner', Malpas maner', Barton terr' &c., Chirton terre &c., Rughe Cristleton terr' &c., Home Cristelton terr' &c., Borewardesley reddit', Yeiton maner', Walefeld terr' &c., Oldecastell bosc', Wevercote terr' &c., custod' pacis ib'm, Shokelach de uno judicatore in Cestr' comitatu, Goldebourne hundr', and Dekynton terr' &c.

[2] The importance of this will appear later, when we come to deal with Rhodri's son and successor. Montgomeryshire antiquaries have not been very successful in their enquiries into the origin of the Cherletons. An article on "The Feudal Barons of Powys" in the first volume of *Montgomeryshire Collections*, contains no reference to the first John de Cherleton of Powys' possessions in Cheshire. The following entry, however, shows him as having a large interest in the very estates, a share of which had been held in dower by Beatrix, the wife of Rhodri :—

"3 Ed. III. John de Cherleton, and master John de Hildeslegh, clerk. Fine—castle and hundred of Malpas, manors of Shokelache, Bradeleye, Ageton, a moiety of the manor of Chirchecristelton, a moiety of a third part of the mill of Barton, a fourth part of the manor of Rowecristelton, and of the serjeantry of the peace of Malpas, and three-parts of the advowson of the church of Malpas. The said manors, &c., being held of the earl of Chester in capite, a licence of alienation was granted to John son of Richard de Sutton, to enfeoff John de Hyldeslegh, clerk, and Peter de Rithre, clerk, of the

We next come to the following :—

27 Ed. I (1299). Fulk le Strange, Bogo de Knovill, and Alianora, his wife, *v.* Rotheric son of Griffin, Katherine his wife, and Cadugon de Hadelegh. Dispute respecting a pool. (*Fine Rolls*, 27 Ed. I, No. 58.)

28 Ed. I (1300). Ellen, who was the wife of Thomas de Arderne, *v.* Roderic son of Griffin, and Katherine his wife. Dower of 4 messuages, 7 bovates of land, 80 acres of wood, 120 acres of pasture, and 10 solidates of rent in Northbury near Meerbury. (*Plea Rolls*, 27-28 Ed. I, *m.* 2 ; 28-29 Ed. I, *mm.* 6, 7.)

28 Ed. I (1300). The said Roderic and Katherine vouch to warranty Thomas son of Thomas de Arderne. (*Ib.*, 28-29 Ed. I, *m.* 8.)

28 Ed. I (1300). Leuca, who was the wife of Richard Faber of Wildeleg', *v.* Roderick son of Griffin, and Katherine his wife. Dower of one messuage and 20 acres of land in Little Egge, and the said Roderick vouches to warranty Urian de St. Pierre. (*Ib.*, 27-28 Ed. I, *mm.* 6d, 7.)

33 Ed. I (1305). Rotheric son of Griffin, and Katherine his wife, *v.* Eignon ap Ithel, and Alice his wife. One messuage, eight acres of

---

castle, hundred, manors, &c., mentioned in the above fine, to hold the same to them and their heirs for ever, together with the reversion of the manor of Yeyton on the death of Robert de Sutton ; with license to the same John and Peter to give the same castle, hundred, manors, &c., to John de Chorleton for life, with remainder to John son of John son of Richard de Sutton and Isabel daughter of the aforesaid John de Chorleton, his wife, and the heirs of their bodies, and them failing, to the right heirs of the aforesaid John de Chorleton, and to grant that the manor of Yeyton, on the death of the said Robert, should remain to John de Chorleton in perpetuity." (*Chester Plea Rolls*, 2 and 3 Ed. III, *m.* 11, 1329-1330. *See* also *Rot. Pat.*, 1 Ed. III, *p.* 2, *m.* 25.)

It is true that throughout this entry de Cherleton is nowhere described as "of Powys", and his name is consistently spelled "de Chorleton." But that they are the same is clear from the following entries upon the patent roll of three years earlier :

"John, son of Richard de Sutton, lord of Malepas, acknowledges that he owes to John de Cherleton, lord of Powys, £3,000 ; to be levied, in default of payment, of his lands and chattels in co. Stafford.

"The said John de Cherleton acknowledges that he owes to the aforesaid John son of Richard, £3,000 ; to be levied, in default of

land, three acres of wood, three acres of heath, and the third part of
the third part of a mill in Masefin. (*Ib.*, 33 Ed. I, No. 75.)

33 Ed. I (1305). Rotheric son of Griffin, and Katherine his wife,
v. Philip de Cawordyn, and Eva his wife. Manor of Masefen, except
four messuages, four bovates of land, six acres of wood, six acres of
heath, and two parts of a mill in the same manor. (*Ib.*, 33 Ed. I,
No. 76.)

By these fines Rhodri and his wife, Katharine, must have
acquired almost the whole of the manor of Masefen. A
township of this name is situated in the hundred of Malpas,
but it does not appear either as manor or vill in the
frequent enumerations of the properties held with the
barony of Malpas. It is described at p. 660 of vol. ii of
Ormerod's *History of Cheshire* (ed. Helsby). The manor of
Althurst, in the hundred of Nantwich (Ormerod, iii, 462),
which will be found later on to belong to Rhodri's
descendants, may also have been acquired by him, but no
evidence is at present forthcoming to that effect.

This concludes the review of Rhodri's Cheshire possessions and interests. He had also lands at Tatsfield or

payment, of his lands and chattels in co. Salop." (*Rot. Pat.*, 20 Ed. II,
m. 1*d.*; January 1327.)

The occasion for this transaction is not apparent, but the entries
upon the various rolls exhibit the point which I am at present
desirous of emphasising, namely, that Rhodri ap Gruffudd and
his son Thomas, with whom we shall deal presently, were without doubt brought into contact with John de Cherleton, lord of
Powys, by reason of their common connection with several of the
most important families of West Cheshire. The remainder to John
de Cherleton under the above fine never operated, because John de
Sutton, the younger, who had married de Cherleton's daughter, had
issue (*see* recovery entered on the plea roll for the 19th Hen. VIII).
De Cherleton married Hawys, the great-granddaughter of Gwen-
wynwyn, prince of Powys, in 1309 ; he died in 1353. No reference to
his earlier marriage, nor to Isabel, his daughter by that marriage,
appears in an article on "The Feudal Barons of Powys" in *Montgomeryshire Collections*, i, 261.

Tattelesfield in Surrey; but as, beyond the single reference to Roderic fitz Griffin, lord of the manor of Tates-
field, as having presented to the rectory of Tatsfield in
the year 1309-10, the evidences of his connection with
Surrey are obtained from entries relating to his son, we
will not enter upon them at this point.

Rhodri ap Gruffudd died in or soon after the year 1315.
He had been granted a sum of £40 per annum by Edward I
(*Rot. Pat.*, 20 Ed. I, *m.* 5; August 1292). Twenty-three
years later, for some unknown reason, this payment was
found to have got into arrear, and an order was then issued
that the deficiency should be made up (*Rot. Claus.*, 8 Ed.
II, *m.* 8; May 1315). Unfortunately no enquiry seems to
have been made into his possessions at his death. His
second wife, Katherine, whom he must have married soon
after the death of Beatrix de Malpas, survived him. He
left by her a son named Thomas, and it may be inferred,
from the total absence of evidence to the contrary, that
he had no other issue.

Thomas ap Rhodri, or Thomas son of Retherick, as he
is most frequently termed, seems to have obtained livery
of his father's estates in the ordinary course. He was
therefore over 21. Katherine, in right of dower, had eight
messuages and 17 acres of land in Newton, near Cudding-
ton, and her right as against Thomas is entered upon the
Cheshire plea roll of 9 and 10 Ed. II, *m.* 17, 1316. In the
next year he was party to a fine levied upon a tenement in
Horton, near Malpas (*ib.*, 10 and 11 Ed. II, *m.* 5*d*); and in
1318-9 we meet with his name upon the recognizance roll
of Chester for that year as surety for William de Burstow,
the chamberlain of Chester (*m.* 1*d* [13]). This is the
last we hear of him in connection with Cheshire, and he
seems between this period and that of his death in 1364 to

have parted with all his property in that county,[1] with,
perhaps, the exception of the manor of Althurst. His
name, however, is to be frequently met with upon the
close and patent rolls for the next few years in connection
with his Surrey estate of Tatsfield. These entries are for
the most part acknowledgments of monies borrowed
from different individuals,[2] who, for their greater security,
had the transactions noted upon the public records, and
it is clear therefrom that Thomas was not flourishing in
Surrey. He nevertheless seems to have made Tatsfield his
usual residence, for we find him a witness to a conveyance
of land in the vicinity in October 1331 (*Rot. Pat.*, 5 Ed. III,
p. 1, *m.* 4*d*). A John de Stoket, of Oxsted (*Rot. Claus.*,
14 Ed. II, *m.* 10*d*) also attests the same deed, and with
this person Thomas had several transactions. A grant of
the year 1324, by Thomas filius Rethericus de Tatlesfelde,
to John Stokete and his son John in fee tail, of certain
lands in Tatlesfelde, is amongst the Harley Charters
(56 H. 21) in the British Museum; and a release, dated
31 Ed. III (1358), by Thomas Rethery, of 7*s.* 7*d.*, part of a
rent arising out of certain tenements in Tattlesfeld,

---

[1] In *Ancient Deeds*, iii, 392 (No. C. 3644), is the following:—"Demise
by Robert de Huxleyg to Urien de Eggerton of all the lands and
tenements which he had in Neuton by Holdecastel of the demise of
Thomas son of Rotheric de Tattlesfield, with all liberties &c., in the
wood of Holdecastel belonging to the said lands. A.D. 1333."

[2] Gilbert de Balsham, of London, "soler," £20 (1320); John de
Mockyng, of Somerset, fishmonger of London, £32 (1325); Thomas de
Evenefeld, of London, "spicer," 100 marks, (1325); Andrew Aubrey
and other executors of the will of William de Evenefeld put in their
places William de Wyckewane to prosecute the execution of a recognizance for 100 marks made to him in chancery by Thomas son of
Rotheric de Tatelesfeld (*Rot. Pat.*, 3 Ed. III, *m.* 36*d*; Feb. 1329);
Adam de Sarum, of London, "spicer," puts in his place William de
Wykewan to prosecute the execution of a recognizance for 100 marks
made to him in chancery by Thomas son of Rotheric de Tatelesfeld (*ib.*, *m.* 35*d*; Feb. 1329).

to one of the same John Stokets is amongst the Cotton Charters (xxix, 8) in the same institution. The latter document still bears the seal of Thomas, thus described in the British Museum *Catalogue of Seals:* " A shield of arms ; quarterly, in each quarter a lion rampant. Between, three pairs of sprigs." The inscription is very indistinct, but it is tolerably certain that the name inserted in the deed followed the form upon the seal, and that the inscription is therefore to be read " S. Thome Rethery." It is difficult to recognise in Thomas Rethery the nephew of prince Llewelyn ap Gruffudd, but there can be little doubt that Thomas, at all events in his capacity as a Surrey landowner, had forsaken the Welsh method of ancestral nomenclature, and had adopted the English mode of forming personal names. The arms upon the seal are those ascribed (with doubtful accuracy) to his uncle, prince Llewelyn.

Whether Thomas's position in Surrey may have been a declining one, or not, he held this property at his death, and it may be that his borrowings upon the security of the Tatsfield estate were expended in the purchase of lands elsewhere. For we next find that he had obtained the small manor of Budefeld, or Bidfield, in the county of Gloucester. This is a mesne manor, a member of the manor of Bisley in the hundred of the same name. Atkins, in his *History of Gloucestershire* (p. 147), observes of Bidfield : " Owen de Roderick was seised of Bidfield, in the reign of king Edward the Third ; but he being attainted for rebellion, Bidfield was granted to Mary Herney, widow of William Herney, 47 Ed. III." Fosbrooke's *Abstracts of Records and Manuscripts respecting the County of Gloucester* (1807) has the following additional particulars :—

" *Bisley.*—This large place contains Avenage, Bidfield, Bussage, Chalford, Ockerige, Tunley, Dennaway, Steanbridge, Troham or Throughgham, a separate manor. In an extent of the lands, which were Rich. de Clare's, Earl of Gloucester, Busseley, with appurtenances and liberties, is valued at £32 6s. 8d. per ann. (Esc., 47 Hen. III, No. 35). Hugh le Despencer, (who had marr. Eleanor, a co-heir of the Earldom of Gloucester), Joan, wife of Humphr. de Bohun, and Hugh Cerne, of Bisley, held the M[anor] and Hund. 9 Ed. I (Nom. Villar.) . . . . Upon Despencer's attainder, Roger de Mortimer, for services done to Q. Isab. had a grant of a mess. and 10 librates of land (Pat. 1 Ed. III). . . . . Not long after, Edw. son of Hugh le Despencer, Earl of Glamorgan, who had a release of the lands of his mother's inheritance, held this M[anor], i.e. what had not been granted to Mortimer (Pasch. Fines, 41 Ed. III). Humphr. de Bohun, Earl of Essex, Hereford, and Northampton, died seized of part of a fee here, which Edw. Earl of March, held, and of the advowson of the second turn of presentation to the church, whose temporals were worth per ann., with accidents, 20 marks (Esc., 46 Ed. III, No. 10). Owen ap Thomas Hetherwicke, a traitor, joining with the French, held a mess. caruc. and a half, of the Earl of Heref. in Budefield, there being 3 acr. of wood, 18 of mead[ow], and 36s. per ann. rent of assize from free and customary tenants, with pleas and perquis[ites] of court (Esc., 43 Ed. III, pars ii), which lands were gr[anted] to Mary Hervey, wid. of Will. Hervey, 47 Ed. III (Sir R. Atkins)."

Attention is particularly directed to the fact that Thomas here comes into contact with the powerful houses of Despenser and Hereford, but no official record breaks the silence upon the relations that existed between them.

So far as I have been able to discover Rhodri had no interest in Wales at the time of his death. Thomas, on the other hand, by means which are not apparent, became possessed of a small estate in Montgomeryshire. He also made an unsuccessful effort to obtain some of the patrimony of his ancestors by claiming directly as the eldest surviving male descendant of the line of Gruffudd ap Llewelyn ap Iorwerth.

I have said that during his lifetime Thomas must have parted with practically the whole of his lands in Cheshire, for the inquisition taken after his death, which will be set forth presently, makes no reference to any property in that county; though it may be that the enquiry

into this portion of his estates would be conducted by the
escheator of the earl of Chester (and prince of Wales),
and returned into the earl's exchequer at Chester. We
know, also, that between A.D. 1320 and 1340, John de
Cherleton of Powys, was acquiring lands in Cheshire
in the interest of his daughter Isabel de Sutton. It
is quite probable that an exchange may have been effected
with Thomas ap Rhodri, by which the latter relinquished
his Cheshire estates for the manor of Dynas, a mesne
manor within the manor of Mechain Iscoed, a part of the
inheritance which John de Cherleton enjoyed in right of
his wife, Hawys, the last of the line of Owen Cyfeiliog.[1]
De Cherleton may have been glad of the opportunity of
introducing into a region which was the scene of constant disagreement and tumult between himself and his
relation by marriage, Griffin de la Pole, a Welsh proprietor who should have almost as strong sentimental
claims to the adhesion of his tenants as one of their own
Powysian lords. Be this as it may, we find Thomas in the
year 1333 in possession of the manor of Dynas.[2] The

---

[1] The history of the commote, afterwards the manor of Mechain
Iscoed, presents great difficulties. An article upon the "Ancient
Lords of Mechain" in the first volume of *Montgomeryshire Collections*,
exhibits these difficulties, but, unfortunately, does nothing towards
their dispersal. "A history of the parish of Llanfechain" in vol. v
of the same publication gives no help upon the point of how the
manor came into the hands of Hawys and de Cherleton. However, it
was almost certainly in their possession in the year 1313 (*Rot. Claus.*,
6 Ed. II, *m.* 18), and, notwithstanding the efforts of Griffin de la Pole,
uncle of Hawys, who held it for a time by virtue of the king's order
(*Rot. Claus.*, 12 Ed. II, *m.* 26 ; October 1318), it still remains (with
the exception of the mesne manor of Dynas) in the barony of Powys.

[2] The present name of the manor is Plas yn Dinas. The author
of the "History of the parish of Llanfechain" (*Mont. Coll.*, v, 203-
284) observes (p. 253) that "all the southern, and a great portion of
the northern part of the parish [of Llanfechain] is in the manor

following entry finds him in that year not only exercising
full proprietary rights there, but also reveals him as a
married man :—

"Licence for Thomas ap Rotheryk to enfeoff John Stoket of the
lands in Dynas and Megheniskoyt in North Wales, which he holds in
chief, and for the said John to re-grant them to him, Cicely his wife,
and their heirs." (*Rot. Pat.*, 7 Ed. III, *p.* 1, *m.* 29; Jan. 1333.)

He was not permitted to remain long in peace.
By an undated petition, but which is of the year 1337-8,
Thomas complains to the king and his council that he has
been disseised of his lands by John de Cherleton ; he has
started an action against the aggressor, but de Cherleton
has been able to stay the proceedings, wherefore he,

of Plas yn Dinas, now [1872] in the possession of the Rev. W. C. E.
Kynaston, of Hardwick. It is called a mesne manor, within the
manor of Mechain Iscoed ; and, in fact, is not substantially a manor,
being parcelled off from the above lordship. Sometime previous to
A.D. 1568, a claim had been made by Edward Kynaston, of Hordley,
an ancestor of the late Sir J. R. Kynaston, of Hardwick and Hordley,
to the title and possessions of the Charletons and Greys, Lords of
Powys, on the ground of the alleged illegitimacy of Edward Grey,
then in possession. The suit was compromised by the surrender of
the portions of Mechain Iscoed called Plas yn Dinas and Trewern
with all their rights, liberties and seigniorities, to Kynaston, and the
deed bears date 10 Eliz. 1568. . . . . Where this Dinas was has
never been satisfactorily shewn. The old entrenchment by the river
Efernwy can scarcely be thought so. This is a construction of very
early date, and has not on it the least vestige of any buildings,
which could scarcely have failed to exist, had there been any, in
10 Eliz. 1568. The word ' Plas,' prefixed, will serve to show that
there was a residence, a mansion existing somewhere in the manor,
at the time ; and Welshmen will remember that ' Plas ' is a comparatively modern term, never applied to the fortified and stronger
abodes of the ancients. The origin of the name, Plas yn Dinas, and
the site, are matters still to be sought for." Elsewhere in the same
article the writer, speaking of the farm called " Ty Coch," says that
it is " in the very heart " of the manor of Plas yn Dinas.

Thomas, prays redress. The petition is in the following terms :—

(*Public Record Office: Ancient Petitions. No.* 10310.)

" A n're seign'r le Roi 't son conseil monstre son bacheler Thomas Rotherik q' come il porta vue assise de nouele disseisine v[ersu]s Johan de Cherleton' 't Hawise sa fem'e 't Johan le fitz Johan de Cherleton' 't aut's de son f[r]aunk ten[auntes] en g'aunt Molencok 't aut's villes en la Marche de Gales, la quele assise feut delaie g'uunt temps auant lan unzisme, quel an le dit Johan de Cherleton' p[ar] cause qil estoit ordine Justice Dirlande pa[r]chacea un bref a les Justices des assises a continuer la dite assise tanq' il demorast issint en Irlaund, et puis ap's se vonie en Engla'de les ditz Johan 't Hawise responderent come tenant, 't le dit Johan fitz Johan 't touz les aut's nomez en le bref firent defaute p' qi defaute lassise feut agarde deu's eux, et puis p' excepcions 't alleggances compassez nient v'itablement feurent ajournez en com'un Bank ou plede feust alassise 't la dite assise remande en pais a p'ndre come piert p' le teno'r de la dite assise qest cosu a ceste peticion, et ore en le men temps le dit Johan fitz Johan compassant a delaier la dite assise plus auant, 't est ale outre meer, 't ad p'rchace un bref a les dites Justices a continuer lassise tanq' il dem'ra la outre, 't puis son aler le dit Johan de cherlton ad feffe le dit Johan fitz Johan 't aut's, la ou ils ne ancient riens deuant en les ditz tenz, p' qoi les dites Justices ne ont mie volu de aler a lassise. Dont le dit Thomas p[ri]e p[ar] dieu remedie qil ne soit desherite p' cieux faux compassementz."

Thomas's plaint is borne out by the following abstract of an entry upon the patent rolls for 1338 :—

" To the justices of the [Common] Bench. Order to continue in the same state in which it now is the assize of novel disseisin which Thomas Retheryk arrained before William de Shareshull and his fellow justices of assize in co. Salop against John de Cherleton, whom the king has appointed justiciary of Ireland, who is staying in that land, and Hawisia his wife, and others contained in the original writ, concerning tenements in Great Melencok, Thledreth, Kithleveno, Stradeneroy, Thlanershemereys, Bodenwal, Thlannegheyn, Doluaur, Codwynnayn, Roulas, Garthloulgh, and Pymyrth, which assize is adjourned before the justices on account of certain difficulties in it, while John is staying in the king's service in accordance with the ordinance made at Nottingham." (*Rot. Pat.,* 11 Ed. III, *p.* 2, *m.* 8*d.*)

It would seem that the quarrel resulted in Thomas's favour. At any rate he continued in legal if not physical possession of the manor; but fresh arrangements were soon entered into, as appears by the following :—

"Licence in consideration of a fine made by John de Cherleton, the elder, for Thomas Rotherik, knight, to enfeoff William de Lake, chaplain, and Robert de Blakenhale, chaplain, of the manor of Dynas, held in chief, and for them to regrant the same in tail to him and Cicily his wife, with remainder in tail to the said John and Hawisia his wife, and reversion to the right heirs of Hawisia. By fine of £20 paid in the hanaper." (*Rot. Pat.*, 15 Ed. III, *p.* 2, *m.* 46; 4 June 1341.)[1]

This is practically the last we learn of Thomas in connection with the manor of Dinas, until we come to the inquisition into that property taken after his death in A.D. 1364.

There is, however, one interesting event in Thomas's career which has been brought to light by these researches, namely, his claim to succeed to the cantred of Lleyn (co. Carnarvon) as next heir to his uncle, Owen ap Gruffudd. It is necessary to devote our attention to this incident, since its failure may have engendered feelings of resentment towards the English in the mind of Thomas or of his son.

Owen ap Gruffudd has always been regarded as having been the eldest son of Gruffudd ap Iorwerth, Llewelyn coming next, David next, and Rhodri last, with possibly a Gruffudd coming between David and Rhodri.[2] The

---

[1] Entries connected with the same transaction will also be found upon the Originalia Roll for the 15 Ed. III, and in the Inq. post mortem for the same year.

[2] We learn from the patent roll of the 3rd Edward III, that there was also a sister named Margaret, who is altogether unknown to our writers of history, a circumstance which may be commended to those who are clamouring for the teaching of Welsh history in our colleges. According to the Record Office *Calendar* she had lands in Bodenham and Thlen, places which are indexed as Bodenham and

masterful temper of Llewelyn soon gave him the lead over his brothers, with the almost necessary result, under the tribal form of political and social administration, of driving Owen and David into strong opposition. By the compact with Edward the First in 1277, the English king compelled Llewelyn to consent to admit both Owen and David into the overlordship, the one of the cantred of Lleyn, the other of the 'dominium' of Snowdon; but whether the arrangement was actually carried out, or how the particular divisions were allocated, is recorded by no chronicle or record so far as I am aware.[1] But we do learn from the documents now to be submitted that Lleyn had, at some time, come into the possession of Owen. He is not mentioned as having taken any part in the last struggle of Llewelyn and David, and the silence of the chroniclers has led to the inference that he was already dead. This was probably not the case. It is more likely that by standing aloof from the unexpected

Thleu, respectively, without suggestion that they relate to Wales. Thleu is, of course, a misreading for Thlen=Lleyn; but it is more difficult to identify Bodenham or Bodeneham. Two places in the adjoining commote of Gaflogion appear in the *Rec. of Caernarvon* as Bodenael (p. 27), and Botenytheth (p. 30). It may be well to mention that in the same index 'Margaret' does not appear under the letter M, but is referred to under 'Llewelyn.'

[1] In the early part of his life David had possessed Lleyn, or some part of it, for in 1252, as dominus de Cwmwd Maen, he entered into a composition with the abbot and convent of Bardsey (*Rec. of Caernarvon*, 252). He was probably despoiled of this property by his brother Llewelyn during one of their frequent fraternal quarrels. So late as the year 1316 we find a release to the abbot and convent of Cymmer of a sum of 39s. which had been unjustly extorted from them by David ap Gruffud, brother of Llewelin, prince of Wales, and lord of the Cantred of Thleyn. (*Rot. Pat.*, 9 Ed. II, *p.* 1, *m.* 4.) This entry provides us with a date for some of the important petitions included in the *Record of Caernarvon*, p. 217 *et seq.*, which, in the preface to that work (p. iv), appear to be attributed to the 33 Ed. III.

and, in the main, unjustifiable outbreak of his brothers,
he secured the commendations and rewards of Edward,
and either received or was continued in the lordship of
Lleyn. He died before the year 1307. At some period
after the accession of Edward the Third (1327) his nephew
Thomas presented a petition to the king and his council
praying that directions should be given to the justices,
(presumably of North Wales), to enquire into his right to
succeed the said Owen as his next heir. The petition runs
as follows :—

(Public Record Office : Ancient Petitions. No. 6790.)

" A le Roi 't a son conseil monstre Thomas Rotheryk' qe p[ar]
la . . . . dit Thomas ad suy p' diu[er]ses petitions . . . .
parlementz 't de s[ur] celes petitions ad eu diu'ses briefs as diu'ses
Justices denquere p'r le heritage de dit Thomas cest assauoir p'r les
t[er]res de Thlen en Northwales les queux lui dussent descendre
auxicom le droit de . . . . cle . . . . p'schein heir cest assauoir
Owayn ap Griffith m[our]ust en son demeigne com de fee
't a la f . . . . dit seign'r le Roi d'au[oir] c[er]tifie la Court des
choses contenus en les dites briefs . . . . queux Justices rien
ne volemt faire ne c'tifier . . . . a n're dit seign'r le Roi a son
conseil qils voillent comander briefs as Justices denquere si le dit
Owayn m[ou]rust come au[an]t est dit, et si le dit Thomas soit heir
pluis p'schein com auant est dit 't s'r ces ret'rner [l]enquest essent q'
le dit Thomas ne soit . . . . es delaye de son droit."

A writ of the king was accordingly issued in these
terms :—

(Ancient Petitions. No. 6791.)

" Rex ad Camerarium nostrum de Northwallia vel ejus locum
tenentem, Salutem. Monstravit nobis Thomas filius Rotherici ap
Griffith per peticionem suam coram nobis . . . . apud North[1] con-
vocato exhibitam quod cum Audoenus ap Griffith aunculus predicti
Thome cujus heres ipse est dudum tempore Edwardi Regis Angliæ avi
nostri tenuisset Cantredum de Thlen in Northwallia ut hereditatem
suam et inde obiisset seisitus ad fidem ipsius . . . . et post

---

[1] Northampton. Parliaments of Edward the Third were held here
in 1328, 1336 and 1338.

cujus mortem dictus avus noster Cantredum prædictum eo quod de dicto avo nostro tenebatur in capite capi fecit in manum suam per quod dictus Rothericus frater et heres præfati Audoeni per peticiones suas in diversis parliamentis dicti avi nostri exhibitas sequebatur de seisina cantredi prædicti habenda, et quod in prosecucione sua hujusmodi antiquam seisinam Cantredi prædicti assecutus fuit [die quo] obiit per quod dictum Cantredum in manu dicti avi n'ri et postmodum in manu domini E. nuper Regis Angliæ patris n'ri hujusmodi occacione extitit et adhuc in manu n'ra existit super quibus idem Thomas per peticionem suam prædictam nobis supplicavit ut sibi super liberacione Cantredi prædicti justiciam facere curaremus : Nos igitur eidem Thomæ in hac parte fieri volentes quod est iustum vobis mandamus quod per inquisiciones inde faciendas et aliis viis et modis quibus melius poteritis nos diligenter informetis si dictus Audoenus fuit seisitus de Cantredo prædicto in dominico suo ut de feodo die quo obiit. Et si dictum Cantredum ad manum dicti avi n'ri per mortem ipsius Audoeni devenit et adhuc in manu n'ra existit ut prædictum est et qualiter et quo modo et si dictus Thomas propinquior hæres ejus sit et cujus ætatis et quantum Cantredum prædictum valeat per annum in omnibus exitibus et de eo quod inde inveniri contigerit nos distincte et aperte sub sigillis vestris et sigillis eorum per quos facta fuerit inquisicio in Cancellaria n'ra sine dilatione reddatis certiores. Teste, etc."

It is possible that a return was made to this writ, and that it may be entered upon the rolls of some branch of the administration that have not yet been examined. It has not yielded itself up to a diligent search, and we are accordingly left with a half-told tale. We do know, however, that Thomas did not obtain the object of his petition.

Thomas died in May 1363, having survived his wife a little less than two years. The king's writ to the escheator of Salop, dated Westminster, the 1st of June in the 37th year of his reign, for the customary inquisition into his estate, is prefixed to the return, which is as follows :—

(*Inquisitiones post mortem.   37 Ed. III, No. 59, first nos.*)

" Inquisitio capta apud Salop' coram Ph'o de Lutteley escaetore domini Regis in comitatu Salop' ac marchiis Walliæ eidem comitatui adjacente, septimo die Junii anno regni Regis Edwardi tercii post conquestum tricesimo septimo virtute brevis domini Regis huic inquisitioni consuti per sacramentum Iuain ap Ior', Eyno' ap Ior',

Eyno' ap Griffri, Ior' ap Tud'r, Ior' ap Griffri, ll' ap Griffri, Ieua' ap Ior' ap D'd, Dauid ap M'ed', M'ed' ap Tud'r M'ed' ap Gruffud, Mad' ap Ken' et Cad' Vagha', Qui dicunt super sacramentum suum quod Thomas Rothery chivaler defunctus in brevi contentus non tenuit aliquas terras seu tenementa de domino Rege in capite in dominico suo ut de feodo die quo obiit in balliva mea, nec de aliquo alio, sed dicunt quod prædictus Thomas tenuit die quo obiit manerium de Dynas de d'no Rege in capite sibi et Ceciliæ uxori ejus et heredibus de corporibus ipsorum Thomæ et Ceciliæ exeuntibus, et si predicti Thomas et Cecilia obierunt sine herede de corporibus suis exeunte, tunc post decessum ipsorum Thomæ et Ceciliæ prædictum manerium cum pertinentiis integre remaneret Johanni de Cherleton seniori et Hawisiæ uxori ejus et heredibus de corporibus ipsorum Johannis et Hawisiæ exeuntibus, tenendum de d'no Rege et heredibus suis per servicia quæ ad prædictum pertinentin perpetuum, secundum tenorem cujusdam finis in Curia domini Regis levati prout in prædicto fine plenius continetur. Et dicunt quod prædictus Thomas tenuit manerium prædictum de domino Rege in capite in forma prædicta per servicium quartæ partis unius feodi militis. In quo quidem manerio est unum capitale messuagium quod nichil valet p' annum ultra repris'. Et sunt ibidem decem acræ t're arabiles in d'nico quarum quælibet acra valet p' annum viijs. Et sunt ibidem duæ acræ prati quarum acra valet p' annum ijs. Et est ibidem quidam boscus separalis cujus herbagium valet p' annum ijs. Et subboscus ejusdem nullus. Et sunt ibidem duo molendina aquatica quæ valent p' annum xxs. Et est ibidem de redditu assisæ liberorum tenentium et nativorum decem marcæ p' annum solvendæ ad f'm omnium sanctorum. Et opera custumaria ibidem in autumpno ad messionem bladorum d'ni valent p' annum iiijs. Placita et perquisita Curiæ ibidem valent p' annum xls. Item dicunt quod prædictus Thomas obiit xxix die Maii ultimo prædicto [præterito] sine heræde de corporibus ipsorum Thome et Ceciliæ uxoris ejus exeunte. Et dicunt quod prædicta Cecilia obiit xij die Septembr' anno regni Regis Edwardi tercii post conquestum tricesimo quinto. Item dicunt quod prædictum manerium de Dynas cum suis pertinentiis integre remanere debet Joh'i de Cherleton' chivaler d'no Powisiæ filio et herædi Joh'is de Cherleton' chivaler filii et herædis Joh'is de Cherleton' senioris et Hawisiæ qui sunt partes finis prædicti, eo quod prædicti Thomas Rothery et Cecilia uxor ejus obierunt sine herede de corporibus ipsorum Thomæ et Ceciliæ exeunte. Et dicunt quod prædictus Joh'es de Cherleton' chivaler hic [? fil'] prædicti Joh'is de Cherleton senioris dominus Powisiæ est ætatis viginti sex annorum et amplius. In cujus rei testimonium huic inquisitioni juratores prædicti sigilla sua apposuerunt." [The seals are not now appendant.]

Two points of importance in this document call for remark. Firstly, it will be noticed that Thomas is said to
have held no land of the king in chief except only the
manor of Dynas, a statement corroborated by a later
inquisition which will be dealt with presently. Tatsfield
he had parted with, and Budefeld he held of the earl of
Hereford. The Cheshire manor of Althurst would be
held of the prince of Wales as earl of Chester. The
second point is that he is described as leaving no heir,
whereby the manor of Dynas passed to John de Cherleton
in virtue of the fine that had been levied. Now, were this
statement correct, the hypothesis upon which we have
proceeded would instantly be seen to be baseless, and our
entire argument would collapse. But it can be demonstrated by the following most interesting entry upon the
rolls of the court of Chancery that the jurors at Salop
were mistaken :—

(Public Record Office : Placita de Cancellaria. No. 67.)

" Placita coram domino Rege in Cancellaria sua apud Westmonasterium in crastino sancti Martini anno regni Regis Edwardi tercii a
conquestu tricesimo nono.

" Dominus Rex mandavit breve suum vicecomiti Salop' in hæc verba ;
Edwardus dei gratia Rex Angliæ, dominus Hiberniæ et Aquitaniæ
vicecomiti Salop', Salutem. Cum per inquisicionem per Philipem de
Lutteleye escaetorem nostrum in com. prædicto de mandato nostro
factam, et in Cancellaria nostra retornatam sit computum quod
Thomas Rotheryk' chivaler, defunctus, tenuit tam in dominico quam
in servicio die quo obiit manerium de Dynas cum pertinentiis in
Marchia Walliæ de nobis in capite per servicium militare, et quod
Audoenus filius prædicti Thomæ est heres ejusdem Thomæ propinquior
et est plene ætatis, quodque Johannes de Chorleton' chivaler, dominus
de Powys clamans jus in manerio prædicto post mortem prædicti
Thomæ per finem inde in curia nostra levatum supponendo ipsum
Thomam fore mortuum et nullum heredem de corpore prædicti
Thomæ procreatum esse superstitem, eo quod idem Audoenus tunc
in longinquis partibus existit seisinam de manerio prædicto cum
pertinentiis a nobis prosecutus fuit et nobis homagium pro eodem
manerio fecit et exitus et proficua inde hucusque percepit, per quod

E

idem Audoenus nobis supplicavit ut cum manerium prædictum cum
pertinentiis præfato Johanni in ipsius Audoeni exheredationem
liberatum existit velimus ei super hoc de remedio congruo facere
providere, Nos volentes in hac parte fieri quod est justum tibi
præcipimus quod scire faciatis præfato Johanni quod sit coram nobis in
Cancellaria nostra in crastino S'ci Martini proximo futuro ubicunque
tunc fuerit ad ostendendum siquid pro se habeat vel dicere sciat quare
manerium prædictum cum pertinentiis in manum nostram resumi et
præfato Audoeno ut filio et propinquiori heredi ejusdem Thomæ
liberari nobisque de exitibus ejusdem manerii a tempore mortis
ejusdem Thomæ per ipsum Johannem perceptis responderi non debeat
et ad faciendum ulterius et recipiendum quod curia nostra con-
sideraverit in hac parte. Et habeas ibi nomina illorum per quos ei
scire feceris et hoc breve. Teste me ipso apud Westmonasterium
decimo die Octobris anno regni nostri tricesimo nono.

"Ad quem diem prædictus Joh'es de Chorleton' per Johannem de
Lancastre clericum attornatum suum venit et dicit quod quidam finis
levatus fuit in curia domini Regis apud Westmonasterium a die
sanctæ Trinitatis in xv dies anno regni Edwardi regis Angliæ tercii
a conquestu xv, coram Rogero Hilary et sociis suis tunc justicariis,
etc. inter Thomam Rotheryk' chivaler et Ceciliam uxorem ejus
quærentes et Willelmum de Lake capellanum et Robertum de Blake-
male capellanum deforcientes, de manerio prædicto cum pertinentiis
quod quidem manerium est in Marchia Walliæ per quem quidem finem
prædictus Thomas recognovit manerium prædictum cum pertinentiis
esse jus ipsorum Willelmi et Roberti ut illud quod iidem Willelmus et Robertus habuerunt de dono prædicti Thomæ, pro
qua quidem recognitione fine et concordia iidem Willelmus et
Robertus concesserunt prædictis Thomæ et Ceciliæ prædictum
manerium cum pertinentiis et illud eis reddiderunt in eadem
curia habendum et tenendum eisdem Thomæ et Ceciliæ et heredibus de corporibus ipsorum Thomæ et Ceciliæ exeuntibus de
domino Rege et heredibus suis per servicia que ad prædictum
manerium pertinenda inperpetuum, ita quod si iidem Thomas et
Cecilia obierunt sine herede de corporibus suis exeunte quod . . . . .
manerium prædictum cum pertinentiis integre remaneret Johanni de
Chorleton' seniori et Hawisiæ uxori ejus et heredibus de corporibus
ipsorum Johanni [et Hawisiæ] exeuntibus, tenendum in forma
prædicta, etc. Ita quod si iidem Johannes et Hawysia obierunt sine
herede de corporibus suis exeunte manerium prædictum cum
pertinentiis integre remaneret rectis heredibus ipsius Hawisiæ
tenendum in forma prædicta, et dicit quod prædicti Johannes
et Hawisia obierunt et ipse Johannes de Chorleton' junior est
consanguineus et heres prædictorum Joh'is et Hawisiæ videlicet

filius Joh'is filii prædictorum Joh'is de Chorleton' senioris et Hawisiæ
et heres ipsius Hawisiæ in forma prædicta, et dicit quod tempore mortis
prædicti Thomæ et per plures annos antea prædictus Audoenus fuit in
partibus longinquis, ita quod de esse ipsius Audoeni non habebat
noticia prout per inquisitionem virtute cujusdam brevis domini Regis
de diem clausit extremum post mortem prædicti Thomæ coram
Philipo de Luttcleye escaetore domini Regis computum fuit per quod
prædictus Johannes de Chorleton' junior virtute finis et inquisitionis
prædictorum per debitum processum in Cancellaria domini Regis
factum ut consanguineus . . . . prædicti Johannis de Chorleton'
senioris et Hawisiæ seisinam et liberationem de manerio prædicto
optinuit, et sic salvo sibi et heredibus suis vel suo virtute finis
prædicti per jus de remanere juxta tenorem finis illius non dedicit
quin prædictus Audoenus . . . . et heres prædictorum Thomæ
et Ceciliæ de corporibus ipsorum Thomæ et Ceciliæ et ei dictum manerium per mortem prædicti Thomæ patris sui . . . . . Audoeno
ut filio et heredi præfati Thomæ liberari debet, per quod consideratum
est quod prædictum manerium . . . . Audoeno liberetur, salvis
Regi exitibus de eodem manerio tempore mortis prædicti Thomæ
perceptis de . . . . ad scaccarium suum."

The insuperable obstacle with which we were confronted
turns out, therefore, to be no obstacle at all; but, were it
not for the fortunate preservation of the above document
it would have been impossible ever to have proved the
identification of Owen of Wales with the family of Griffith
ap Llewelyn ap Iorwerth. Thomas ap Rhodri died leaving
a son, and that son succeeded in making good his claim to
his father's estate. Owen was away in foreign parts, and
probably did not hear of his father's death until many
months after its occurrence.

Now, it is clear that in order to prepare and present his
petition to the king Owen must have returned to this
country probably at least six months before November
1365, when the decree of the Chancellor was pronounced
which restored the manor of Dynas to its rightful owner.
But if it was double the length of time (and it could not
well have been more) it cannot be said that he had suffered
much by the law's delays. It is possible that he had to

take legal proceedings for the assertion of his claim of
succession to the little estate in Budefeld, and to his
reversionary rights in Tatsfield ; or it may be that the
decision of the Chancellor in his favour in respect of the
most important of his possessions was at once accepted as
applicable to the rest.   How long he had been away from
England, or what had been his career, it is impossible to
conjecture.   Froissart says that Owen de Galles had come
to the court of France quite a youth, had become a favourite
with the king, and had fought, presumably (though by no
means necessarily), upon the French side at Poictiers
(A.D. 1356).   It is somewhat difficult to credit the last
statement, as it is improbable that he would have ventured
back to England a few years later, unless, indeed, upon
learning of his father's death he had made his peace with
the English king and his council.   And had he been known
to have fought in the ranks of the French it is probable
that some remark thereupon would have been made in the
record of the proceedings before the Chancellor.   But the
evident fact that his existence was quite unknown to the
jurors who served upon the inquest taken at Shrewsbury
upon his father's death, points to the conclusion that he
had been long absent from England.   The jury upon that
occasion was formed entirely of Welshmen, several of whom
at least, from the necessity of obtaining local information
respecting the character and value of the property, would
have come from the manor of Dynas.   They may have been
coerced by fear of de Cherleton, who was upon the spot,
but the difficulty could have been got over by returning
what is termed an open verdict.   It is, indeed, impossible
to resist the conclusion that they knew nothing of Owen ;
and if they, the tenants of Dynas, knew little, how much
less the rest of the Principality.

  Events were peaceful in England, and the quiet life of

a country gentleman probably did not accord with the restless and adventurous spirit of Owen. In less than six months he had turned his back upon England, which he was destined never to see again. According to his own statement, made a few years later, he proceeded to divers foreign courts, pouring into unsympathetic ears the story of his wrongs, and dragging

"at each remove a lengthening chain."

So long as he continued the heart-breaking course of a political refugee the English authorities appear to have taken no heed of him.[1] He at last determined upon renewing his acquaintance with the French court, and thither he proceeded.

The affairs of France were at their worst when the accession of Charles the Fifth, in April 1364, aroused hopes in the partizans of that country that a policy of more determined resistance to the English would be adopted. Owen's previous acquaintance with the young nobles of the French court would naturally lead him to side with them in the struggle that everything portended was soon about to be re-opened; or he may have joined one of the bands of Free Companies that were impartially preying upon the territories of both parties. Preparations had been going on for some time, and on the 29th April 1369 war was declared

---

[1] Woodward, *History of Wales*, ii, 564, says that Owen "served under Duguesclin in the war respecting the possession of the throne of Castile between Peter the Cruel and Henry of Transtamare." There is no evidence that Owen took part in the Spanish war of 1366-7, and the fact that his English estates were not then confiscated proves that he was not known to be fighting against the Black Prince in that campaign. Woodward is also wrong in stating that, "in the course of this war it happened that the earl of Pembroke and some of his knights were made prisoners by the French; whereupon Yvain, hearing of it, went and taunted the earl," &c. This incident took place, as we shall see, several years after the Spanish war.

between France and England. Whatever may be thought of the nature of Owen's position amongst the French prior to this date, it is clear that his continuance with them, and open and active hostility to their enemies, transformed him, from the English point of view, into a traitor and enemy to the English king. His property in this country was forfeited, and in order to know its character and extent the following inquisitions were taken :—

(*Public Record Office: Inquisitiones post mortem. 43 Edward III, Part 2, No. 4 second numbers.*)

[The writs issued to the several escheators are in identical terms. They commence]—"Quia pro certo didicimus quod Owinus ap Thomas Rotherik inimicis nostris de Francia est adherens et cum ipsis inimicis nostris contra nos et fideles nostros in partibus transmarinis de guerra equitavit contra fidem et ligeanciam suam, per quod omnia terræ et tenementa bona et catalla sua infra regnum nostrum Angliæ et alibi infra potestatem nostram ad nos tanquam nobis forisfacta dignoscuntur pertinere, Nos volentes, etc.

"Inquisitio capta apud le Pole [Welshpool] coram Willelmo Banastre de Yorton, escaetore domini Regis in comitatu Salop' et Marchiis Walliæ eidem comitatui adjacente xxiij° die Decembris anno regni regis Edwardi tercii post conquestum quadragesimo tercio virtute brevis domini Regis huic inquisitioni consuti per sacramentum Willelmi Scherer, Ricardi Symmes, Joh'is le Smyth, Ricardi Rot', Meredith ap Griffith, Howel ap Tudur, Morgan Loyd, Eynon ap Ior', Madok ap Ken'uic, Madok ap Howel, Yevan Scholayg, et Madoc Says, Qui dicunt super sacramentum suum quod Owinus ap Thomas Rotherik inimicis domini Regis de Francia adherens habuit et tenuit die adhesionis videlicet xx° die Octobris ultimo præterito manerium de Dynas cum pertinenciis in Marchiis Walliæ prædicto com' Salop' adjacentem in feodo talliato secundum formam cujusdam finis in curia d'ni Regis levati prout continetur in quadam cedula huic inquisitioni consuta.[1] In quo quidem manerio de Dynas est unum capitale[m] messuagium quod nichil valet p' annum ultra reprisas.

---

[1] A copy of the final concord is appended to the inquisition, but as its terms are accurately set forth in the Chancery proceedings already dealt with, it is omitted here.

Et est ibidem una carucata terræ que val' p' annum   xxs.

„ quedam placea prati que val' p' a'm   xiijs. iiijd.

„ quoddam molendinum aquaticum dimissum
ad firmam pro   xxs.
p' annum solvend'ad terminos Annunc' b'te
Mariæ et S. Mich'is equis porcionibus

„ quidam boscus vocatur Fryth Dynas cujus
herbagium val' p' a'   ijs.

„ quedam placea pasturæ separalis subtus
boscum prædictum quæ val' p' a'   vs.

„ quidam alius boscus vocatur Garthboulch
cujus pastura val' p' a'   iiijs.

„ de redditu assisæ tam liberorum tenentium quam nativorum p' a' solvend' ad
f'm S. Martini   vjli.

„ quidam redditus frumenti viij^{xx} hop' p' a',
solvend' ad f'm S. Martini quorum quilibet
hop' valet iiijd.   [liijs. iiijd.]

„ de putura equorum d'ni quolibet anno de
nativis quinque gogerettas aven' solvend'
ad f'm S. Martini quorum quilibet gogerett'
val' ijs.   [xs.]

„ de putura Raglot' p' a' solvend' ad f'm Puri-
ficationis beatæ Mariæ   [xs.]

„ de putura equi Raglot' v quart' aven'
p' a' quarum quodlibet quart' valet ijs.   [xs.]

Et sunt ibidem de redditu gallinarum de nativis ibidem
xl gallinæ solv' ad f'm Natalis D'ni pretium
gallinæ jd. ob'.   [vs.]

Et est ibidem quidam redditus Kylchwyr   xxs.
p' a' solv' ad f'm Pur' b'tæ Mariæ

„ quidam redditus Caousty [caws-dy]   xs.
p' a' solv 'ad f'm Apostolorum Philippi et
Jacobi

Et sunt ibidem v opera unius hominis per unum diem[1] in
autumpno, precium operis per unum diem
et unius hominis ijd.   [xvjs. viijd.]

Placita et perquisita curiæ ibidem val' p' a'   cs.

Et dicunt quod dictus Owinus non habuit nec tenuit aliqua alia
terras vel tenementa nec habuit aliqua bona seu catalla in comitatu

---

[1] A total of 100 works is required to make up the full amount.

seu Marchiis prædictis die adhesionis prædicto. In cujus rei testimonium presentibus juratores prædicti sigilla sua apposuerunt die et
loco et anno supradictis."

[endorsed] " Summa valoris particuloris manerii
infrascripti [per annum] xx*li*. xix*s*. iiij*d*."

" Inquisitio capta apud Kyngefeld in comitatu Surrey coram Johanne
de Bisshopeston escaetore domini Regis in comitatu prædicto xix die
Novembris anno regni regis Edwardi tercii post conquestum xliij°
virtute cujusdam brevis domini Regis huic inquisitioni consuti per
sacramentum Joh'is Coddeston, Walteri Colgrim, Joh'is Bodesham,
Ricardi Parker, Ricardi Carbonel, Ricardi Daas, Joh'is atte War',
Henricus atte Herne, Willelmi Taylor, Willelmi Perham, Willelmi
Snowte et Jacobi de Enyngfeld, juratores, Qui dicunt super sacramentum suum quod Owynus ap Thomas Retherik in brevi contentus
non habuit aliqua terras seu tenementa bona nec catalla in com'
prædicto die quo adhesit inimicis d'ni Regis de Francia et cum ipsis
contra d'num Regem et fideles suos in partibus transmarinis de
guerra equitavit contra fidem et ligeanceam suam. Dicunt enim quod
idem Owynus discessit a partibus Angliæ circa festum Annunciationis
beatæ Mariæ anno regni Regis nunc quadragesimo et postea cum
dictis inimicis conversatus est et eis adhesit et adhuc est adherens
ut intelligunt. Dicunt tamen quod tempore quo discessit ab Anglia ut
præfertur nulla habuit terras seu tenementa bona seu catalla in
com. prædicto ut prædictum est. Set dicunt quod Thomas Retherik
pater prædicti Owyni fuit quondam seisitus de manerio de Tatlesfeld
et cum advocatione ecclesiæ ejusdem manerii cum pertinentiis in
dominico suo ut de feodo in com' prædicto, qui quidem Thomas
manerium et advocationem prædicta cum pertinentiis concessit
Stephano Bradepul parsone ecclesiæ de Tatlesfeld, Rogero de
Stanyngdenn et Alano Lambard ad terminum vitæ eorum, et postea
dictus Thomas relaxavit dicto Rogero imperpetuum totum jus et
clameum quod habuit in revertione manerii et advocationis prædictorum
et prædicti Stephanus Bradepul et Alanus Lambard attornaverunt se
dicto Rogero de revertione manerii et advocationis prædictorum. Et
postea prædicti Stephanus Rogerus et Alanus concesserunt manerium
et advocationem prædictum cum pertinentiis d'no Thome Dovedal et
heredibus suis, habendum et tenendum prædicto d'no Thome et heredibus suis ad terminum vitæ eorundum Stephani Rogeri et Alani. Et
dicunt quod diei postea vid' die Martis in festo Sancti Blasii
[3° Februarii] anno xl° d'ni Regis nunc prædictus Owynus antequam
sese recessit ab Anglia ut prædictum est similiter relaxavit dicto
Rogero et heredibus suis de se et heredibus suis totum jus et clamium

(*sic*) quæ habuit vel habere potuerit in revertione manerii et advocationis prædictorum. Et dicunt quod dictum manerium tenetur de
Archiepiscopo Cantuariense per fidem ut de manerio de Otteford et
quod valet per annum in omnibus exitibus juxta verum valorem
ejusdem vij. *li*. In cujus rei testimonium tam prædictus escaetor
quam prædicti juratores huic inquisitioni indentato sigilla sua alter-
natim apposuerunt. Datum die anno et loco supradictis.

" Inquisitio capta apud Gloucestr' coram Willelmo Auncell escaetore
d'ni Regis in com' Glouc' et Hereford' et Marchiis Walliæ eisdem com'
adjacent' xxº die Januarii anno regni Regis Edwardi tercii post conquestum xliijº virtute brevis d'ni Regis huic inquisitioni consuto per sacramentum Joh'is Hatherleye, Rogeri leYonge, Joh'is Pygace, Simonis
Brokworth, Thome Lesty, Walteri Lydeneye, Joh'is Stonehouse,
Hugonis Clyffale, Joh'is Maldon, Willelmi Walsshe, Joh'is atte Halle
et Joh'is Keck, Qui dicunt per sacramentum suum quod Owynus ap
Thomas Retheryk in brevi nominatus qui est adherens inimicis d'ni
Regis de Francia et cum ipsis inimicis d'ni Regis contra d'num Regem
et fideles suos in partibus transmarinis de guerra equitavit contra
fidem et ligeanceam suam tenuit die adhesionis prædicte unum
messuagium et unam carucatam terræ et dimidiam cum pertinentiis
in Budefeld in prædicto Com' Glouc' que valent per annum xs. quando
seminantur, et quando non seminantur nihil valent per annum quia
jacent in communi et nunc jacent frisce et inculte in dominico suo ut
de feodo de comite Hereford' per servicium militare. Item sunt
ibidem quatuor acræ bosci quæ nihil valent quia erat prostratus [*sic*]
per prædictum Owynum, et jacent in communi. Item tenuit ibidem
xviij acras prati quarum quælibet acra valet per annum xij*d*. quando
fulcari et levari potest, et herbagium ejusdem prati post falcacionem
nihil valet per annum quia jacet in communi. Item tenuit ibidem
in forma prædicta de redditu assisæ tam liberorum tenentium
quam custumariorum xxxvjs. per annum solvendos ad terminos S'ci
Martini, Annunciationis beatæ Mariæ et Nativitatis S'ci Johannis
Baptistæ equis portionibus. Et dicunt quod placita et perquisita
curiæ ibidem valent per annum xij*d*. Et dicunt quod prædictus
Owynus non tenuit aliqua alia terras seu tenementa de d'no Rege in
capite nec de aliquo alio die adhesionis prædicte in com' et Marchiis
prædictis. Et dicunt quod idem Owynus non habuit aliqua bona seu
catalla prædicto die adhesionis in com' et Marchiis prædictis. Et
dicunt quod adhesit inimicis d'ni Regis de Francia xiijdie Octobris
ultimo præterito ut intelligunt. In cujus rei testimonium præsenti-
bus juratores prædicti sigilla sua apposuerunt die et loco et anno
supradictis."

It will be observed that the senior male representative
of the ancient line of North Wales princes—if Owen was
really such—had sunk very low. According to the most
liberal methods of computation his entire estate could not
have amounted to more than £500 per annum of our
present money. His only place of residence was the
paltry house at Budefeld with its carucate and a half of
land in the common fields of the manor. The capital
messuage of Dynas was in such a condition as to swallow
up its value in outgoings. After a youth spent amid the
increasingly luxurious appointments of the French court
and the excitement of its constant occupation, Owen,
upon his return to his mean patrimony and quiet days in
England, must have felt his occupation gone. His mind
was soon made up. The jurors who met at Welshpool
date his defection from the 20th October 1369; those of
county Gloucester return it as having taken place on
the 13th of that month, as they understand; but those
of county Surrey state that he withdrew from England
about the date of the feast of the Annunciation of the
blessed Virgin, that is, the 25th March 1366, and by reason
of the business upon which he had returned, namely, the
legal recovery of his property, and the probable fact that he
had been born and brought up at Tatsfield, it is likely that
his movements would be better known to the residents of
that manor than to those of the other places where his
interests lay.

Owen ap Thomas ap Rhodri, of the princely line of
Gwynedd, never returned to his native land. Whether he
went entirely alone, or whether he was accompanied by a
few followers to whom his lineage was known, and upon
whom the glamour of a great name, and the fascination
of a lost cause, still held sway, it is impossible to say. The
curtain falls upon Owen ap Thomas, but rises again upon

the fortunes of him who was known to his French friends
as Owen of Wales.[1]

We have already given Froissart's narrative of the exploits of Owen ; but a brief sketch of the events in which
we know him to have taken part is essential, in order to
bring the personal details noticed by the French chronicler
into relation with the circumstances in which they were
manifested.

As has been said, war between England and France was
declared on the 29th April 1369, and from the very outset
it proceeded with ever brightening prospects for the French.
In the hope of relieving his country of its horrors by re-
moving its operations to that of his enemy, the French
king projected an invasion of England, and to carry out
his intention collected a large fleet at Harfleur. The plan
was in great measure frustrated by a counter descent of
the English upon the northern coast of France. The
French preparations were well known in England, where

---

[1] Christine of Pisa, in his *Vie de Charles V* (Panthéon Littéraire:
Chroniques et Mémoires), says that Owen was accompanied by a
relative (parent) named Jehan de Vuin (Ieuan Wyn) and that their
presence in the French ranks was the signal for the defection of a
number of Welshmen who had been serving with the Prince of Wales.
Christine's words are as follows :—" Item en cel an dessusdit
[1369] arriva en France Yves de Gales, noble escuyer, lequel
estoit, comme en disoit, droit heritier de la princée [*al.* prin-
cipauté] de Gales ; et pour la renommée susdicte du bon roy
Charles, avoit relainqui [*al.* laissé] les Anglois, et s'estoit venu
rendre au roy de France, avec luy un sien parent et compaignon,
moult vaillant escuyer, qui jadis avoit esté de la bataille des trente,
du costé des Angloiz, appelleé Jehan de Vuin, dit le Poursuivant
d'amours, avecques autres Galois moult beauls hommes, nonobstant
fussent compaignous du prince de Gales, filz du roy d'Angleterre, et
eussent son colier, considerans euls estre par les Angloiz desherités
de leur propre terre et seigneurie ; par quoy naturellement les héent
[*al.* haissant], relainquirent tout, et avecques autres Françoiz arrivent
vers La Rochelle en l'isle de Marene."

steps were at once taken to strengthen the sea coasts. An
order, dated the 24th December 1369, was issued to John
duke of Lancaster, and to seventeen of the majores barones
who held lands in Wales or the Marches, as well as to the
sheriffs, keepers of the royal castles, and other officers of
the Principality, to safely guard that portion of the realm.[1]
One of the commanders of the French squadron was Owen
of Wales, whose name we now meet with for the first time
as a combatant, and upon an element where we should
hardly expect to find him. Nothing appears to have been
done upon the sea during the year 1370, but towards the
end of that year another and almost identical proclamation
issued by the king of England to the great barons having
lands in Wales or the Marches (*Fœdera*, vi, 663) shows
that an invasion by the French was again apprehended.
The year 1371, however, seems to have passed in inactivity,
so far as the fleet at Harfleur was concerned, and it is not
until 1372 that Owen comes well to the front. On the 8th
May of that year king Charles ordered the commissioning

---

[1] They were ordered to be prepared to resist "maliciæ inimicorum
nostrorum predictorum si qui ingredi presumpserint partes illas et
omnes homines suspectos in dictis dominiis vestris dictis inimicis
adherentes vel de coniva auxilio consilio aut favore suo quomodolibet
existentes arestari et sub aresto detineri faceretis. Ita quod nobis et
regno nostro aut ligeis nostris ibidem per dictos inimicos nostros seu
sibi adherentes dampnum vel periculum non eveniret quoquo modo ac
idem per diversos inimicos de die in diem nobis declinantes pro certo
didicimus quod dicti inimici nostri cum multitudine navium ac
hominum ad arma et armatoria jam supra mare existunt et infra
dictum Principatum applicare eundem Principatum subjectio' et
dominio suo attrahere ac nos et dictos ligeos nostros pro posse suo
nisi celerius et virilius eis manu forti resistatur totalitis destruere et
subvertere proponunt et se parant." (*Fœdera*, vi, 642.) It will be
noticed that the issue of this proclamation synchronizes very closely
with the proceedings taken against Gruffudd Says as an adherent of
one Owen Lawgoch, a traitor and enemy of the king, as related in the
Record of Caernarvon.

of a naval force which was to be commanded by Yevain de Galles (*Froissart*, ed. Kervyn de Lettenhove, viii, 435-7, notes), and two days later Owen issued a declaration, which is given in the appendix to Thierry's *Histoire de la Conquête de l'Angleterre par les Normands* (notes et pièces justificatives, No. 7), and of which the following is a translation :—

"Evain de Gales, to all those to whom these letters shall come, Greeting. The kings of England in past times having treacherously and covetously, tortuously and without cause and by deliberate treasons, slain or caused to be slain my ancestors, kings of Wales, and others of them have put out of their country, and that country have by force and power appropriated and have submitted its people to divers services, the which country is and should be mine by right of succession, by kindred, by heritage, and by right of descent from my ancestors the kings of that country, and in order to obtain help and succour to recover that country which is my heritage, I have visited several christian kings, princes and noble lords, and have clearly declared and shown unto them my rights therein and have requested and supplicated their aid, and have latterly come unto the most puissant and renowned sovereign Charles, by the grace of God king of France, dauphin of Vienne, and have shown unto him my right in the aforesaid country and have made unto him the afore-named requests and supplications, and he having had compassion upon my state and understanding the great wrong that the kings of England have done unto my ancestors in former times, and that the present king of England has done unto me, and of his beneficent and accustomed clemency in which he is the singular mirror and example amongst christians of justice, grace and mercy to all those that are oppressed and require comforting, has granted me his aid and the assistance of his men-at-arms and fleet in order to recover the said realm, which is my rightful heritage, as has been said ; know all ye, therefore, that in return for the great love that my said lord the king of France has shown unto me, and is truly showing by his expenditure of three hundred thousand francs of gold, and more, as well in the pay of men-at-arms, archers and arbalisters as in [the provision of] ships and the pay and expenses of the sailors, in harness and other matters and in various expenses, the which sum I am at the present time not able to furnish, I promise loyally and by my faith and oath upon the holy evangelists, touched corporeally by me, and for my heirs and successors for ever, the aforesaid sum of three

hundred thousand francs of gold I will return and wholly repay, or
my heirs and successors or those who may claim through them (ou
ceul qui auront cause d'eulx), or by their will or command, without
any other terms ; and I herewith have made and entered into, for me
my heirs and successors and for all my country and subjects for ever,
with my said lord the king of France for him and his successors and
for all their country and subjects, a good and firm treaty, union and
alliance, by which I will aid and assist them by my person, my
subjects and my country, to the utmost of my power and loyalty
against all persons alive or dead (contre toutes personnes qui povent
vivre et mourir). In witness of which I have sealed these letters with
mine own seal. Given at Paris the 10th day of May, the year of
grace one thousand three hundred and seventy-two."

In this document Owen sets forth both his wrongs and
his claims in their most extravagant form, and to these we
will return presently ; in the meantime we will follow his
active career.

Disaster after disaster overtook the English cause
in France, amongst those of most serious consequence being
the death of Sir John Chandos at the close of 1369, and with-
drawal of the Black Prince at the opening of 1371. In the
spring of 1372 king Edward determined upon a great effort
to recover his lost ground, and preparations were made for
the increase of the English forces in France. One fleet
was destined for Rochelle, where the castle was strongly
held by the English, though a considerable body of the
townsmen were known to be partizans of the enemy.
Henry of Trastamare, who had become king of Castile in
spite of the English opposition, placed his ships at the
disposal of the king of France, and so dilatory were the
English that the Spanish fleet was in position before the
town when the former arrived. The battle that ensued
resulted in the total defeat of the English, and the
capture of the earl of Pembroke, their commander. The
victors at once set sail for their own country, taking
their captives with them.

Meanwhile, Owen had sailed from Harfleur with a portion of the French fleet that had been assembled there, and with four thousand men-at-arms. Whether England was his real aim, and the coast of Wales his intended destination, it is impossible to say; at any rate, he got no further than the isle of Guernsey.[1] Here he landed his troops, speedily over-ran the island, and compelled the English garrison to seek shelter in the castle of Cornet.[2] The siege of the castle was being pushed briskly on when events transpired elsewhere which caused Owen's talents to be temporarily diverted to the sphere of diplomacy.

[1] The Baron Kervyn de Lettenhove states that, according to the chronicle of du Guesclin, Owen's plans were for a descent upon England, but that the delay in the sailing of the Spanish fleet, which was to have joined his own, caused him to direct his attentions upon Guernsey.

[2] The *Chronique des Quatre Premiers Valois* is the fullest authority for the attack upon the island, and records an incident in the struggle which Froissart has missed. The story is as follows :—" Le roy de France, pour domagier les Anglois en plusieurs lieux et en plusieurs manieres et sur plusieurs marches, fit une armée en mer d'environ quatorze barges et moult d'autres vaisseaulx. Et en furent chiefz Yvain de Galles et Morelet de Mommor, en leur route bien six cens hommes d'armes, sans les mariniers des vaisseaulx, qui estoient bons guerroiers et hardiz, et sans l'autre menue gent. Et partirent de la fin de la riviere de Seyne, et singlerent vers les ysles de Guernesy. Et comme cil des ysles securent que les Françoiz faisoient armée, ilz le firent scavoir au cappitaine de Saint Sauveur le Viconte. Lequel y envoya hastivement des gens jusquez à quarante hommes d'armes, et autant d'archiers ou plus. Comme ilz furent venuz es ysles, ilz mistrent la gent en conrroy sur le port. Et les Françoiz singlerent à plain tref vers les ysles pour pourprendre terre là où estoient la gent du pais armés de telz armes comme ils avoient. Et sachiez que jeunes femmes et les bois-selettes des dictes ysles avoient en ce printemps de lors fait chapeaulx de flours et de violettes et les avoient donnés aux jeunez hommes, et leur disoient que cil se devoient bien deffendre qui les avoient à amies. Et cuidoient ceulx des ysles qu'il n'y eust eu navire de France que mariniers et gens d'eaue. Et comme les Françoiz parvindrent à pourprendre terre, ilz saillirent des vaisseaulx et des barges tres ysnelement et vigereusement armés de toutes

The king of France was quick to perceive the importance of the great naval victory which the Spaniards had just won, and saw his opportunity of capturing the town and

pieces, et vindrent courre sus à ceulx des ysles. Et là oult une dure bataille et pesant. Yvain de Galles et Morelet de Mommor mistrent leur gent en deux batailles, et par force d' armes pristrent terre."

Owen's descent upon the isle lived long in popular remembrance. It formed the subject of song and story even to our own day. A publication entitled *The Guernsey and Jersey Magazine*, which flourished in the thirties, in the course of a series of articles upon the history of the islands, observes :—" Notwithstanding the several truces agreed upon at different times between the English and French, they were so ill observed that the war may be said to have continued till the 8th of May 1360, when a definitive treaty of peace was signed between the two nations, by which king Edward ceded to the French the province of Normandy, but specially reserved to himself the possession of the Channel Islands. This treaty was respected up to the year 1369, when king Charles the Fifth, coming to the French throne, declared war against king Edward, the close of whose reign was not so marked by victory as the early period. Charles, receiving intelligence that the earl of Pembroke had sailed with a fleet of forty ships, to protect the town of Rochelle, which still held out for the English, fitted out a considerable naval armament, of which he gave the command to Yvon de Galles, a pretended Prince of Wales, whose father (it was said) had been put to death by Edward, when he annexed that principality to England. Henry, king of Castile, sent, at the same time, some vessels to join the French, and their united force, meeting the English, gained some advantage over them. Yvon de Galles (as it is said), missing the French fleet, made a descent on Guernsey, popularly called from tradition ' La descente des Saragousais,' from which it is probable that he had not missed them, but attacked the island both with the French and Spanish divisions. However, there were several warm engagements, and a great number of men killed on both sides, and the ground on which New-Town is built is still known by the name of ' La Bataille,' being the scene of one of these encounters. Some French authors have alleged that Yvon de Galles met a body of Englishmen in the island, and not only killed four hundred of them, but also forced the remainder to take shelter in Castle Cornet, after which he plundered the island. Others make no mention of any Englishmen being present, nor of any plundering at all, but admit that four hundred men were killed, as well as confirming the retreat

castle of Rochelle. He accordingly sent in haste to Owen
to raise the siege of Cornet, and to follow the Spanish ships
with the view of obtaining the king of Castile's consent

of the remainder into Castle Cornet, adding that Yvon de Galles laid
siege to it ; but that soon afterwards he raised it, and sailed to Spain.
. . . . There is an old Guernsey ballad on this invasion, which we
shall insert in our next number, as possessing some local interest, but
it is to be observed that the poet has borrowed most of his facts
from his imagination." In a succeeding number is given the ballad
entitled "Owen of Wales." It is poor stuff, but the following stanzas
may contain an echo of the effect created by Owen's unexpected
visit :—

> "O listen, listen, gentles all,
>   My tale's not over long,
> And whether ye be great or small,
>   Attend unto my song.
>
> "I sing of Owen, prince of Wales,
>   A chief of royal blood ;
> He loves a dance in whistling gales,
>   Far o'er the briny flood.
>
> "His merry men grow old in sin,—
>   For plunder is their duty,—
> Cut, slash and dash, through thick and thin,
>   Wherever there is booty.
>
> "Norman, French, Arragonian, Turk,
>   They're of all sorts and sizes,
> Black and white villains of all work,
>   Like rogues at the assizes.

*   *   *   *   *

> " Owen of Wales, of royal kin,
>   The leader of the foe,
> Sighed for new laurels in the din
>   Of carnage and of woe.
>
> "Dangers the hero loved and dared,
>   By disappointment vext ;
> No peril of this world he feared,
>   Nor cared he for the next.

F

to their return to Rochelle. Contrary winds had delayed
the Spaniards, so that (according to Froissart) their fleet
and Owen's vessel arrived at the port of Santander upon
the same day.¹ The English prisoners were disembarked,
and it was here that Owen had his dramatic meeting with

> "Yet in our isle he found, I ween,
>   A garter on his thigh;
> 'Twas neither silk nor velvet sheen,
>   Though scarlet was the dye.
>
> "For nigh the mill of La Carrière,
>   As the rash leader came,
> Stout Richard gashed him with a spear
>   That never missed its aim.
>
> "Then whirled in air a trusty brand,
>   And felt his bosom glow,
> Yet only hacked Sir Owen's hand
>   With a tremendous blow.
>
>   *   *   *   *   *
>
> "Eighty good English merchant men
>   Arrived at close of day,
> And old king Charles' merry men
>   For mercy 'gan to pray.
>
>   *   *   *   *   *
>
> "Nettled with rage at this defeat,
>   Sir Owen, full of cares,
> Now gave the word—the hostile fleet
>   To Sampson's harbour steers.
>
> "Then to St. Michael's priory,
>   Ellen, his lady fair,
> Hastened in all bravery,
>   And found sweet welcome there.
>
> "(Sir Owen woo'd the lovely dame,
>   In Gravelle's wealthy land ;
> Proud heiress of a noble name,
>   She claimed a prince's hand.)"

¹ The writer of the letter in the *Arch. Camb* (3rd Ser. vi, 62) makes
it clear that Owen was at Santander in the month of July 1372. He
there drew out a receipt to which is appended a seal described as
bearing " four lions rampant gardant," the arms of Thomas Retheric

the earl of Pembroke. Owen's mission was completely successful, and the Spanish fleet once more sailed for Rochelle, where they anchored before the castle to await its surrender. The principal military commander of the English, the Captal de Buch, was in the neighbourhood of Soubise, a strong fortress at the mouth of the river Charente, not many miles from Rochelle. With admirable promptitude, Owen placed 400 men in barges, which were rowed as far as Soubise. Here he surprised the English by a night attack; slaughtered or took prisoners the entire party, and captured their leaders, the Captal de Buch and Sir Thomas Percy.[1] An incident characteristic of mediæval

of Tatsfield. The version given by the writer of the *Chronique des Quatre Premiers Valois* is that Owen having failed to subdue the island of Guernsey, sailed away to Spain in search of the Spanish fleet. He makes the king of France's commission to Owen to be received whilst the latter was at Santander, and asserts that the Spanish ships of war were requested for a descent upon Wales, a proposal which led to almost a mutiny. His words are—" Yvain de Galles et Morelet de Montmor alerent au roy Henry et lui requistrent qu'il leur voulsist delivrer navire et l'armée comme il avoit promise au roy de France. Maiz les Espaingnolz distrent au roi Henry : 'Sire, envoiez nous en la terre desvoye, en Grenate, en Persic, oultre les destroiz de Marroc ou où il vous plaira fors en Galles. Car là ne yrons nous point par nulle maniere.' Ce fut dit à Yevan. Par quoy il se parti d'Espaingne moult yré, pour ce qu'il avail failli à son emprise." As a matter of fact, Owen did not fail in his mission.

[1] Sir Thomas Percy was taken prisoner by a Welshman, said to have been a priest and Owen's chaplain, whose name is given in some editions of *Froissart* as David House (ed. Luce, viii, 69), and in others as David Honnel (ed. Buchon, 649), the latter, of course, standing for Honnel=Howel. M. Luce (*loc. cit.*) has the following note to the passage :—" Thomas de Percy sénéchal de Poitou, fut pris en effet par un Gallois, mais ce Gallois ne portait pas le nom indiqué par Froissart ; il s'appelait en réalité Honvel Flinc [Howel Flint]. Par acte daté du château du Louvre le 10 janvier 1373 (n. st.) Thomas de Percy, chevalier d'Angleterre, reconnut qu'il était 'prisonnier à Honvel Flinc, de Gales, lequel nous avoit pris en la bataille qui a esté ceste presente année où

methods of warfare is related by the writer of the *Chronique
des Quatre Premiers Valois* in connection with this encounter. During the struggle an English knight or
soldier shouted " Where hast thou got to, false traitor,
Yvain de Galles, false renegade ; the king of England and
of France shall be avenged upon thee." To which Owen
replied " I am here," and ran upon the Englishman,
whom he felled to the earth with the blow of his battle-axe.[1]
The castle of Soubise immediately surrendered, and the
practical result of this daring action was the extinction
of the English power in Saintogne. Rochelle fell soon
afterwards, and Owen was ordered to conduct his prisoners
to the king at Paris. The war continued, with an
occasional English success to relieve the almost unbroken
series of disasters, but the chroniclers do not record any

nous sommes (la pièce est datée de 1372 ancien style) devant la ville
de Soubise, ou pais de Guienne en laquelle bataille fut aussi pris par
les gens de très noble et très puissant prince Charles, par le grace de
Dieu roy de France, monseigneur Johan de Gresly, appellé le captal
de Buch.' (*Arch. Nat.*, J. 362, No. 2.)" After the death of Owen in
1378, Howel Flint joined the corps of Ieuan Wyn, and signs a muster
roll of the 1st May 1381, as the first man in the company. (Thierry,
Hist. de la Conquête de l'Angl.; pièces justificatives, No. 5.)

[1] The entire passage is as follows :—" Les Françoiz se assemblerent
de toutes pars et vindrent au logeiz de Yvain de Galles et se mistrent
en conrroy. Et avoient jà les Angloiz desconfit aucuns Françoiz et
chassé jusques au logeiz de Yvain. Et lors les Geneuois et les
arbalestriers Françoiz pristrent fort à traire contre les Angloiz, et
moult en occistrent et navrerent. Là oult moult dure bataille et
pesant. Ung Angloiz prist a crier : ' Où es tu allé, faulx traistre
Yvain de Galles, faulx regnié ? Huy sera vengié le roy d'Angleterre
et de France de toy.' Lors dit Yvain : 'Veez me ça !' et couru sus
à l'Angloiz et le fery d'une hasche si fort qu'il l'abati à terre, et
aucuns autres l'occistrent. Et adonc apleurent Françoiz de toutes
pars" (p. 239, ed. Luce).—Though the story may owe something to
the imagination of the chronicler, it is proof of the reputation that
Owen had gained as a fighting man.

particular action of Owen, though we hear of his activity as a naval commander. The fear of foreign invasion was constantly present with the English council, repeated orders being issued for the defence of the maritime districts of England. Both countries were exhausted, and were glad to agree to a truce, which was several times renewed, and which it was hoped would terminate in a lasting peace. There can be little doubt that Owen's inveterate hatred of the English kept him active in the work of their destruction, and he would seem, from the *Life* of du Guesclin, already referred to, to have taken part in the struggle for Brittany under that great captain in the years 1374-5. His name is met with in the French muster rolls for the years 1373-4-5, in company with that of his fellow-countryman and kinsman, Ieuan Wyn. The twelve-months' truce agreed to on the 27th June 1375 was fairly kept, but the period of enforced idleness could not have been congenial to the restless spirit of Owen, and he seems to have turned to an altogether different quarter in search of the military adventure which had now become his passion.

Tschudi (1505-1572), the historian of Switzerland, when dealing with the irruption of Enguerrand de Coucy and a body of free companies into that country in the year 1375, quotes the following folk-poem which, without doubt, preserved to his day an episode that had keenly excited the popular imagination :—

> " Der Herz Graf Ingram von Guison
> Wolt Statt und Burg nemmen inn
> Er wondt das wär alles sin
> Sin Schwächer von Engelland half Im
> Mit Lib und Gut
> Herzog Yffo von Calis mit
> Sim guldinen Hut."

" The . . . . count Enguerrand de Coucy
Would city and fort take possession of,
He fancied the land was all his own,
His father-in-law of England helped him
With blood and treasure
Duke Iffo de Galis with
His golden Hat."

Now, there can be little doubt that in Yffo von Calis we should recognize Owen de Galles[1]; but, in any event, the Swiss enterprise was merely an episode. We find Owen back in France in the year 1376, and again in the service

[1] The Rev. Robert Owen (*The Kymry*, 94) identifies Iffo with an Ieuan ap Einion, but gets no further, whilst the late Mr. Charles Ashton (*Gweithiau Iolo Goch*, 149) makes Ieuan ap Einion to be of Bron-y-foel in Eifionydd, and the hero of an elegiac poem by Iolo Goch. The Rev. R. Owen's remarks are as follows: " Few, perhaps, are aware that the English Company of Enguerrand de Coucy, defeated by the Swiss on January 13, 1376, at Buttisholz, was commanded by Ieuan ab Einion ; whom an old song of the period styles ' Hertzog Yffo von Callis mit sim guldinen hut,' the chief Evan of Wales with his golden hat. Enguerrand was a son-in-law of Edward III, and held fiefs in Wales, which explains his having a Welsh lieutenant "—but does not explain the real point requiring explanation, namely, why Iffo wore a golden hat. Prof. Dändliker, in his *Short History of Switzerland*, refers to this incident in the following terms:—" A long period of fear next followed, during which both parties [of Swiss] recruited their strength, and even joined hands in friendship, being unexpectedly united by the presence of a common foe. Baron Ingelram von Coucy, grandson of Leopold I of Austria, and son-in-law of Edward III of England, required the dukes of Austria to give up Aargau, which he claimed in his mother's right ; and not obtaining it, he invaded Switzerland in 1375 with a numerous army of French and English mercenaries [Note : These troops received the nickname of " *Gugler* " on account of their headgear resembling a cowl (Swiss-German, ' Gugel')]. Terror and dismay were universal at the devastation wrought by these undisciplined troops. Wherever they went crops were destroyed, men and cattle butchered, and villages, churches, and monasteries set on fire. In this emergency Austria sought reconciliation with the Confederates, and renewed the Peace of Thorberg. She also concluded an offensive and defensive alliance with the towns, from which, however, the country districts

of Charles the Ninth, for Thierry has printed (*Hist. de la conquête de l'Angl. par les Normands :* pièces justificatives, No. 4) a list of his company dated at Limoges, the 8th of September. This list is highly interesting, but it has been produced in so corrupt a form that, pending the opportunity of visiting the national library at Paris, it is not reproduced here. The truce, which terminated on the 26th June 1376, saw both sides prepared to renew the conflict, but no important movement took place during that or the succeeding year. Of Owen we hear nothing until his arrival at Mortagne-sur-Garonne, where he met with an untimely end at the hands of his squire, John Lamb, as has already been related in the pathetic and picturesque narrative of Froissart. Death came to him when he was in the prime of life, and at the height of his

held aloof out of hatred to Austria. The Confederates advanced immediately against the " Guglers "; in Dec. 1375, a few troops from Lucerne, Entlebuch and Unterwalden repulsed one division of mercenaries at Buttisholz in the district of Sursee; troops from Berne and Fribourg attacked another division at Ins (or Jens), and the Bernese alone finally gained a brilliant victory over the main army near the monastery of Fraubrunnen. The rest of the invaders, partly owing to these defeats and partly to the want of provisions and the severity of the winter, were compelled to withdraw without attaining their object." (Miss E. Salisbury's Translation, p. 63.) The difficulty is to know whether the poetical reference to Yffo's golden hat is a satirical or far-away allusion to the 'gugel,' by which the mercenaries of Enguerrand de Coucy were distinguished; or whether Owen wore some headdress which he had adopted to set forth his pretensions ; or whether, indeed, the words are intended to be no more than a poetical allusion to those pretensions which must have been well known throughout Southern France and its confines. It is difficult to imagine that Owen would have flaunted his claims so ostentatiously whilst in the train of the king of England's son-in-law, but de Coucy had important interests on both sides and fluctuated accordingly. He was earl of Bedford in the English peerage, and held fiefs in Wales only as, at this time, 1375, holding the wardship of the young earl of March.

resources. He must have been about the age of forty, and
probably a few years below rather than a few years above
that period.

Let us now take up the questions with which we started,
and to which we are better prepared to reply.

(1) Is the Owain Lawgoch of Wales the same personage
as the Yeuain de Galles of Froissart?

Notwithstanding that upon not a single occasion do
we find Yeuain, or Owen, de Galles, distinguished by
any form of cognomen which might stand for or be
assumed to represent the Welsh "Llawgoch,"[1] it is
submitted that the facts bearing upon this point, when
taken together with those which have more direct
reference to our second question—Who was Owen of
Wales?—are sufficiently strong to warrant us in returning
to our former query an unhesitating affirmative. There is,
in the first place, the total absence of any other personage
bearing the name of Owen whom the testimony of contemporary English records and French chronicles demonstrate
to have been at a particular moment of time (the year 1370)
an enemy of the king of England and—from the English
point of view—a traitor to his country. Secondly, there is
the immense weight of tradition. Not the tradition of
centuries in the course of which names have been so altered
and circumstances so reversed that it has become directly
opposed to irrefutable record; but the tradition that, in an
absolutely literal sense, embodies the story "our fathers
have told us." In this connection, I would draw particular
attention to the subsequent portion of this paper, which
has been contributed by Mr. J. H. Davies. His researches
into Welsh mediæval poetry prove how valuable those

---

[1] It is curious, however, that the Guernsey ballad, already given,
should represent Owen as being wounded in the hand in the encounter on the island.

otherwise largely worthless effusions may be, as the only depositories of the thoughts of a community upon contemporary or nearly contemporary occurrences, and of names and incidents which are beneath or beside the notice of officialism. It is impossible to read the poem of Llewelyn ap Cynwrig ddu o Fôn without acknowledging that its testimony is ample as to the identity of Owain Lawgoch with Owen of Wales.

(2) Who was Owen of Wales?

With respect to this, our second question, we have more abundant evidence upon which to frame our reply. Up to the day when Owen unsuspectingly went out to his death we have been able to trace his career. His still unobliterated footprints on the sands of time are few and far between, but they have enabled us to construct a fairly consistent and consecutive story. The most sceptical critic cannot doubt that the Owen of Wales "filz à un prince de Galles" (*Froissart*), for whose murder John Lamb was rewarded, is the Owen Retherrik "qui se disoit prince de Galis", whose follower, Bleddyn ap Ynian, returned to his allegiance eighteen months after his leader's assassination. If so, then all else follows, as the night the day. The one defective link, that is, the identification of Owen ap Thomas ap Rhodri with Owen Lawgoch, though morally certain, is rendered absolutely so by the same old poem of Llewelyn ap Cynwrig ddu, to which we have already alluded; for the bard, in addressing the red-handed Owen, distinctly styles him the son of Thomas and grandson of Rhodri. It must also not be forgotten that the seal of Owen de Galles bears the same heraldic device as that of Thomas [ap] Rotheric, a fact the full force of which will be recognised by those who know that this is a far more reliable source of identification than the designation of an individual as written by a mediæval clerk.

The above was already in print when, during the process
of cataloguing the manuscripts relating to Wales in the
Harleian collection of the British Museum, the following
hitherto unnoticed entry was alighted upon :—

(*British Museum: Harleian 2076*, old folio 98, modern 63*b*, note *g*).

" M'd' that S'r Thomas Rotherick, kn't, father to Owen Logate lord
of Marebury, and of Althurst in Marebury parish pr'tended without
title to haue beene Prince of Walles, and then was tooke and putt in
Prison and there died, and Owen aforesaid went into Denmarke of
purpose to haue wedded the king's daughter, and his owne chamb'-
layne slew him, the said Owen, and came to the king of England and
tould him the forecast of the said Owen, and then the king seized all
his lands in Cheshire and beside London and all other places, and
exiled the said Chamb'laine for y't hee was false to ye said Owen his
m'r."

The volume containing this entry forms one of the
immense collection of the family of Holme of Chester,
which is for the most part devoted to pedigrees and
genealogical and historical memoranda relating to the
county of Cheshire in particular, and, more generally, to
the adjacent parts of both England and Wales. Standing
by itself, unsupported as it is by the quotation of a single
authority, the entry would not carry us very far ; but,
carefully examined, it will be found to supply the one link
that was wanting to our chain of evidence connecting
Owen Lawgoch with Owen ap Thomas ap Rhodri. It is also
clear that without the enquiries into the possessions and
patrimony of Owen, which have cost so much labour and
appeared to return somewhat inconclusive results, the
full significance of this brief entry would never have
become apparent. For who would have recognised Owen
Lawgoch in " Owen Logate, lord of Marebury and of
Althurst in Marebury parish "? The very mixture of
fiction (in those details which the writer of the note drew
from tradition or the reports of others) and of fact (in the
circumstances which he was acquainted with from his own

knowledge or obtained from contemporary documents) gives the notice an importance for us that it would not have possessed had it been confined to facts alone. It should be observed, first of all, that the source and, perhaps, the form of the entry is earlier in date than the manuscript from which it has been extracted above. This is a series of notes upon Cheshire properties and their early proprietors, drawn, there can be little doubt, from the many sources that would be open to an accredited officer of the college of arms. If we could regard them as the production of one person, we might assume (from the name at their commencement) that their author was Sampson Erdeswick, a celebrated Cheshire herald of the sixteenth century, many of whose pedigree collections came into the possession of the Holme family. Be this as it may, it is obvious that the original writer, whoever he may have been, or in whatever form he recorded his information, was chiefly concerned with the devolution of the Cheshire manor of Althurst. A violent break occurred in the possession of this manor, as we know from the patent rolls of the 4th year of Richard II,[1] though no reference to that, or, indeed, to any other transaction relating to the manor, appears upon the official palatinate rolls. But the events which had permitted the intrusion of a new owner were vaguely known to the genealogist. The fact that a lord of Althurst

---

[1] " Grant, for life, to Roger atte Gate, king's esquire, of the manor of Althurst, co. Chester, in lieu of £10 yearly granted to him by letters patent of the king's father dated 20 February, 46 Edward III, from the same manor, forfeited by Owen Rothcrik, as it appears by inquisition that the value of the manor is only £10 2s. yearly but he is to render the surplus of 2s. at the exchequer of Chester." (*Calendar Rot. Pat.*, 4 Ric. II, *p.* i, *m.* 17; 29 Sept. 1380.) This forms the only evidence I have been able to discover of the possession of this manor by Owen or his ancestors.

had been a traitor would linger long in the public memory,
and the actual circumstances of his death in a foreign
land, though generally known at the period of their
occurrence, would become more and more obscured as the
story passed from generation to generation. That the
above entry has not been abstracted from Froissart, but is
altogether independent of the chronicler's version, is
manifest; whilst its striking agreement with Froissart's
statement that Owen's father had suffered death at the
hands of the English king, is calculated to make us ponder
whether we have yet unravelled the fate of Thomas. Since
we do not know the source of the above extract, it is useless
to speculate upon the devious course by which " Lawgoch",
or " Y llaw goch", became "Logate". Sufficient is it for
us, that by reason of that happy amalgam of fact and of
fiction to which we have adverted, we need feel no hesitation in accepting the entry as supplying the link hitherto
required to unite Owen Lawgoch, Owen ap Thomas ap
Rhodri, and Owen of Wales in one indissoluble entity.

As a corollary to the above questions arose the
problem of the true value of Owen's claims; and in order
to estimate these aright it became necessary to trace his
ancestors, from whom he derived his pretensions to "the
throne of Wales." This has been effected with thoroughly
satisfactory results, and has been productive of what I
trust will be acknowledged to be a substantial addition to
the stock of our historical knowledge of the fortunes of
certain members of the family of Llewelyn " ein llyw
ola'." The relationship of Owen to the chiefly line of
Gwynedd has been established, and a number of minor,
but hardly less interesting points have been brought into
prominence for solution by others, or await a more
convenient season.

The oft-repeated truism that a chain is no stronger than

its weakest link, is, of course, as applicable to the moral as
to the material sphere; and I am well aware that there are
regrettable lacunæ in the train of reasoning I have presented. But there does not seem to me to be any insuperable
obstacle or any impassable gap in any part of the route
lying between the extreme points of the problem; and
when remembrance is had of the distant period in which
the persons who have been the subject of our enquiry
lived and wrought—from six to seven centuries ago—it is
remarkable that the breaks in the evidence should be so
few and non-essential.

Having thus brought together into one personality
Owain Lawgoch—Owen ap Thomas ap Rotherick—Owen
of Wales, let us endeavour briefly to set forth what manner
of man he was.

So slight are the materials at our command that any
estimate we may form of Owen's character must be
imperfect and, perhaps, erroneous. That he had great
capacity for war is clear, as well from the admiration
he commanded from his friends, as from the fear in which
he was held by his enemies. His outburst against the
earl of Pembroke at Santander would seem to point to the
possession of a passionate nature, and in the heat of
combat, as in the attack upon the English before Soubise,
he appears to have been terrible. But the same enterprise
proves his capacity for organization and intuitive knowledge how best to obtain the desired end, which are
amongst the highest qualities of a military commander.
The agreement of contemporary writers as to the universal
feeling of regret with which his death was received
denotes a bright, frank, and generous nature, at least
towards those who were his friends; and the picture which
old Froissart draws of him, glad of the converse of his
squire because they spoke of Wales and of the great

doings there would be in that far off country when its
prince should come into his own again, touches our hearts
and engages our sympathy amid the common-place sur-
roundings and sordid considerations of our own day.

This brings us to the point, How far were Owen's pretensions based upon actual fact, and how far did he believe
in them himself? The capacity for self-delusion seems so
inherent and inexhaustible in some minds that an answer
to the latter half of the query is difficult. Froissart's
account of the mental impression made upon Owen by
Lamb's true and untrue tidings, " for he made him believe
how all the country of Wales would gladly have him to be
their lord," should not be accepted too readily; it is one
thing to describe the actions of a man for which testimony
is abundant—and yet Sir Walter Raleigh discovered how
hard it was to state these with perfect fidelity; it is quite
another thing to record the motives and portray the
emotions of the closest of friends. The claims that Owen
had openly put forward not only to the king of France,
but to all who would lend him ear, would probably induce
him to listen with confidence and self-complacency to the
fictions of Lamb; and as he had started by asserting that
he had been deprived of his rights, he would probably
be only too willing to believe that there existed those who
would perish with him in their maintenance.

Fictions assuredly they were which brightened the hope
and clouded the judgment of Owen. If we endeavour to
arrive at a verdict that is not biased by the sense of our
common nationality or coloured by the kindly influences
of natural sympathy, we can come to but one conclusion,
namely, that there existed no good grounds for Owen's
assertions that he had himself been cruelly and unjustly
treated by the English king, or that his ancestors had been
treacherously murdered and their country, the principality

of Wales, wrongfully seized by that king's predecessors. The ethics of kings and counsellors, particularly those of the middle ages, do not as a rule extort our admiration, and it would be folly to appraise them by the precepts—the less said about the practice the better—of this century. The small portion of Wales that in the year 1282 retained the shadow of a former independence lost even that reflection in a struggle that was probably inevitable. It is no source of gratulation to a Welshman, it never can be, that the slowly expiring light of Welsh national independence was for ever extinguished in 1282; but it is a subject of pride, whence springeth comfort, that its last prince died an honourable death. The impartial student of history must recognize that Owen's frame of mind, though a perfectly natural one from the point of view of sentiment, was not based upon sober reality, and it is with the latter alone that we, as historical students, are here concerned. Owen was himself the grandson of a man who had to flee from Wales into England for liberty and probably life. We have followed the devious course of his father and grandfather, so far as records that are inexpugnable in their veracity will permit, and the conclusion to which we are forced is that not a shade of reason existed for Owen's unhappy delusion, apart from the distorted fancies that brooding over a lost cause is only too prone to engender.[1]

[1] It was the apparent impossibility of accounting in a rational and convincing manner for the occasion of Owen's bitter hostility to England, and for his assertion that his ancestors (Froissart says his father, which is calculated to put an enquirer upon a wrong scent) had been done to death by the English king and certain of his nobles, that led the writer in his lecture to reject Owen's kinship with the princely house of Gwynedd, and to assert his connection with Llewelyn Bren, who was unquestionably of the royal line of Morganwg. I have elsewhere (*Western Mail*, 2 May 1898), I think conclusively, shown that Llewelyn Bren's name was Llewelyn ap Griffith, the same as that of the last prince of Gwynedd, with whose

Still more difficult is it to comprehend the ground of his assertion that he himself was the subject of injustice on the part of the English king. Whatever may have been his career abroad during his father's lifetime, he had but to return to his native land—for I have little doubt that he was born at Tatsfield—to obtain the restoration of all his father's patrimony, and upon the date at which his adhesion to the enemies of England was clearly proved he is found to have been in possession of every acre that his father had held at his death.

That his own death was accomplished by one of the blackest acts of treachery ever perpetrated, and that

latter years he must have been contemporary. Now, the Morganwg Ll. ap Griffith, after an abortive rising in the year 1316, was captured by a body of troops which had been assembled under the earl of Hereford and lord Despencer—the ancestors of the very noblemen named by Owen of Wales in his tirade against the earl of Pembroke at Santander (" and also the earl of Hereford and Edward [de]Spencer, for by your fathers, with other counsellors, my lords my ancestors (*messires mes pères*) were betrayed ")—imprisoned in the Tower, released and again captured by Despencer, and hanged by him at Cardiff Castle. Ll. Bren is not stated to have had a son named Owen, but he had one named Roger, which might (but not probably) be the Anglicised form of Rhodri. Had Owen really been a descendant of this family, his animosity against the ruling powers of England, and, especially, against the descendants of the de Bohuns and the de Spencers, would have been explicable. But I have abandoned this view, and have now, I trust, satisfactorily proved, in agreement with my friend Mr. J. H. Davies's consistently expressed opinion, that Owen de Galles was of the princely line of Gwynedd. If Owen knew anything of events in Wales, either from his father or from others (for he was not born when Ll. Bren was hanged), he must have heard of that shocking contempt of justice on the part of the younger Despencer, and it seems possible that he may have assumed the undoubted wrongs of another family to bolster up the fictitious injuries under which he believed he himself laboured. The rising of Llewelyn Bren has been neglected by our writers of history, and as its elucidation, when attempted, will involve considerable research into unpublished records, its present unsatisfactory condition will probably long continue.

this act was directly instigated, as it was welcomed and rewarded, by the English authorities, is morally if not absolutely certain. Greatly as it advantaged his enemies, there were no doubt many in the English ranks who, like the brave Soudic of Lestrade, exclaimed when the details of the assassination became known " We shall have rather blame thereby than praise." But Owen has had his revenge. Whether during his life he had absorbed the history and assumed the character of another it is difficult for the historian to determine. It is otherwise with the student of popular traditions. Professor Rhys has shown that the failures of this world may find redress in the realm of romance. By his meteoric career and his pathetic end Owen established a sway over the imaginations of his countrymen which has proved more enduring than any material kingdom which he could hope to have won. He has displaced even the glorious Arthur from some of the latter hero's most charming retreats in the domain of popular fancy, and so long as Welsh romantic literature has its exponent or its votary so long will the name of Owen ap Thomas ap Rhodri smell sweet and blossom in the dust.

*(The following section is contributed by
Mr. J. H. Davies, M.A.)*

The story of Owen ap Thomas ap Rhodri, as narrated by the graphic pen of Froissart and as recorded in the contemporary documents of the English Courts, has been told; nothing now remains but to string together in some kind of order the few confirmatory facts gleaned from Welsh sources. Unfortunately, no Welsh records of the period survive in prose, if any ever existed. We have therefore

G

to turn to the evidence supplied by Welsh poetry. But before dealing directly with the references to Owen found in the poetry of the period, it may be well to supplement the few data we produce by giving a description of the class of poetry in which this evidence is found.

From the earliest times it may be presumed that the Welsh people were fond of speculating as to the future, and the professional prophets or seers amongst them were treated with awe and respect. We accordingly find that Taliesin and Myrddin, in the poems attributed to them, made forecasts of the future, and quite a considerable proportion of the poetry in our oldest existing MSS. is concerned with such prophecies. Mr. Stephens, in his *Literature of the Kymry*, has proved that some, at any rate, of the prophecies attributed to Myrddin were concoctions of a later age. For our purpose, however, that is of little consequence, as we only intend to note the prophecies grouped around the name of Owen written or composed before the year 1350. By this means we hope to eliminate from the poetry which contains references to Owen ap Thomas all the legends which may be referred to an earlier person of the same name. The prophecies relating to Wales, as distinct from those common to other countries, group themselves into periods. It will be convenient to tabulate them in the following way :—

I. Prophecies attributed to Taliesin and Myrddin.

II. Prophecies said to be written about the end of the 13th century.

III. Owen ap Thomas prophecies.

IV. Prophecies relating to Owen Glyndwr.

V. Prophecies written between 1415 and 1485, the period during which penal laws were put into force against Welshmen.

VI. Prophecies of the 17th century.

Far and away the most prolific period is that between 1415 and 1485. The poetry of this period breathes a spirit of hatred towards the Saxon, which cannot be matched in that of any other period.

In the present state of our knowledge of the early literature of Wales, it is very difficult to make any statement concerning, or express any opinion upon, the prophecies of Taliesin and Myrddin.

We have, however, the fact that the *Black Book of Carmarthen*, written in the 12th and early 13th centuries, the *Llyfr Taliesin*, written about 1275, Peniarth MS. 3, and the *Red Book of Hergest*, part of which was written early in the 14th cent., contain a number of prophecies attributed to these two bards.

In the *Black Book*, on fol. 25 there is a verse which is thus translated in Skene's *Four Ancient Books of Wales*, p. 371:—

> "Sweet apple tree, and a yellow tree,
> Grow at Tal ardd, without a garden surrounding it;
> And I will predict a battle in Prydyn,
> In defence of their frontier against the men of Dublin;
> Seven ships will come over the wide lake,
> And seven hundred over the sea to conquer.
> Of those that come, none will go to Cennyn,
> Except seven half-empty ones, according to the prediction."

Here we have the earliest mention in Welsh poetry of the legend that seven ships and seven hundred men were to come over from Dublin.[1] In the *Red Book of Hergest*, col. 577 *et seq.*, we find the following dialogue between Myrddin and his sister[2] :—

> 73. "When Lloegyr will be groaning,
>   And Cymir full of malignity,
>   An army will be moving to and fro.

---

[1] See also *Black Book*, fol. 28; *Skene*, vol. ii, 23.
[2] For the text see *Skene*, vol. ii, 227, and translation vol. i, 470.

74. "Myrddin fair, gifted in speech,
Tell me no falsehood ;
What will be after the army ?

75. "There will arise one out of the six
That have long been in concealment ;
Over Lloegyr he will have the mastery.

76. "Myrddin fair, of fame-conferring stock,
Let the wind turn inside the house,
Who will rule after that ?

77. "It is established that Owein should come,
And conquer as far as London,
To give the Cymry glad tidings.

78. "Myrddin fair, most gifted and most famed,
For thy word I will believe,
Owein, how long will he continue ?

79. "Gwenddydd, listen to a rumour,
Let the wind turn in the valley,
Five years and two, as in time of yore.

80. "I will ask my profound brother,
Whom I have seen tenderly nourished,
Who will thence be sovereign ?

81. "When Owein will be in Manaw,
And a battle in Prydyn close by,
There will be a man with men under him."

The portion of the *Red Book* containing this poem is
supposed to have been written after 1318. Here we have
a traditional Owen, who has long been in hiding, coming
forth to conquer the Saxon. He is again mentioned in
the *Red Book*, col. 1051, a poem translated in *Skene*, p. 491.

"And Owein will be the ruler of the kingdom,
A ruddy man in the ruddy scene, the joy of Gwynedd,
Of brave ancestors, the progeny of Mervyn, the bulwark of
sovereignty.
A crowned young hero, on the point of effecting deliverance."[1]

---

[1] Written in the *Red Book* about 1376, but probably composed
at a much earlier period.

In the second period we class such poets as Adda Vras and Y Bardd Cwsg.

These bards also refer to an Owen whose advent was expected, but as we have not seen any MSS. of their works earlier than 1350, it is not possible to ascertain whether these references occur in the original poems or not. As far, however, as they repeat the stories already found in the works of the earlier bards, they are presumably genuine compositions.

There can be no doubt, as we shall show later on, that these prophecies, with their references to an Owen who was to be the deliverer of his nation, exercised a potent influence on the Welsh, and prepared the way for the gallant enterprises of Welshmen like Owen Glyndwr and Henry VII, the grandson of Owen Tudor.

To illustrate this we shall quote a few passages attributed to these poets in Welsh MSS. The extracts are taken for the most part from a MS. written by Lewis Morris in 1726, copied from an older MS. of which Lewis Morris gives this description : "It is of a fair character, with a Saxon or old British Letter at y⁰ beginning of each Cowydd; and by its orthography I guess it might be written about y⁰ time of Henry y⁰ Eight. It hath been sometimes In y⁰ hands of the famous Mr. William Jones, Mathemat. of Llanbabo (formerly Secretary to the Lord Chancellour of England), for I find his name of his own handwriting therein, and [also] some annotations in the margin written y⁰ year 1597."

> "Mi a stynaf yr haf yn oleuaf i le
> Ag yn deccach nog i bu haf o'r Hafe
> Mi anfona rad i bob gwlad rhag eisie
> Mi a ollynga ofyn i'r Dyffryn mawr i ddryge
> Mi a dynna y Ddraig wen o uwch ben 'r holl ddreigie
> Mi a dystia 'n gyntaf yr haf hirfelyn
> A phob dyffryn yn llawn or grawn dinewyn

A goreseyn llydan gan hudol llwydwyn
Llydaw, ar naid ai blaid o'r Gorllewyn
Llew goruchel rhyfel yn goreseyn
A gobeitho rhagllaw y daw llawenydd
A phob deynudd yn ymgweiriaw
Gwyr a meirch marchogion Llydaw
Llychlyn ar gychwyn a dytyn i Fanaw
Saith gan llywydd llynges ar des yn hwyliaw
Ag ir wen ynus, ynus Lydaw
Llwydion farchogion y Mon yn tiriaw
Ag Owain ai wyr i bob tir a ddaw."

Y Bardd Cwsg.

Owing to the modern orthography, one would be inclined to attribute this poem to a later date than 1300, were it not that the references to the seven hundred ships coming over the sea are found in the *Black Book of Carmarthen*, p. 25, as stated before. Though the spelling has been modernized, there is no reason to doubt that the poem itself may be the genuine work of Y Bardd Cwsg.

Here is another poem by the same author :

"Daw byd anhyfryd i Saesson
Rhag maint i gallu ni allant fyddon[1]
Er hyd fo'r coed cadarn nis cuddion
Na dim ni bydd wrth i boddion
Cyfud o gudd gwr a wna budd oi obeithion
Ag Owain fydd i henw honaid gyfrangon
Llew glew a glywir i adchwelon
Llyngesau 'n ddian a ddaw i Aberon
Aberoedd a fu ufuddion
A Chymru yn hy ynghaerfrangon
Caffant wledd gylanedd oi gelynion
Owain a fu, Owain a fydd, Owain a fydd etto'n
Ag Owain a rydd gwared am i tir i Frython.[2]"

These prophecies, together with the others quoted from earlier sources, are sufficient evidence of the fact that the Welsh people were looking forward to the coming of an

---

[1] fudion. [2] See also *Cat. Hist. MSS.*, Mostyn MSS., p. 104.

Owen from over the seas who would re-conquer the lands
they had lost. Originally they may have referred to Owen
ab Edwin or Owen of Manaw, as Stephens suggests,[1] but
as time went on they were made applicable to Owen ap
Thomas, Owen Glyndwr, and even Henry VII, the grandson of Owen Tudur. So great was the influence of these
vaticinatory poems that it is said Welshmen sold their
goods and belongings in order to buy horses and armour in
readiness for the new leader they were expecting. As
recently as the 16th century the people of Anglesea,
influenced by the dark sayings of the Welsh seers, did not
trouble to plough and sow, expecting the end of the world,
as the following extract shows :—

"Sion Brwynog, neu Sion ap Hywel ap Llywelyn ab Ithel oedd
fardd o Fon, a flodeuodd rhwng 1520 a 1560. Yn ei amser ef yr
oedd y werin yn myfyrio mwy ar y Brudiau nag ar lyfrau buddiol, a
thrigolion Mon y pryd hyny yn peidio aredig na hau, gan ddisgwyl
diwedd y byd "Hau i bwy"? meddent. Am hyny canodd Sion
Brwynog yr Englyn canlynol.

"Arddwn, gweddiwn bob ddau—yn gefnog
  Nog ofnwn y Brudiau;
  Tirion hedd, tariwn i hau
  Tra fo un o'r terfynau."   *Gutyn Peris*, 1836.

But the most interesting proof of the all-absorbing
interest taken by the Welsh in these prophecies is found
in a poem by Meredydd ab Rhys, who lived about the
middle of the 15th century, which we give here at length.

The bard had neglected his farm, and sold his cattle,
buying instead horses and armour "like a soldier". For
nine years he had watched the sea, expecting the hosts of
the deliverer, only to be disappointed. At last he had to
sell his horses and armour, and even his shirt, to make
peace with the king. All this causes him to curse the

---

[1] *The Literature of the Kymry*, 1849, p. 216.

book of prophecies which had misled him. The book is
then supposed to address him and to remonstrate with him
on his incredulity, but he persists in his disbelief to the
end.

" Y brad llwyd kymysc brud a llaid[1]
Brud hen llyfr y Brytaniaid
brwydyr ar dir kamber ydwyd
brychliw dwrch brycheulud wyd
brath groen hyfr brith grwn hyfedr
byrkutan tal llydan lledr
beth a dal ym dy obeithiaw
yn boeth y bych hen beth baw.
Eddilwch ym dy ddilid
1 ddiawl gwent i ddel gid
y neb ai yscifen au
a lenwis dy ddolenau
am roi ynvyt gerdd Ferddin
yn llowdwr krwth o henlledr krin
a tarw moel llyna goel gwan
in twyllo on tai allan.
Ffol yw dy siarad brad brec
ffol o eiriau ffilorec
a ddaw ir bobol a wyddym
fyd ta a heb ddowod tym ?
kred fi na rown welldyn krin
er myrdd o eiriau Merddin.
Mae ynod bragod bregeth
gyfrinach gwion bach beth
y gwr a ddyfod geiriau
gwir gynt heb draythu gair gau
bellach ni chair gair ogan
digelwydd rwng dau galan
sores am bob gair saruc
oth ben lyfr fferen ffuc
ni chawn er a wnawn o nod
oer gwynyn air gwir ynod
hwyr ddadyl herwydd a ddoydy
hen bortias Adda fras fry.

---

[1] *Addit. MSS.* 31057, p. 39.

Bod yn anhwsmon bydol
ar dasc a weythym ar dol
gwerthu r gwarthec mowrdec man
a ffrynu meirch a ffrwynau
prynais fal milwr gwr gwrdd
rif amyl or arfau ymwrdd
gwilio i bum ar gil heb wedd
am y lan es naw mylynedd
ar feder wrth ymarfodi
symyd fyd i somed fi
gorfod gwerthu r graic arfau
ar meirch rygorol or mau
a gwerthu r bais rac trais trin
i brynu heddwch brenin.
A brydais yt y bryd serth
a brydaf yt yn brydferth
ffailiedic lyfr ffol ydwyd
ffeiliest ar iawn ffalster wyd
ffugiol o hen henol brych
ffugiol fyth poed ffagal fyddych.
Taw dy fardd nid ta dy foes
tirion rroed Mair yt hir oes
Och fi grist pann na chaf gred
am i ham lyfr myhumed
och wr drwc wyd o chware
chwerw a ffrom na chair ffrae
Drwc yw fal dirawio gwr
Dy ddyll nid wyd ddeyallwr
Deyall hyn Duw ai llynia
i daw y byd hyfryd ta
edrych a welych o waith
a wnel Duw erbyn eilwaith
Gad ym f arglwydd gydymaith
atteb ith wyneb oth iaith
Maer drin wedi eginaw
yn gwyr drud yn Lloyger draw
pan fo aeddfed yw fedi
yn amser yr R ar i
y mae gyfyrbyn a Mon
ar i oddef arwyddion
ynnynu tan ymanaw
a fydd ruw ddydd a ddaw
i ddiawl pe lloscai Ddulyn
oedd ddim mwy ol i ddyn

taw, taw a ddaw eiddil
hwt, hwt, dos yscwt yscil
temel gau twyll odlau lledlyth
iti ni choiliaf fi fyth."

Meredydd ap Rys ai kant.

We now come to the prophecies in which reference is
made to Owen ap Thomas. The first poem was written
by Iolo Goch and was printed by Mr. Ashton in his
edition, p. 239. The text in his book is, however, so
corrupt that we append another version taken from a MS.
written about the middle of the 16th century. Mr. Ashton
takes for granted that the Owen referred to in the poem
is Owen Glyndwr, but we think this assumption is in-
correct.

In the third and fourth lines the author gives the name
of the person whose praises he sings as Y and N and I
and W, which form YWIN or YWAIN. In line 7 Ywin
is called a sailor, a description by no means inapplicable
to Owen ap Thomas or Ywain des Galles, but hardly
applicable to Owen Glyndwr. In lines 21 and 22 the bard
refers to the killing of two of Owen's uncles. Now, we
do not think there is any record of the killing of two
of Owen Glyndwr's uncles by the English, but the two
brothers of Owen ap Thomas's grandfather Rhodri, *i.e.,*
the two last princes of Wales, Llewelyn and David ap
Gruffydd, received their death blows at the hands of
the English, so that the reference would be quite correct
in his case. In lines 27, 28, and 29 there are references
to Owen's coming from over the sea, another fact incon-
sistent with the history of Owen Glyndwr. On the whole,
therefore, we are inclined to think that this poem, since
it undoubtedly refers to some historic personage contemporary with Iolo Goch, must refer to Owen ap Thomas
ap Rhodri.

The latter part of the poem is simply a repetition of the
older poems mentioned above, but we know of no reference
in these older poems to the slaughter of two uncles of the
traditional Owen, and this fact alone seems to us to be
primâ facie proof that our hero is referred to here.

    " Rodded tuw ras kwmpas koeth[1]
    Gair hwylddawn ir gwr haelddoeth
    Y ac N ywr kymhenddoeth
    I ac V ddwbl ywr kwbl koeth
5 Mae yni fryd wryd aer
    Ruthro engyl rrethri anglaer
    Morgenau nid amheuir
    ymorol flaidd hoiw radd hir
    Blwyddyn yw hon gron gryno
10 Ir ddraic wen roi iffen ar flo
    Ar ddraic koch lwybr wrth groch lid
    Ai hamlwe ffagl ai hymlid
    Llithred eira llethrid araul
    Gan ddeheuwynt ne hynt haul
15 Pan ddel ior kynyddfor kain
    Gwr o lendid i gaer Lundain
    Ang hyfion y kyssonir
    O Rufain damwain i dir
    Efo a ddial ddeudal ddic
20 Bore rwng Dofr a Berwic
    Na bu iawn ddygyn greulawn wedd
    Weithred ladd i hewythredd
    Fflamblaid Loegr bobl goegras
    Yn fflam dan a mwe glan glas
25 Dan ddyrnodiau blifiau blwng
    Glod astud ai glud ostwng
    Ni wybyddir o hir hynt
    Ar for gwyrdd las gwynias gwynt
    Oni ddel tarw ryfel taer
30 Ymyse engil ymwase anglaer
    Trwy Gymry lle treir llew trin
    Yno i bydd yn naw byddin
    Myrdd ar for gwyrdd a fwrw gwynt
    Lwgwr ddeffro i Loegr ddyfrynt

---

[1] *Addit. MSS.* 31057, f. 102*b*.

35 A chanto bwiall eillmin
    Llychlyn llwybr tremic trin
    [Fyniw dir ne Fon y daw
    Leder ar bobyl o Lydaw
    A chantaw er blinawr blaid
40 Llynges o naw kan llongaid
    Llong a ddaw gar llaw ffawydd
    Llongesawe o fachawe fydd
    A llong fraith a lleng frython
    A llynges gar mynwes Mon."

                    Iolo Goch ai kant.

But if there is any doubt about this poem, there can be
none about the one that follows, which is a remarkable
instance of the light thrown on current events by Welsh
Poetry.[1] The poem is variously attributed to Llywelyn ap
Cynfrig ddu o Fon, Llywelyn Meurig ddu, Llywelyn
ap Owain, and others. There are copies of it in the
following MSS.: British Museum *Additional* 14887, f. 47
(17th cent.), 14994, f. 58*b* (O. Myfyr), 31057, f. 44 (16th
cent.) and f. 115*b*, and in the *Lewis Morris MS.* before
referred to. All these MSS. differ in minor details, which
we shall refer to when necessary. The bard begins by
referring to the Brudiau, or prophecies, of Myrddin
Amhorfryn, Myrddin Emrys and Taliesin. In line 32
there is a mention of Owen Lawgoch, but we have quite
failed to gather its meaning or make out its connection
with the three preceding lines. The MSS. differ slightly
in their readings.

    Addit. 31057, f. 44, has

            " Tridydd ormes Taliessin[2]
             trethu a wnai truth oi fin

---

[1] In Pen. MS. 94, p. 180, it is called "Marwnad Ywein Tudyr," but
this is clearly wrong.

[2] The three "Armes Taliesin" will be found in the *Myf. Arch.*
(Geo's ed.), pp. 45, 72, 119.

Ni day oi ben grechwen groch
Awen lwgwr Owain lowiwgoch."

The Lewis Morris MS. has

"Trydydd ornes Taliesin
traethai oi fodd truth oi fin
Nid ac oi ben grechwen groch
Awen lewgur Owen Lowgoch."

The poet then refers to the prophecies of Adda Fras and Y Bergam, who had taught the people to be on the watch for the coming conqueror. Consequently they had watched the shores and had bought horses and arms in readiness for the fray,[1] only, however, to be disappointed.

"The grandson of Rhodri came not, and great was our grief, alas that he came not, may the devil who murdered him be himself killed."

This reference in line 46 to the murder of Owen by an assassin shows how the news was received in Wales. All the MSS., however, do not agree as to the reading.

Addit. 31057, f. 44, has

"Lleddid y diawl ai llwyddawd."

Add. 14887, f. 47, has

"Lleddid y dewl ai lladdawdd."

The line is omitted in the *Lewis Morris MS.*

The bard then proceeds to lament his loss and calls him "the son from Aberffraw in Anglesea," Aberffraw being the seat of the Gwynedd princes. But he continues, "Though the noble Owen of Gwynedd, the son of Thomas, be slain, there is another Owen who is his heir, and all the signs which the bards said were to herald the coming of the deliverer have not yet been seen; Owen is still abiding his time, but when he really comes, we shall have war throughout Wales."

---

[1] Cf. the poem of Meredydd ab Rhys, above.

We suggest that this is the drift of the poem, but
confess that some of the lines are difficult of interpreta-
tion. The reference to another Owen may, of course, be
to Owen Glyndwr, but it may also refer to the Owen who,
according to the old tradition, is still sleeping with his
men in a great cavern, from which he will some day
emerge to win back the lands of his forefathers.[1]

[CYWYDD I OWEN AP THOMAS AP RHODRI.][2]

"Kyfriw ardal kowirdeb
Kof helaeth ni wnaeth neb
Kablur brud kwbwl aur Brydain
Kof y byd kyfrwyddyd kain
5   Dilis goro chwedyl yn oedd
Am a fu ac am a fydd
Am bob chwedyl ir genedl gain
Ywr brud i wr o Brydain
Eraill fal dyna arwydd
10   Ysydd gelwyddoc i swydd
Merddin wyllt hagr orwyllt haint
Amhorfryn amau hwyr fraint
Kerdd wemal am ofalu
Gynt o goed a gant yn gau

---

[1] The following lines out of a poem attributed to Llywelyn ap
Owain ap Cynwrig refer to the same event:—

"Rai a fydd yn ryfeddu
Hir orwedd mewn bedd i bu
Goir mewn pridd yn gyhyd
I gorff yn gyfan i gyd
Yn gyhyd diwyd awen
Kan mlynedd rrinwedd ren
Y Gwr ai duc or gweryd
or bedd yw ddangos ir byd
Na cheisient wiwrent wared
Ni chan na heddwch na ched
Oni fo ymwthio maith
Aer feinios ar o vain aith."

Ll. ap Owain ap Kynwric.

Addit. 31057, f. 66, and at f. 96.

[2] *Addit. MSS.*, 31057 p. 115b.

15 Yw borchell ddiysbell gas
     Ai fedwen fal ynfydwas
     Merddin Emrys am treisiawdd
     Ai fawl pell hawl nid pwyll hawdd
     Ai son wrth frenhinawl sud
20 Gwrtheyrn yn gwrthaud
     Hwn a beris hen burawr
     Lladd y dewinion ir llawr
     A gillwng nid o galledd
     Y ddraic wen ddirowioc wedd
25 Oi chwsk yn ol iach esgud
     I wlad Rufain os hyn osud
     Ynfyd koel or anfad kudd
     Ai law lle roysan ludd[1]
     Trydedd ormes Taliesin
30 Traethu a wnai truth oi fin
     Nid ai oi ben grechwen groch
     Awen lwgwr Owain Lowgoch
     Eryr Kaer Septon[2] arab
     Ai gwrs ar ol gwersi yr ab
35 Adda Fras goweithas gain
     Byrgwd ffals y bergain
     A ddysgodd ini ddisgwyl
     Beunydd bwy gilidd bob gwyl
     Gwiliaw traethau yn ieufank
40 Gorllanw ffrwyth gorllwyn[3] Ffraink
     Prynu meirch glud hybarch glod
     Ac arfau ar fedr gorfod
     Yn ol oiri[4] yr aeth ini
     Er edrych am WYR RODRI
45 Llyna och ym lle ni chawdd
     LLEDDID A DIAWL AI LLADDAWDD
     Ni chan groiw ruw loiw lef
     Uwch fym hen o nen yn nef.
     O druan o bleith yr anwyd[5]
50 O ddyn ai ynfydu iddwyd
     Kyd ddarlleud hud hoiw dryw
     Y gerdd oll ac arwydd yw

---

[1] See *Red Book*, vol. i, p. 98.
[2] See *Myf. Arch.* (Gee's Ed.), p. 561.   [3] *al.* gorllewin.
[4] *al.* ocr ir aeth.   [5] *al.* o ble ir hanwyt.

Mae modd ni wyddud myn Mair
Dull iowngof deall ungair
55 Na graddau nac arwyddion
Y MAB or BERFFRO YM MON
Ni ddoeth diben ych penyd
Ni ddaw byth oni ddel byd
O LLAS OWAIN GAIN GWYNEDD
60 FAB TOMAS FFUREIDDWAS Y FFYDD
MAE GAN GRIST GYFIAWN WISGALL
AWEN AER OWAIN ARALL
Ni ladd dur ruw natur rus
Nowtawdd pryd ystin atus[1]
65 Ni chanwyd kyrn ni chenynt
Kynwr ymhorth Kyllwr gynt
Ni ddoeth nid wyd toeth hyd hyn
Diliw dros gaerau Dvlvyn
Nid mawr angerdd y Werddon
70 Ni bu lud ymud ym Mon
Ni ddialodd gwahodd gwych
Gwm minod gamau mynych
Ni chan bugeilydd yn chwoc
Koel chwerw kil y chwaree
75 Ni sengis ffflowr ddelis fflwch
Brenin Aber bryn ebwch
Ni syrthiodd y seren bengrech
Ir llawr mae Owain yn llech
Pan ddel o drais i geisiaw
80 Owain o dre Rufain draw
Aur dalaith ar daith i daid
O randir i orhendaid
Di argel fydd ryfel rrwy
O Lyn Kain i Lan Konwy."

Llywelyn ap Kynfric Ddu o Fon ai kant.

In *Mostyn MS.* 133, p. 174*b*, there are the following
lines :—

"Pan vo rrvdd rredyn
pan vo koch kelyn   } ai bwiall awchliw.
y daw gwyr Llychlyn

---

[1] *al.* prodestinatus.

Gidag Owain Lowgoch ⎫
Ai baladr rryddgoch ⎬ Ynghors Vochno."[1]
i gyro Sayson val moch ⎭

In the same *Mostyn MS.*, p. 379, is the following enigmatic saying :—

"A lion shalbe generat out of the bere by the full strength an nature of a dunn cow, &c.   Owain Lawgoch."[2]

We find references to Owain Lowgoch in the works of the later poets also. It is not always clear whether they refer to him as a historical or legendary personage, but it is certain that some of the poets who lived a century after his day speak of him in the former character. Tudur Aled, who wrote in the last quarter of the fifteenth century, mentions him in one of his poems, and so do Lewis Glyn Cothi and Lewis Mon. The two extracts which follow are taken from poems by Tudur Aled :—

"Sant ar y vaink Sion tra vych[3]
rruw vylaidd mewn rryfel oeddych
Mwy bw y kad y mab koch
gan Loegr noc Owain Lowgoch
ewch i'r maes gida cheirw Mon
Aros drin ar estronion."

This poem is addressed to John Puleston, who flourished about 1500. The poet speaks of his fierceness in the battle-

---

[1] One of the great battles was to be fought by Owen at Cors Vochno (near Borth, North Cardiganshire). The battles are thus mentioned in *Addit. MS.* 31057 :

" Llyma y prif gadau :
Kad Nan Konwy a Chad Withon
Kad Kors Fochno a chad y Mon
Kad Kwannud a chad Kaerleon
Kad Abergwaith a chad Withon
Ac felly y terfyna."

[2] See *Cat. Hist. MSS.*, vol. i, pp. 106, 110.   [3] Pen. MS., 110, p. 37.

field, and says that his enemies feared him more than the
English people feared Owen Lawgoch.

> "Aeth hwnt air ith anturwyr[1]
> Od a dail ydiw dy wyr
> Llai genym y lle i ganu
> Lle doeth Llyr Lledaith a llu
> LLOWGOCH wyt llaw a gwayw chwyrn
> Llwyth Owen llew a theyrn
> dy wayw yn ddellt neu'n dan a ddaw
> dy gynyw chwyrn da gwnewch arnaw."

In these lines, also addressed to Puleston, the poet
compares his hero to Llawgoch, and then says that he is
of the lineage of Owen, lion and sovereign. Whether this
Owen is Owen Lawgoch or Owen Glyndwr is not clear, but
the Pulestons were descended from a sister of Glyndwr.

Lewis Mon, in a poem to Owain Meurig of Anglesea,
begins by saying:—

> "Awn i Loeger OWAIN LOWGOCH[2]
> Amheirig cainge or mor coch
> I waith ryfel ith rifent
> I dynnu rrwyd hyd yn rrent."

Lewis Glyn Cothi, in addressing Owain ab Gruffydd ab
Nicholas, says :—

> "Ni weled o'r maen bedydd[3]
> Henw sy well n'or hwn sydd;
> Henwau a roed hen ar wyr,
> A hyn mal henwau milwyr ;
> Ban y rhoed bob un o'r rhain,
> O dy Dduw ydoedd Owain.
> Cri OWAIN RHODRI lle'r oedd
> Aeth ei ofn i eithavoedd ;
> Owain y Glyn hen a'i gledd ;
> Owain Nic'las ai naweledd ;
> Owain Gwynedd, llin Gynan " &c.

---

[1] Pen. MSS., 110, f. 44-5.   [2] Addit. 14978, f. 162b.
[3] Lewis Glyn Cothi's Works, p. 139.

The bard praises the name of Owen, and proceeds to
enumerate the celebrated persons who had borne the
name, saying that the fear of Owain Rhodri reached the
furthest limits of the world. Owain Rhodri is here, we
are of opinion, no other than Owen Lawgoch in another
guise.

The "tribanwyr" of Glamorganshire in a later age
reproduced the stock prophecies in verse, but to them
Owen Lawgoch was merely a name, and it is probable that
his connection with Owen ap Thomas had been completely
forgotten. The herald-bards *(arwydd-feirdd)* of North
Wales it is true, as has been already shown in the earlier
part of this paper, did know that he was the same person,
but even their information goes no further than a bald
statement of the fact.

Thomas ab Ieuan ab Rhys, the Twm Gelwydd teg of the
Iolo MSS. (pp. 200-3), who is said to have reached the
patriarchal age of 130 in 1604, wrote a long prophecy
(*cwndid*), in the course of which the following verse
appears :—

"Fe ddaw Owain dros y dwr
a dan gynghorwr ganddo
a'r fran ddu o blith y sêr
ag fe ddaw peder atto."

" Owain with his two councillors will come from
over the water, and the black crow from the
stars, and four others will come to him " (*sic*).

Another song, written in 1668, has the following verses :—

"Ceir clywed cloch hen Arthur yn canu'n fawr ei rhwysg,
I maes o dref Caerlleon yn ymyl Dyffryn Wysg,
Yn seinio dan arwyddion yn erbyn Owen draw,
Medd llyfr y d'roganau sy'n warrant yn fy llaw.

" Ceir gweled Owen law-goch yn d'od i Frydain fawr,
Ceir gweled newyn ceiniog yn nhref Caerlleon-gawr,
Ceir gweled Towi'n waedlyd, a chlwyf ar Edmwnd Goch,
Waeth bod yn Aber-Milffwrd o blaed i'r Saeson moch."

This song was published at Carmarthen in the 18th century and has been reprinted several times, the last occasion within the last two or three years. In the later editions, another song has been added to it called "Dechreu Darogan Myrddin", but we have not seen any edition of this previous to the one printed at Carmarthen by M. Jones. This song also contains references to Owen :—

> "Dan llywodraeth Brenin Owen,
> Hwn wladeidda ynys Brydain :
> Wrth Ffynon-enlliw rhoddant battel,
> Nes cwympo llawer o'r ddwy genel.
>   *   *   *   *
> "A'r Llithynwyr ânt yn amlwg
> Hyd y llo a elwir Colbrwg,
> I gwedd a gwyr y cywyr Owen :
> Hwn wladeiddia ynys Brydain.
>   *   *   *   *
> "Yna cerddant hwy ac Owain,
> A chwmni ar frys i ddinas Llundain ;
> A gosodant hwn yn enwog,
> Yn wyr frenin gwych calonog.
>   *   *   *   *
> "Yr Owen hwn yw Harri'r nawfed,
> Sydd yn trigo yn ngwlad estroniaid :
> Pe bai 'r bleiddiaid wedi ei fwyta,
> Fe ddaw hwn i wlad Brydania."

It is clear that in these later songs the Owen of the *Black Book* prophecies has become confused with Owen Lawgoch and perhaps Owen Glyndwr. The fact remains, however, that the name of Owen Lawgoch is still preserved in a popular song, which has gone into a new edition within the last few years. We have not met with the name Owen Lawgoch in any poetry written before the year 1370. It may be that to the Welsh of the 14th century, the word Llaw-goch was equivalent to the English Red-hand, and had the secondary meaning of outlaw. Were this so, it would explain why Owen ab Thomas should have been thus designated.

APPENDIX I.

An interesting episode illustrative of the attitude of the English government towards Owen of Wales is recorded by the St. Alban's writer of the *Chronicon Angliæ*, 1328-1388, which has been edited under that title by Sir E. Maunde Thompson in the Rolls Series. In his preface the editor observes that about the end of 1376 or 1377 " John Menstreworth, a soldier who had deserted to the French, was brought prisoner to England. It should be remarked that in his confession he speaks of assisting an unknown pretender to the throne of Wales. He was condemned to death, but before execution wrote a private letter to the king, filling ' maximam partem folii papyri regalis,' which he delivered into the hands of lord Henry Percy. This letter was never seen again. Something in it that touched the consciences of lord Percy and the duke [of Lancaster : John of Gaunt] is suggested as the cause of its suppression " (p. lvii).

The chronicler's narrative runs as follows :—

"*De captione J. Menstreworthe et morte ejus.* Per idem tempus captus est quidam miles, nomine Johannes Menstreworthe, qui proditiose exercitum deseruerat Anglicanum, eo tempore quo dominus Robertus Knollis, mandato regis Angliæ, cum multa turba magnatum, missus fuerat ad invadendum vel subjugandum suo nomine regnum Francorum. Hic itaque Johannes et ingenio providus erat et manu promptus, sed ambitiosus plurimum ; multosque in eadem expeditione duxit valentes et fortes. Unde contigit, cum cerneret eundem Robertum alios quoque dominos ejus consilia parvipendere, ut indignatus campum desereret [*another MS.* deferret] et eosdem relinqueret inter manus hostiles, ea præcipue tempestate qua maxime ejus auxilio indigebant. Factumque est, ut tali occasione et exercitus noster magna dispendia pateretur, et ipse ad regem Franciæ iret transfuga mente perversa. Cujus consilio idem rex usus, multa mala intulit genti nostræ. Tandem captus est in Navaria a quodam Vasconensi armigero, dicto Lodowico de Sancto Egidio, juxta urbem Pampilionem, dum literas et mandata regis Francorum deferret versus Hispaniam, ad colligendum ibidem tam copiam armatorum

quam navium, ad regnum Angliæ invadendum : quorum omnium ipse
fuerat dux decretus. Advectus in Angliam et ad confessionem
compulsus, fatebatur quod circa Pascha cum   , [Note : Blank in
the Harl. MS.] qui se dicit heredem Walliæ, venisset ad invadendum easdem partes, quatenus, propriis restitutus, avita hereditate
gaudere ejus auxilio potuisset, et ipse ad regem Franciæ iterum
remeasse. Iccirco post paucos dies condempnatus morte turpissima,
cum cerneret nullam omnino evadendi viam, postulavit calamum et
papyrum, quos dominus Henricus Percy præcipit afferri : scripsitque
maximam partem folii papyri regalis, et signavit illud, rogans ne alius
quam ipse dominus rex illud signaculum removeret. Quod suscepit
de ejus manibus dominus Henricus Percy ; sed quis sigillum amoverit,
quisve contenta perspexerit, soli, ut dicitur, dux et ille sciverunt.
Unde creditum est, quia ad lucem illud scriptum non est venire
permissum, eo quod quædam ibidem contenta perspexerint soli, ut
dicitur, dux et ille, et alterius vel amborum conscientias contingebant.
Idem vero Johannes, postquam talia conscripsisset tractus et
suspensus, ac decapitatus, necnon in quatuor partes sectus, satis, ut
dicebatur, pœnitens, proditoribus provenientes fructus collegit."

There can be little doubt that the personage who
called himself the heir to [the crown of] Wales, and
who talked of invading the principality for the purpose
of resuming his hereditary rights, was Owen of Wales,
but the fact that the chronicler did not know his name
leads to the inference that his personality was not well
known to English writers, though his name, his fame, and
his claims were well impressed upon the minds of the
English officials in France. Poor John Menstreworth or
Minstreworth was executed, and in accordance with the
horrible custom of the times, his body was dismembered,
the quarters being consigned to the towns of York, Newcastle, Bristol, and Carmarthen. The portion destined for
the last mentioned town was entrusted to a David ap
John, who contracted for its conveyance to its destination,
and whose account therefor has survived.[1] In another

[1] The portion for Bristol had to be made into an innocent looking
parcel and shipped "with other merchandise." The Baron de
Kettenhove (*Froissart*, ix, 508 note) gives the following from our

recension of the same chronicle John Minstreworth is
said to have been a Gloucestershire man (in comitatu
Gloucestriæ oriundus). He was in the English ranks, and
is said to have joined the French in the year 1370, after a
quarrel with Sir Robert Knollys. It is possible that he
had heard the story of Owen's departure from Budefeld,
and it is clear that the two became associated. However
that may be, a partially illegible inquisition post mortem
at the Record Office, of the 20th Jan. 47 Edw. III, enables
us to say with certainty that Minstreworth held lands
in Usk.

II.

No effort has been made in the above paper to explain
the rise and development of the legend of Owain Lawgoch.
This is no part of the duty of the historian; but, were it
otherwise, he would have found himself forestalled and
out-distanced by Professor Rhys. A word or two may,
however, be permitted, not in explanation of the peculiar
localisation of the legend, or, rather, the limited area
within which Owain Lawgoch has become its protagonist,
but as an aid to others more capable of offering such
explanation. The country of Owain Lawgoch may be
said to comprise the modern county of Carmarthen, the
central theatre of his exploits being the romantic neighbourhood of Dinefwr, the chief seat of the South Wales
princes of the line of Rhys ap Tewdwr. The legends
with which Owain is expressly connected are, or recently were, current in other portions of South Wales

public records :—"Johanni Pole mercatori eunti cum aliis mercatoribus
cum tertio quarterio ejusdem Johannis versus Bristol, et illud in-
volvit infra unum fardellum inter alia mercimonia sua pro eo quod
nullus inde sciret causa amicorum ejusdem Johannis commorantium
in partibus illis et quia aliquem alium invenire non potuit ad execu-
tionem ejusdem quarterii faciendum, et vix prædictum Johannem
causa supradicta ex conventione inde facta cum Johanne, 73 s. iv d."

(especially the uplands of Glamorganshire, the country of Llewelyn Bren), but curiously enough they are not found in North Wales, where Arthur retains the position from which elsewhere in Wales he has been ousted. This being the case, it would be natural to look for Owen in the line of Deheubarth chieftains. So far, however, as I have been able to learn there is no such personage in the pedigrees of the Dinefwr families. But an Owen Goch was a great man in Carmarthenshire in the first half of the fourteenth century, though I have been able to discover nothing about him beyond his name. This appears in an entry upon the patent rolls of the 13th Edward III (A.D. 1339), where, in a grant to Rhys ap Gruffudd of Dinefwr, are included certain lands of Lleucu (misread Llengu in the printed *Calendar* of the Public Record Office) daughter of Owen Goch. It would be quite in accordance with the principles of mythopœic development to find that this person, having become notorious for his hidings in caves, had lent his name to a greater Owen; though it is historically impossible that he could have been the Owen of Wales who was murdered in the year 1378. I am informed by Mr. W. Llewelyn Williams, barrister-at-law, that Owen Lawgoch is usually spoken of in the valley of the Towy as Owen Goch Lawgoch; and Mr. J. P. Owen, of 72, Comeragh Road, W., tells me that his mother used to relate the pedigree of a great Carmarthenshire family in which an Owen Goch figured. It may not be inappropriate to mention that in a pedigree which I have only just come across in British Museum *Harleian* 1969, Thomas ap Rhodri is given a daughter (not named, but *quære* Elin, see the pedigree from *Hengwrt* 351, *ante* p. 25), said to have been married to Meredydd ap Gruffudd (*alias* ap Owen) ap Gruffudd ap yr arglwydd Rhys of Dinefwr.

The South Wales genealogies are in a terrible tangle, and not one of them can be accepted for historical purposes without correction and corroboration from the public records.

III.

In the second volume of *Feudal Aids*, recently issued by the Deputy Keeper of the Public Records, under the county of Gloucester, at p. 251, is the following entry relating to the year 1303 :—

"Hundredum de Byseley. De Botherico (*rectius* Rotherico) filio Grifyny pro quarta parte un[ius] f[eodum] m[ilitis] in Budefelde." (De eodem comite [H. de Bohun], sed per forisfacturam accidit regi. *added.*)

Further on (p. 286) is the following, of the date of 1346 :—

"Hundredum de Byseleye. De Thoma Rotherwyk pro quarta parte un. f. m. in Budefeld quam Rothericus (filius Grifyny), pater suus, quondam tenuit ibidem, x*s.*"

The first of these entries proves that the small estate of Budefeld had been enjoyed by Rhodri ap Gruffudd, and the passages at p. 39 of this paper require modification accordingly. It would also seem that Thomas did not succeed to the manor by hereditary right, his father Rhodri's grant appearing to be for life only. Thomas obtained a re-grant, and was in possession in A.D. 1346.

CORRIGENDA.

P. 19, 8th line from bottom, alter " to John de Neville " into " of John de Neville", and *dele* " by John de Neville " in last line but one of same page.

P. 23, 12th line from bottom, *dele* the square bracket.

P. 37, last line, and p. 44, line 15, the year 1364 should be 1363 ; *vide* Thomas ap Rhodri's inq. post mortem, p. 47.

P. 40, 6th line. The date of the returns called *Nomina Villarum* is the 9th Ed. II, not Ed. I.

P. 44, 12th line from bottom, for " Gruffudd ap Iorwerth", read " Gruffudd ap Llewelyn ap Iorwerth ".

CANU PENILLION.[1]

GAN Y

PARCH. W. H. WILLIAMS (Watcyn Wyn).

Pa fodd y dechreuwyd canu geiriau, canu llinellau, canu penillion? Yr wyf bron meddwl mai adrodd wedi codi i hwyl ydyw, siarad wedi angerddoli,—

"Ymadroddion ar dân
Yw geiriau ar gân."

Y mae barddoniaeth yn y meddwl, a cherddoriaeth yn y llais yn galw ar eu gilydd ac yn ateb eu gilydd o hyd. Beth yw'r "Hwyl Gymreig" ond siarad ar gân, a chynghorwn bob un i ofalu nad aiff i "hwyl" os nad all e' ganu,—ond yr wyf yn ofni fod rhai yn gwneyd.

Credwn mai y syniad cyntaf o ganu geiriau yw, ymollwng i adrodd yn naturiol nes codi i hwyl a gwres, a phriodi seiniau cydnaws a'r geiriau beth bynag fyddont. Y mae hyn yn amlycach yn ein hen gerddoriaeth nag ydyw mewn cerddoriaeth ddiweddar, ac y mae yn amlwg iawn yn y "canu gyda'r tannau", oblegid y darnodiad o hwnw yw "adroddiad ar gân". Fel hyn y dywed Idris Fychan mewn llyfr ar ganu gyda'r tannau, sydd wedi ei gyhoeddi gan Gymdeithas y Cymmrodorion; "nid canu yr alaw y bydd y dadgeiniad, ond rhoi adroddiad ar gân; y delyn sydd yn canu'r alaw". Yr offeryn sydd yn

---

[1] Read before the Honourable Society of Cymmrodorion, at 20, Hanover Square, on Wednesday, the 11th of April, 1900. Chairman: Mr. William Jones, M.P.

cyfeilio y'nghaneuon y dyddiau diweddaf hyn, a'r llais
dynol yn canu'r alaw, ond gyda'r tannau yr offeryn sydd
yn canu'r alaw, a''r dadganwr yn cyfeilio. Fe all y
dadganwr gyda'r tannau gymeryd digon o ryddid, os bydd
yn deall ei waith, dim ond iddo ofalu am bum peth—
mesur, acen, cynghanedd, amser, a thonyddiaeth.

Y mae y gelfyddyd yn myned dan dri enw gwahanol,
sef Canu gyda'r tannau, Canu gyda'r delyn, a Chanu
penillion. Canu gyda'r tannau mae'n debyg yw'r hen
enw, a'r enw cyflawnaf, am fod yna offerynau llinynol
eraill gan yr hen Gymry heblaw y delyn.

Yr oedd y crwth mewn bri neillduol fel offeryn Cymreig.
Y mae un o'r hen feirdd Gryffydd ap Hywel wedi canu
cywydd "Y Crwth Chwechtant", ac y mae yn werth
ei ddyfynu i ddangos yr offeryn :—

> " Prenol teg, bwa a gwregis,
> Pont a bran, punt yw ei bris,
> A thalaith ar waith olwyn
> A'r bwa ar draws byr ei drwyn ;
> Ac o'i ganol mae dolen,
> A gwâr ŵyr megis gwr hen,
> Ac ar ei frest cywir frig
> O'r masarn fe geir miwsig ;
> Chwe yspigod os codwn,
> A dyna holl dânau hwn,
> Chwe thant a gaed i fantais
> Ac yn y llaw yn gân llais,
> Tant i bob bys ysbys oedd
> A deudant i'r fawd ydoedd."

Gwelir felly y gall canu gyda'r tannau feddwl canu gyda'r
delyn, neu gyda'r crwth, neu ryw offeryn llinynol arall.

Nid oes angen esbonio canu gyda'r delyn, y mae yn
esbonio ei hun.

"Canu penillion,"—dylem ddweyd gair ar hyn. Yr
oedd yna offerynau cerddorol eraill, heblaw y delyn
deirhes, a'r crwth chwechtant gan yr hen Gymry, megis y

crwth trithant, y bibgorn, a'r tabwrdd, ac os na allai dyn feistroli un o'r offerynau hyn gallai gael pastwn, a gelwid ef yn "gerddor pen pastwn". Tebyg mai oddi wrth hyn y mae y term "pastynfardd" ein dyddiau ni yn dod, ac feallai mai tylwyth o'r un teulu ydynt.

Gallwn feddwl mai rhywbeth yn lle dawnsio oedd y pastwn yma, os na allai dyn chwareu a'i law, na dawnsio a'i droed, celai gynyg ar y pastwn. Y tro diweddaf y bu "cystadleuaeth ben pastwn" wirioneddol yn yr Eisteddfod Genedlaethol oedd yn Llangollen yn y flwyddyn 1858. Bu yno le difrifol yn ol yr hanes, pump neu chwech ar y llwyfan yn pastyno am y goreu! Ab Ithel mae'n debyg oedd y pechadur cenedlaethol ddygodd hyn i fewn, a bu rhai o'r gwyr selog am "drefn a dosbarth" yn bygwth ei bastyno yntau am wneyd hyn. Ond diangodd; tebyg fod ofn y pastynau eraill arnynt.

Mae'n debyg mai y delyn deirhes oedd y delyn Gymreig. "Y delyn droed", neu y "pedal harp" yw telyn y Sais, ac yr oedd y diweddar Mynyddog yn arfer dweyd mai y gwahaniaeth rhwng Cymro a Sais yn canu telyn oedd fod y Cymro yn chwareu a'i law, ond fod y Sais yn rho'i ei droed ynddi bob tro y byddai yn cynyg. Mae'n debyg mai telyn deirhes oedd y delyn gyntaf enillodd Pencerdd Gwalia, a'r hyn oedd yn rhyfedd yn hono oedd fod y *bass* ar ochr y llaw dde, ar *air* ar ochr y llaw chwith, a'r peth cyntaf wnaeth y telynwr cyflym oedd, newid y tannau, er mwyn i'r llaw dde gael canu *air* a'r llaw chwith ganu *bass*. Ond y mae yn chwith genym feddwl, fod y Pencerdd medrus, wedi "rho'i ei droed ynddi" er's llawer dydd!

Mae'n debyg fod perthynas agos gynt rhwng y bardd, a'r telynwr, a'r dadganwr,—yr oedd y tri yn un. Yr oedd yn rhaid i'r pencerdd fod yn benbardd, a'r penbardd, yn bencerdd. Pe delai yr hen drefn yn ol, byddai genym lai o brif feirdd nag sydd, ac ni byddai y pencerdd mor aml hefyd. Yr oedd yn rhaid i'r pencerdd gynt yn llys tywysogion Cymru Fu, allu gwneyd telyn, cyweirio telyn, canu telyn a'i law ei hun, gwneyd ei farddoniaeth ei hun, a chanu ai lais ei hun, ac yna celai ei dalu; ac yr oedd hi yn werth talu dyn felly—yr oedd yn dalentog mewn gwirionedd. Eithaf peth fyddai cael yr hen drefn yn ol, er mwyn i'r bardd chwilio am ei lais, a'r cerddor am ei awen, ac atal eu tal os na allant wneyd hyny.

Mae'n debyg mai mewn cystadleuaeth y dechreuwyd canu penillion. Yr oedd yr hen Gymry yn enwog iawn am gystadlu. Yr oedd ganddynt bedair-camp-ar-hugain mewn chwareu, pedair-cainc-ar-hugain mewn miwsig, a phedwar-mesur-ar-hugain mewn barddoniaeth. Pwy all esbonio dirgelwch y rhif "pedwar-ar-hugain" yn Llyfr Dadguddiad ein hen genedl ni?

Yn amser Hywel Dda, pan fuasai y pencerdd farw cystadleuid am ei gadair yn y llys. Os buasai mwy nag un teilwng yn cynyg yr oedd yn rhaid penderfynu drwy gystadleuaeth, a chystadleuaeth galed oedd hi, am fod y sefyllfa yn urddasol a'r tal yn dywysogaidd, ar dynion mwyaf athrylithgar a gwrteithiedig yn y wlad yn cynyg am y swydd.

Wedi colli nawdd y tywysogion, a chefnogaeth bonedd y wlad y dysgwyd canu penillion gan y werin. Credwn mai yn canu penillion, ac yn dilyn telyn y cafodd ysbryd y deffroad afael yn ei gyweirnod. Wedi i daran dori uwchben y llys, wedi i'r ystorm ddychrynu y pendefigion yn eu palasdai, ac i hen noddfeydd y gân gael eu chwalu y cafodd gwerin Cymru afael yn "y gân a gollwyd". Chwalwyd y gân, ond nid aeth un nodyn i golli. Crewyd discord ond ni ddinystriwyd y gynghanedd. Collwyd y pencerdd, ond cadwyd y gerdd yn fyw. Tarawyd y bardd i lawr, ond dyrchafwyd yr Awen. Wedi peidio talu neb aeth pawb i ganu am ddim, ac "ni bydd diwedd"

byth ar swn y delyn mwy. Credwn mai dyma ddechreu
canu, a dylem ninau fel cenedl feallai "ddechreu canmol"
y rhagluniaeth ryfedd ddygodd hyn i fodolaeth.

Y mae Gweirydd ap Rhys, yn "*Hanes Llenyddiaeth
Gymreig*" yn dweyd; Pan derfynodd cefnogaeth gyffred-
inol y pendefigion i Farddoniaeth, ac y peidiodd a bod yn
grefft i enill arian fel yr oedd hi gynt, daeth penillion a
chaneuon, ac anterliwdiau i gael eu cyfansoddi a'u coleddu
yn fwy cyffredinol"; ond nid dyma y pryd y dechreuwyd
ysgrifenu cyfansoddiadau o'r ansawdd hyn. Yr oedd
cefnogi a chyfoethogi y bobl a phenillion a diarhebion yn
un o hen arferion y sefydliad barddonol.

Yr oedd tai cân a thelyn yn gyffredin y'Nghymru gynt,
ac yr oedd y muriau wedi eu gorchuddio a phenillion, a
thrioedd, a diarhebion; a'r pethau hyn yr oedd yr hen
Gymry yn "papyro y gwelydd",—nid rhyfedd eu bod yn
hyddysg ynddynt. I'r tai hyn y byddai bechgyn a
merched talentog y gymydogaeth yn crynhoi i gwrdd a'u
gilydd, i gystadlu canu a barddoni. Dyma lle tarddodd
y ffrydiau sydd wedi gwneyd "môr o gân" o Gymru i
gyd.

Canent bob math o ganeuon. Y mae Idris Fychan yn
dweyd fod pedwar dosbarth o ganeuon ganddynt, sef (1)
Caneuon gwladgarol, (2) Alawon helbul, (3) Cerddi
dawnsio, ac (4) Alawon bugeiliol a charwriaethol. Yr
oeddynt yn rhanu eu halawon yn *sets*, yr hyn sydd yn
profi eu bod yn deall cerddoriaeth ac yn gallu ei threfnu.

Nid yn unig yr oedd hi yn gystadleuaeth rhwng y
dadgeiniaid a'u gilydd, ond yn gystadleuaeth galed
rhwng y telynwr a'r dadganwr, am fod un yn ceisio bwrw
y llall allan. Gall y dadgeiniad daro i fewn lle y mŷn, ond
peidio taro ar ddechreu'r *bar*, a gall fyn'd lle y myno ond
gofalu bod yn ol i orphen i'r eiliad gyda'r delyn. Os elai
y telynwr allan yr oedd y cwmni yn gwaeddi "Dyna dwll

yn y delyn"; os elai y dadgeiniad allan gwaeddent oll,
"Dyna dwll yn y gân".

Wrth gystadlu celai yr un ar ben y rhes ddewis ei fesur
i ddilyn y delyn, a byddai yn rhaid i bob un y tro hwnw
ddilyn yn yr un mesur. Yr ail dro celai yr ail gychwyn a
dewis ei fesur, a byddai yn rhaid i bob un y tro hwnw ei
ddilyn yntau, ac felly nes myned o gylch i gyd. Yr oedd
hyn yn gofyn côf da a digon o benillion, neu ynte awen
barod a digon o allu gwneyd penill ar unrhyw fesur.

Y mae dau ddull o ganu, dull y Gogledd a dull y De,
ac y maent yn dra gwahanol. Canu "sill am dant", maent
yn y De, a chanu cyfeiliant yn ol dull y Gogledd. [Rhodd-
wyd engreifftiau o'r ddau ddull mewn cân gan Eos Dâr.]
Fel y dywedasom, yn y tai cyffredin, yn hen amaethdai y
wlad,—ar ol colli nawdd llys a phalas,—y dysgodd y werin
ganu penillion, a diamau mai yno yr oedd y canu goreu,
yr oedd yn fwy rhydd, ac yn fwy cartrefol. Teimlad
llawer un o'r bechgyn doniol, ac o'r merched glân wrth
agoshau at ambell hen amaethdy oedd :—

> "Wel dyma'r hen dy wyf yn garu,
> Hen dy canu telyn y'Nghymru!
>   A'r gwellt iddo'n do,
>   A'r drws heb un clo,
> A'r mur ddim rhy falch i'w wyngalchu!

> "A phistyll bach gloew yn disgyn
> Dan ganu wrth dalcen y bwthyn,
>   A'r pistyll bach glân
>   Yn dweyd am y gân
> A glywid o fewn yr hen gegin!

> "A digon o le ar y pentan
> I gynwys y teulu yn gyfan,
>   A goleu tân glo
>   Yn gwneuthur y tro,
> I gadw'r tywyllwch tu-allan.

"A chwmni o'r bechgyn doniolaf,
Yn gymysg a'r merched siriolaf,
    A phob un a'i gân,
    Yn gylch am y tân,
I loni nosweithiau y gauaf!

" Bydd Dafydd a'i law ar y delyn,
A Gwen gyda'i phenill yn dilyn,
        A'r Awen fwyn ddôs
        Yn canu'n y nós
I gadw'r Bwciod o'r gegin,

" A'r Henwr o'i gader heb godi,
Ddystawa y stwr gyda'i stori,
    Mae pob un yn glust,
    A phawb yn dweyd 'ust',
Un doniol yw Newyrth am dani!"

Yr oedd "y stori" yn chwareu rhan bwysig ar yr hen
aelwydydd doniol hyn, weithiau caffai ei hadrodd, bryd
arall ei chanu. Onid "storiau" ar gân yw ein Bugeilgerddi
a'n Rhiangerddi; a'r rheol gynt oedd eu cyfansoddi o'r
dechreu i'r diwedd ar yr un mesur, ar un o fesurau yr hen
alawon Cymreig, er mwyn eu canu gyda'r delyn.

Yr ydym wedi sylwi yn fynych mewn ambell Riangerdd,
neu Fugeilgerdd ddiweddar, mai gwendid awenyddol yw
newid y mesur; y mae y bardd fel yn myned maes o anadl
ac yn newid ei fesur yn sydyn heb ddim yn y byd yn y gân
yn gofyn am hyny, ond tebyg fod y rheswm i'w gael yn y
bardd.

Mae'n debyg mai caneuon serch, a rhyw ganeuon
bugeiliol, oedd yn cael eu canu fynychaf gan y bobl
gyffredin, gan feibion a merched gwlad y delyn. Arthur
yn cydio yn Elen a "braich o gywydd", ac Elen yn goglais
Arthur a rhyw "gynghanedd braidd gyffwrdd",— y rhai
hyn oedd penillion anwyl y beirdd, a'r rhai hyn oedd wrth
fodd calon y merched, yn peri i'w llygaid ddisgleirio a'u
gruddiau wrido o fwynhad! Cariad a Thelyn! Wrth

edrych dros hen benillion telyn, (Casgliad Mr. Jenkyn
Thomas,) dyma y rhai gyfarfyddwn fynychaf o ddigon.
Dyma ychydig o honynt:—

"Llawer gwaith y bu fy mwriad,
Gael telynor imi'n gariad,
Gan felused swn y tanau
Gyda'r hwyr a chyda'r borau.

"Cleddwch fi pan fyddwyf farw,
Yn y coed dan ddail y derw ;
Chwi gewch weled llanc penfelyn,
Ar fy medd yn chwareu'r delyn !

"Ffordd fer i dreulio'r gauaf,
Hir oriau tywydd eira,
Yw cadair fawr o flaen y tân,
A llunio cân ddiddana.

"Dau lanc ifanc aeth i garu,
Noswaith dywyll fel y fagddu,
Swn cacynen yn y rhedyn,
Troes nhw adre'n fawr eu dychryn.

"Os ai di garu dos yn gynar,
Cyn i'r merched fwyta'u swpar,
Ti gai weled yn y gwydyr
Pwy sydd lan a phwy sydd fudur

"Llawn yw'r mor o heli a chregin,
Llawn yw'r wy o wyn a melyn,
Llawn yw'r coed o ddail a blodau,
Llawn o gariad merch wyf finau.

"Lle bo'r cariad, wiw mo'r ceisio
Cloi mor drws na'i ddyfal folltio,
Lle bo'r 'wyllys fe dyr allan
Drwy'r clo dûr a'r dderwen lydan."

Ond waeth heb ddyfynu penillion telyn a serch, y maent
yn ddirif, a chenid hwy yn ddiddiwedd, ac y mae yr hen
fesur hwn yn bur boblogaidd ;. mewn gwirionedd nid oes
un mesur wedi cael cymaint o le yn marddoniaeth Cymru,
y mae t'rawiad naturiol y llinell yn cerdded gyda ni i bob
math o farddoniaeth lleddf a llon.

I

Mesur arall poblogaidd iawn yw y Triban, yn enwedig yn y De, yn Morganwg. Y mae rhai o nodweddion amlwg barddoniaeth Cymru yn y triban, megis yr "odl canol y llinell" a'r "gynghanedd braidd gyffwrdd":—

> "Nid dwli canu telyn,
> Nid anglod crefft gwneyd englyn,
> Mae ambell un heb un o'r ddwy,
> O lawer fwy o lolyn,
>
> " Y genedl ddeil i ganu,
> A'r diddan fo'n prydyddu,
> Ddaw dim un gwarth i dad na mam,
> O'r hanos am y rheiny."

Yr oedd triawdau yn gyffredin iawn wedi eu rhoddi yn y tribanau, megis;

> " Tri pheth sy'n anhodd hynod,
> Byw'n sobr lle bo diod,
> 'Nabod merch wrth wel'd ei gwên
> A thwyllo hen frythillod!"

ys dywedai rhyw hen fardd oedd wedi bod yn pysgota, a ffaelu dala dim drwy'r dydd.

Y mae "ergyd canol y llinell", wedi gwneyd gwaith cryf a phendant iawn yn ein hen farddoniaeth, yr oedd yr hoel yn cael ei tharo ar ei phen yn hwn bob amser, ac ergyd i dre gan law gyfarwydd, a rhyw anadl cynghanedd yn cynorthwyo.

Difyr iawn fyddai olrhain dadblygiad y gynghanedd yn ein barddoniaeth. Yr oedd yr holl fesurau oddigerth dau neu dri yn ein meddiant cyn cynghanedd. Gadawodd Dafydd ap Edmwnd rai o honynt allan, a rhoddodd i fewn dri neu bedwar mesur digon diddefnydd a disynwyr. Wn i a ganodd Dafydd awdyl ar y pedwar-mesur-ar-hugain ar ol yr un yn Eisteddfod Caerfyrddin 1451?

Cymerodd y telynegwyr at y mesurau caethion i'w canu gyda'r delyn, am fod yn dda gan glust y Cymro glywed

swn y gynghanedd. Daeth pedwar-mesur-ar-hugain cerdd
dafod, a phedair-cainge-ar-hugain cerdd dant i alw am eu
gilydd yn foreu, a chafodd y dadgeiniad le iawn i ddangos
ei allu i ddarllen ac acenu yn gywir yn y mesurau caethion,
—ond nid yw pob un o honynt wedi dod yn boblogaidd
—y pigion genir.

Credwn fod llawer o'r duedd i fod yn gywrain gyda'r
delyn wedi codi o'r fan hon; a dichon fod hyn yn cyfrif am
boblogrwydd y gynghanedd, yn enwedig yn y Gogledd.

Y mae amryw engreifftiau dewisol o'r cynghaneddion
i'w gweled yn llyfr Idris Fychan. Dyma benill cynganeddol
prydferth iawn;

> "Tra bo rhew yn dew ar dwyn,
> Iâ'n y cwm, a llwm y llwyn,
> Wyf ddi fraw'n cyweiriaw can,
> Yn fardd hy mewn ty min tan,
> Byw fel hyn mewn bwthyn bach,
> Brenin wyf am bron yn iach."

Rhagorol o beth i ddysgu dyn i ddarllen a geirio ac
acenu yn briodol, yw canu cynghanedd gyda'r delyn.
Byddai'n werth i lawer o ddadganwyr y dyddiau hyn fyned
drwy gwrs o addysg "canu gyda'r delyn" er mwyn dysgu
geirio yn hyglyw a phriodol, a chofio fod swn i ddilyn
synwyr, a'r gair i ledo'r gan. Dylid sefydlu Ysgol Canu
Penillion, os am gadw'r hen genedl a'r hen iaith gyda'u
gilydd y'ngwlad y gân. Nid ydym yn cymeryd arnom
farnu y canu, ond gallwn ddweyd fod y geirio yn cael rhy
fach o sylw o'r haner, a'r feddyginiaeth oreu i hyn fyddai
canu gyda'r delyn.

Tra yn son am ddysgu geirio yn gywir, eithaf peth fyddai
i'n dadganwyr gofio tafodiaith hen gân, a'i chanu yn ol y
dafodiaith yn yn hon y cyfansoddwyd hi. Os bydd y gân
yn ol tafodiaith Gogledd Cymru caner hi felly, ond yn ol
tafodiaith Dyfed allan a hi yn iaith y wlad hono, os yn ol

iaith Morganwg, peidier ar un cyfrif a cheisio ei gwyrdroi.
Gallem nodi "Y Gwenith Gwyn" fel engraifft

> "Pa un a'i fi ai arall Gwèn
> Sydd oreu gèn dy galon"

dyna ddywed y bardd yr ydym yn dra sicr, ond fel hyn
mae y gwelliant diweddar,

> "Pa un ai fi ai arall Gwen
> Sydd oreu gan dy galon"

yr hyn sydd yn dinystrio sill acenol canol y llinell, yr
hen ergyd Cymreig ydym wedi bod yn son am dano.

Felly am "Y deryn pur", y mae y'deryn yn colli llawer
o'i bluf harddaf wrth fod y dafodiaith yn cael ei newid.
Cân bachgen ifanc wedi meddwi ar gariad, ac wedi haner
meddwi ar gwrw yw "Y deryn pur", cân wledig syml
o ran miwsig a geiriau, a gresyn na chelai hi ei chanu
felly bob amser, a rhaid ei chanu felly cyn gweled ei
gogoniant.

> "Y deryn pur a'r aten las,
> Bydd imi'n was dibrydar,
> Brysur brysia at y ferch,
> Lle rhoes i'm serch am hydar ;
> Dos di ati, dwad wrthi,
> Mod i'n wylo'r dwr yn heli
> Mod i'n irad am ei gwelad,
> Ac o'i chariad yn ffaelu a cherad,
> O! Duw faddeuo i'r hardd ei llun
> Am boeni dyn mor galad."

Caner yr hen gân yn rhydd a naturiol heb addurno dim
arni ac heb geisio gwneyd y miwsig na'r geiriau yn rhy
glasurol, a bydd blâs a hwyl arni.

Yr oedd llawer o benillion yn cael eu gwneyd ar y
pryd, os na fuasai digon o honynt ar gôf y dadgeiniad yr
oedd yn rhaid iddo allu gwneyd penill yn fynych neu
golli ei le yn y gân, a cholli y wobr yn y gystadleuaeth.
Yr oedd yna hen alawon a chydgan rhwng pob llinell, er

mwyn rhoi amser i'r bardd a'r dadganwr wneyd llinell
newydd tra buasai y cwmni yn canu y cydgan megis "Nos
Galan", "Hob y deri dando", ac "Ar hyd y nos".

Dyma engraifft o "Nos Galan" gyda'r geiriau "Dyna
ydyw'r gwir, a'r gwir i gyd" ar gyfer y cwmni, yn gydgan
rhwng y llinellau :—

> "Mae y dyn ag arian ganddo,
>   *Dyna ydyw'r gwir, a'r gwir i gyd,*
> Ar holl wlad yn perthyn iddo,
>   *Dyna ydyw'r gwir, a'r gwir i gyd*
> Ond os cyll ei aur a'i urddas,
>   *Dyna ydyw'r gwir, a'r gwir i gyd*
> Aiff yn union heb berthynas,
>   *Dyna ydyw'r gwir, a'r gwir i gyd.*

> "Mi rois goron am briodi
>   *Dyna ydyw'r gwir, a'r gwir i gyd*
> Ni rof ddimai byth ond hyny
>   *Dyna ydyw'r gwir, a'r gwir i gyd*
> D'wedais wers o flaen y person
>   *Dyna ydyw'r gwir, a'r gwir i gyd*
> Mae'n edifar gan fy nghalon,
>   *Dyna ydyw'r gwir, a'r gwir i gyd."*

Hefyd, yr oedd amgylchiadau lleol, a digwyddiadau
perthynol i'r ardal, a chyfeiriadau at rai o'r cwmni, yn
cael sylw neullduol ac arbenig. Nid canu hen benillion o
hyd, ond penillion wedi eu cyfansoddi yn " newydd spon "
ar gyfer yr amgylchiad.

Y mae Eos Dâr wedi gwneyd mwy na neb y gwyddom
am dano yn yr ystyr hyn ynglyn a'r Eisteddfod Genedlaethol, oddi ar Eisteddfod Aberhonddu yn 1889 hyd yn
awr. Y mae wedi canu penillion ar gyfer y lle a'r amgylchiadau y'mhob Gorsedd y bu yn canu ynddi, o hyny hyd
yn hyn.[1]

---

[1] Y mae croniel lled gyflawn o'r cyfryw iw cael yn "Cân a Thelyn",
cyhoeddedig gan B. Parry, Oxford Street, Swansea.

Dyma ychydig enghreifftiau o "benillion achlysur".
[Canwyd hwy yn y cyfarfod gan Eos Dâr.]

CYMRU A LLUNDAIN.

"Beth wnelai Llundain,
   Er cymaint yw hi,
Heb ferched a bechgyn
   O Gymru fach ni;
Am gân, ac am delyn,
   A phregeth gwir yw,
Hen Gymru sy'n cadw
   Tref Llunden yn fyw.

"O Gymru daw'r canu,
   O Gymru daw'r stŵr,
Daw Llunden bron tagu
   I Gymru am ddŵr;
Mae Llunden yn anfon
   I hen wlad y gân,
Am laeth ac am enwyn,
   Am ddŵr, ac am dân!"

TYWYSOG CYMRU A'R BWLEDAU.[1]

"Byw fo Tywysog hen wlad y gân,
Er gwaethaf cawodydd o fwledi tân,
Mae'r delyn yn canu, diolch i Dduw,
Am gadw Tywysog Cymru'n fyw."

W. JONES A. S. A'R GADAIR.

"Pwy allasai lanw'r gadair heno,
Fel y gwna boneddwr glan o Gymro;
William Jones o Ogledd Arfon
Cymro pur, a brwd ei galon."

Y DELYN A'R PENCERDD.

"Beth fuasai Cymru heb ei thelyn?
Buasai fel y gauaf heb y celyn!
A buasai 'r delyn ddigon tila,
Oni buasai bysedd Pencerdd Gwalia!"

---

[1] Cyfeiriad at yr ymosodiad llofruddiog ar Dywysog Cymru yn Mrussel.

Y CYMRODORION A'U HYSGRIFENYDD.

"Beth fuasai'r byd heb Gymrodorion?
Buasai fel anialwch heb frodorion.
Beth fuasai Cymrodorion Llunden,
Heb gael Vincent wrth eu cefen!"

Ar ol y deffroad ydym wedi son am dano, daeth yna
ddirywiad y'nglyn a chanu penillion, a dichon y gallwn ro'i
dau neu dri rheswm am hyny.

Yn gyntaf, y mae y byd yn myned yn fwy prysur, a'r
byd Cymreig yn gorfod dilyn. Adlais o'r "oes ham-
ddenol" yw canu gyda'r delyn. Difyrwch hirnos gaua'r
"amser gynt" ydyw. Oes arall yw'n hoes ni! Yn ail,
y mae yn anhawddach byw yn awr nag oedd. Y mae mwy
o gystadleuaeth afiach a rhaid gwneyd mwy o waith; gan
hyny, mae y canu a'r barddoni wedi myned yn grefft i
enill arian.

"Mae'r bardd yn canu ei ganeuon serch,
Er mwyn y wobr, ac nid er mwyn y ferch.
Mae aur ac arian heddyw'n fwy o swyn,
Na hudol serch, a gwenau cariad mwyn!
Mae llais y galon wedi ei golli'n lan,
Cyweirnod arian yw cyweirnod can!
Mae'r bardd yn canu ei alarnad ddlawd,
Er mwyn ei bres, ac nid er mwyn ei frawd!
Mae mwy o swyn i feirddion Gwalia wèn,
Yn nail y program, nag yn nail y pren!
Mae natur wedi ei cholli dan y ne',
Yr ymarferol sydd yn llanw'i lle.
Mae'r Awen yn cardota'r dyddiau hyn,
Nid byw'n frenhines yn ei phalas gwyn;
Nid canu ar destynau bythol grand,
Ond rhyw geinioca fel rhyw German Band;
Nid canu telyn natur a'i mwynhau,
Ond chwareu giwga am ei bwyd y mae!
Nid canu mwy er mwyn y gerdd na'r gair,
Mae'r delyn wedi myn'd yn delyn aur,
Mae'r delyn gynt fu a'i thânau yn dair rhes,—
Heb ond trithant,—tant arian, aur, a phres!"

Yn drydydd ac yn olaf, oferedd. Rhaid i ni gyfaddef fod y
delyn wedi bod yn ofera, a'r telynwr yn llymeita, a'r bardd
yn yfed, a'r dadganwr yn meddwi. Aeth rhai i wneyd
crefft o honi, a chrefft lawn o demtasiynau, o wledd i
wledd, ac o balas i balas, ac yn y diwedd o dafarn i dafarn,
a gadawodd y cantorion respectable hi oherwydd hyny, ac
yna aeth y canu a'r penillion yn isel.

Buwyd yn canu sothach gyda'r delyn, ac aeth teimlad
Piwritanaidd Cymru yn ei herbyn o achos hyny, ac aeth y
crwth, a'r delyn, a'r bardd, a'r cerddor yn bethau ysgymun
yn ei olwg; ac y maent yn ysgymun bethau hyd y dydd
hwn y'ngolwg llawer o ddynion crefyddol, ac ni fynant
ddod yn ddigon agos iddynt i gael gweled eu bod yn
camsynied. Mae'r bardd Cymreig heddyw mor sobor a'r
un dyn yn y wlad ar gyfartaledd; mae'r delyn wedi ei
dwyn yn ol o lan afonydd Babilon feddw; mae'r penillion
wedi ymlanhau ac ymburo. Y mae y rhôd yn troi, ac y
mae yr hen ganeuon difyr a da yn dod yn ol, a byddai yn
fendith i ganwyr cyhoeddus Cymru wneyd mwy a'r grefft,
er mwyn ei deall a'i harfer.

Dylai pob Cymro sydd yn proffesu bod yn fardd, neu yn
gerddor, wybod rhywbeth am nodweddion Cymreig barddoniaeth a cherddoriaeth ei wlad a'i genedl. Y mae
cynghanedd mewn barddoniaeth, a *chanu penillion* mewn
cerddoriaeth yn nodweddion hollol Gymreigaidd a phagan
o Gymro yw hwnw nad yw yn gwybod rhywbeth am
brydferthwch a chyfrinion y ddwy gelfyddyd. Yr ydym
wedi bod yn wan ac yn ffôl fel cenedl y'nglyn a'n nodweddion Cymreig. Y mae oes o ddiystyru wedi myn'd
dros ein pen, a'n haddysg wedi bod yn hollol gamsyniol;
ond fel y dywedwyd y mae y rhôd yn troi, a'n dynion
mwyaf goleuedig a deallus yn ceisio'n harwain allan o'n
camsynied dybryd. Gadewch i ni ddysgu canu cenhedloedd

eraill, ond ar bob cyfrif beidio esgeuluso ein canu prydferth cywrain ein hunain.

" Gadewch y gofid yn y byd
A dewch i gyd i ganu.
Ni fynwn dro ar ' Ben y Rhaw',
Neu rywbeth ddaw ran hyny,
Ni allwn hwylio fawr a mân
I'r mor o gân sy y'Nghymru !

" Gofalwch am benillion glân,
O gylch y tân yr hwyrnos,
A nithiwch bob rhyw us i ffwrdd,
Rhag dod i'r cwrdd yn agos,
Fel na bo dim o'r pethau hyn
Ond y 'Gwenith gwyn ' yn aros."

WALES AND THE COMING OF THE NORMANS (1039—1093).[1]

By PROFESSOR J. E. LLOYD, M.A.

I PROPOSE in this paper to trace the course of Welsh history during the period which immediately preceded and that which followed the acquisition of the English crown by duke William of Normandy, and especially to discuss the relations between the Welsh and the followers of William in this the first age in which Welshman and Norman, for good and for evil, made each other's acquaintance. To two aspects of the subject I would in particular call your attention—the importance of the reign of Gruffydd ap Llywelyn as a preparation for the struggle with the Normans, and the anomalous course of the struggle during the first twenty years, when considerable progress was made by the barons with the conquest of North Wales, while the South remained almost intact in the hands of its native rulers.

We are all familiar with the manner of regarding the reign of Edward the Confessor as a preparation for the Norman Conquest of England. The story has often been told how Normans flocked to the court of Edward, were settled by him on the land, and were raised to bishoprics,

[1] Read before the Honourable Society of Cymmrodorion at 20, Hanover Square, on Wednesday, the 9th of May, 1900; Chairman, Dr. Isambard Owen.

until the nation grew accustomed to their foreign ways and offered but a half-hearted resistance when they came over in their thousands. The reign of Gruffydd ap Llywelyn, Edward's contemporary, was in Wales a preparation in a very different sense. Gruffydd was the first Welsh prince for many years who had succeeded in uniting the whole race under his rule; he was, as one of the Saxon Chronicles calls him, "king over all the Welsh kin", and vindicated his right to the position by the most active operations against his English borderers. It cannot be doubted that his vigorous personality and independent attitude did much to infuse into his fellow countrymen a greater confidence in themselves, and so helped them after his death to offer a united resistance to the invader. His successes fired them, as the Elizabethans were fired by the triumphs of Drake and the sea-dogs.

During the age which preceded Gruffydd's appearance, the English had pushed their settlements, not only as far as the present boundary of Wales, but also in some places beyond it. I regard Offa's Dyke as a genuine attempt, which I find no difficulty in attributing to Offa himself, to mark off the English from the Welsh sphere of influence; and it proves on examination to be along a considerable part of its course a dividing line between the villages and townships with English and those with Welsh names. Now, I need not remind you that, starting as it does from near Prestatyn (the Prestetone of *Domesday*, and, therefore, simply Preston) and wending its way southward to Ruabon, it cuts off from Wales large parts of our Flintshire and Denbighshire, including the districts of Holywell, Flint, Hawarden, and Wrexham.¹ But be-

¹ Places called "Prestetone" or "Prestetune" are fairly common in *Domesday*, and, in the cases which I have been able to trace, are now represented by Prestons. Such are Preston, near Faversham,

yond this, the evidence of place-names goes to show that, even after Offa fixed his boundary in the eighth century, there was a further westward movement among the men of the march. In the neighbourhood of Montgomery, Edderton, Forden, Thornbury, Woodliston, Hopton— English settlements which date, as *Domesday* shows, from before the time of Gruffydd ap Llywelyn[1]—are all west of the dyke : further south, the border had in the same fashion been crossed by the dwellers in Waterdine, Weston, Pilleth, Radnor, Burlingjob, Kington, and a group of villages on the north bank of the Wye around Eardisley.[2] Nothing shows more clearly the strength of the English settlements on the border at this period than the statement made in *Domesday* that the three royal

Kent; and Preston Wynne, near Hereford. The accentuation of Prestátyn seems to create a difficulty, but Professor J. Morris Jones, to whom I have referred the point, explains that in the transition from the old Welsh accent on the last syllable to the modern accent on the last but one, the Prestetón of the eleventh century would readily become, on Welsh lips, Prestátun in the thirteenth. The shifting of the accent and the change from an unaccented e to a, are illustrated by Selattyn (for the "Suletune" of *Domesday*) and Cornattyn, the Welsh name of Corndon Hill.

[1] The *Domesday* forms are Edritune (*bis*), Furtune, Torneberie, Wadelestun, Hoptune. They will be found in the notice of Montgomery in the Shropshire Survey (Terra Rogerii Comitis). Of these townships, the first four are in the parish of Forden, Thornbury being the one which includes the "Gaer"; Hopton is in the parish of Churchstoke.

[2] Watredene is entered as a vill of Ralph Mortimer's in the hundred of Leintwardine (Shropshire Survey). The Herefordshire lands of Ralph included two hides in Westune and two in Pelelei, which (with others) lay waste "in marcha de Wales". Berchelincope and Raddrenove, vills of "Hezetre" hundred in Herefordshire, were held by King William, who had also two hides in Chingtune. Herdeslege, Witenie, Hantinetune (Huntington), Cicvvrdine (Chickward), Willavoslege (Willersley), and Widferdestune (Winforton)—all in the hundred of Elsdon—may serve as examples of the vills spoken of as lying between Kington and the Wye.

manors of Whittington, Maesbury, and Chirbury together rendered in the time of King Ethelred, *i.e.*, about the year 1000, half a night's ferm. At the death of Edward the Confessor they were waste, and yielded not a penny.[1]

There is nothing in the scanty evidence on the Welsh side to lead us to take a more cheerful view of the position of the Welsh in the latter part of the tenth century and the early years of the eleventh. Maredudd ab Owain in 991 attacks Radnor, where presumably the English were already established; but in the next year his territories of Dyfed and Ceredigion, with Gower and Kidwelly, are harried, as a punishment, by an English force.[2] It is not until the accession of Gruffydd in 1039 that signs appear of a notable turn of the tide.

Gruffydd's father, Llywelyn ap Seisyll, appears to have borne rule over a considerable part of Wales for some five years (perhaps more) previous to his death in 1023. Of what family he came, and what region in Wales was his first home, it is impossible to say[3]; all that is known of the sources of his power is that he married Angharad, daughter of Maredudd ab Owain, who was king of South Wales at the end of the tenth century, and that thus there ran in

---

[1] "Tempore Adelredi patris Edwardi regis reddebant hæc tria maneria dimidiam firmam noctis" (Entry at the end of the notice of Wititone in the Shropshire Survey). This might mean as much as £50 (Round, *Feudal England*, p. 112).

[2] *Annales Cambriæ* and *Bruts*. Maes Hyfaidd is the name of a place, not of a district; accordingly there can be no question, as Woodward (*History of Wales*, i, 203) supposed, of a raid upon Radnorshire.

[3] I have not come across any pedigree of his father Seisyll; his mother Prawst is said to have been the daughter of Elise ab Anarawd ap Rhodri Mawr (Dwnn, *Heraldic Visitations*, ii, 10; see also p. 16). For a very curious story about "the Lady Trawst", wife of "Sytsyllt, a Nobleman and Governor of Hardin Castle", see the article on Hawarden in Carlisle's *Topographical Dictionary of Wales* (1811).

the veins of his son Gruffydd the blood of Rhodri Mawr
and Hywel Dda.[1] Upon his death, Gwynedd reverted to
the old line of Idwal Foel, represented by Iago ab Idwal;
Deheubarth was for a short time held by Rhydderch ab
Iestyn, upon whose reign a Glamorgan scribe looks back
about a century later as a golden age, when there was no
desert spot on hill or plain, and but three hamlets left
solitary in all Wales[2]; it then passed to the descendants
of Hywel Dda once more, Hywel ab Edwin being the
reigning prince in 1039. In that year, Iago ab Idwal is
slain by his own men, and Gruffydd ap Llywelyn reaps the
advantage, whether guiltily or not we cannot tell[3]: he
becomes, at any rate, king of Gwynedd, and, despite the
silence of the chronicles, it may safely be inferred, of
Powys as well.

The great figures of Welsh history are apt to fill the
canvas with ample but misty outlines; their power is
recognised in its effects, but of themselves it is difficult
to get personal knowledge. One is as another; they seem
to lack individuality. The reason, no doubt, is that the
power of character drawing was not, for the most part,
possessed by those who recorded their deeds of might—
"carent quia vate sacro." Let but a Giraldus take up the
pen, and Rhys ap Gruffydd will live before you. Now, no

---

[1] *Brut y Tywysogion*, ed. Rhys and Evans, pp. 296-7 ; Jesus Coll.
MS. 20, as printed in *Y Cymmrodor*, viii, 88.

[2] " In cujus tempore nulla desolatio in montibus nec in plano nisi
tantum tribus uillis per totam gualiam in solitario " (*Liber Landavensis*, ed. Evans and Rhys, p. 253). *Brut y Tywysogion* has a similar
picture of the state of Wales (" or mor py gilyd ") under Llywelyn ap
Seisyll (p. 265).

[3] It will not do to hang any one on the evidence of so clumsy a
translator of his Latin originals as the author of the compilation
represented by *Brenhinoedd y Saeson* in Cleopatra B. v.—the *Brut
y Saeson* of the Myvyrian editors. The deed was done "a suis", say
the Irish annalists.

contemporary writer gives us anything like a character
sketch of Gruffydd—the chronicle of his acts is of the
barest. But it chanced that about a century after his
death a Herefordshire man, who, like most men of position in that county, had a good deal to do with the
lordship of Brecknock, found many legends still current
among the men of Brycheiniog about the great Welsh
chieftain, and, having an interest in such matters, jotted
them down in his scrap book of stories.[1] Walter Map, it
is true, speaks of the king throughout as Llywelyn, and
calls his father Gruffydd; but it is not possible to mistake
the man he has in mind, and the slip was one easily made.
Altogether, the portrait he paints is a strongly individual
one. We must not, of course, look for historical accuracy
in stories passed on, as these were, through three generations; but truth of portraiture, if we allow for a little
heightening of the effects, should not be denied them. A
sluggish lad, needing to be spurred to ambitious thoughts
and daring deeds, with faculties yet slumbering; in the
maturity of his powers a forceful, passionate man, jealous
of rivalry, alike in love and in statecraft, dealing destruction to all who thwarted his purposes, yet with a certain
magnanimity which now and again flashed forth and
relieved the darker colours—such is the picture painted of
Gruffydd in the traditions preserved for us by Map. He
had wit, too, of a grim and biting kind, if we may credit

---

[1] Walter Map's *De Nugis Curialium* was edited by T. Wright from
the unique MS. (Bodley, no. 851) in 1850. The relevant sections are
nos. xxii and xxiii in the second "distinctio". It was clearly from
Brycheiniog the tale told in the former section originally came, for
"stagnum de Behthenio" is Llangorse Lake, and appears in dist. ii,
cap. 11, in the more intelligible form of "stagnum Brekeinauc". The
close connection between Herefordshire and Brecknock during this
period is well brought out in the "Cartulary of Brecon Priory"
printed by R. W. Banks in *Archæologia Cambrensis* for 1882 and 1883.

the story that he justified his ruthless removal of all
rivals from his path by saying that he did no murder, but
only blunted the points of the horns of Wales, lest they
should injure the dam.[1] The story told of his early days
is to the effect that he was then a home-keeping lad, who
sought no adventures. In the only son and heir of a king,
this was deemed disgraceful, and at last his sister drove
him out, one New-Year's Eve,[2] the recognised night for
bold enterprises and weird experiences, to seek his fortune.
He chose to hear it in a way then deemed infallible, by
eavesdropping; and planted himself against the wall of a
house (like all Welsh houses, of slender construction),
where a company were seated around a cauldron in which
were being cooked sundry pieces of beef. "See this piece",
remarked one, as he peered into the bubbling pot; "often
as I push it with my prong below the others, it nevertheless persists in coming to the top."   Gruffydd's fortune
was told, and thenceforth, we are informed, no one had
reason to complain of his lack of energy. His generosity
came out in a parley he held at the mouth of the Severn
with king Edward. The Confessor had come to Aust
Cliff, Gruffydd was at Beachley, not far from Chepstow—
a mile of estuary separated them, and for a time neither
would confess inferiority by crossing to meet the other.
At last Edward, weary of the strife, entered a boat and
made for the Welsh shore. Gruffydd was so overwhelmed
by this condescension that he cast off his mantle of state,
rushed into the stream until it ran breast high around

---

[1] "Neminem occido sed obtundo cornua Wallie ne possint ledere
matrem." I have here and elsewhere checked the printed text by
reference to the manuscript.

[2] Map, or his informant, probably confused Jan. 1 and Nov. 1. the
first day of the Celtic year. Nos Galan Gaeaf was until recent years
a favourite time for "rhamanta" or seeking omens (Elias Owen,
Welsh Folklore, pp. 280, 281, 286, 288, 289).

him, and embraced the royal skiff in a passion of devotion. Then he carried Edward ashore on his shoulders and did homage to the king whose humility, he said, had conquered his pride and whose wisdom had put to shame his folly.

It was, then, no common man who became ruler of North Wales in 1039, and the victory of Rhyd y Groes ar Hafren, in which Edwin, brother of Earl Leofric of Mercia, and two royal thegns were slain by the Welsh under Gruffydd's leadership, opened the new reign auspiciously.[1] It has always been a matter of wonder to me how Mr. Freeman came to the conclusion that this battle was fought near Upton-on-Severn, in Worcestershire, a place at least twenty miles from the Welsh border: one would not have supposed that the arrangements for the defence of Mercia against sudden raids from across the border were so inadequate.[2] In point of fact, Rhyd y Groes ar Hafren was on the *Upper* Severn : it was a spot well known to Welsh mediæval tradition, and forms the scene of a good deal of the action of the Arthurian tale called the Dream of Rhonabwy. For it was the trysting-place where Arthur assembled his men in readiness for the great battle of

[1] Powel failed to see the identity of the battle of Rhyd y Groes and that referred to in the English chronicles (*Historie of Cambria*, reprint of 1811, p. 68). Other writers followed him in separating the two until Woodward (i, 206-7) saw a connection. Not to speak of the identity of date, there is the fact that in Heming's *Cartulary* the death of Edwin is ascribed to "Grifino rege Brittorum" (Oxford, 1723, p. 278).

[2] *Norman Conquest*, vol. i, p. 506 of the third edition. On the occasion of the reading of this paper, Mr. Willis-Bund told the Society that, when staying in the house with Mr. Freeman, at a place called the Rhyd, near Upton-on-Severn, he talked with him about the identification of Rhyd y Groes, and pointed out to the great historian that there was a carn at Hanley Castle, close by where they were staying, and this might be Rhyd y Groes—an identification which he afterwards found, to his dismay, had been seriously adopted.

K

Mount Badon; as Rhonabwy journeyed towards the
ford across the broad meadows of Argyngroeg, the road
was hemmed in for a mile on each side by the tents and
the warlike gear of a busy host.[1] Montgomeryshire antiquaries[2] identify Rhyd y Groes with an old ford near
Munllyn, in the parish of Forden, on what evidence I
have not so far been able to ascertain; if one were to be
guided solely by the language of the romance, it would be
rather in the neighbourhood of Buttington or Welshpool
one would look for it. But that it lay between Montgomery and Melverley is certain, and when the fact is
borne in mind that the Severn was here the boundary
between the two peoples, nothing seems more reasonable
than that Gruffydd's first encounter with the English
should have taken place at a notable ford across the river.
Florence of Worcester speaks of the affair as an ambuscade[3]; this could scarcely have been contrived by the
Welsh at the end of a long march across the Malvern
Hills; at their own doors, as the train of Mercian notables
was crossing into Powys, with no suspicion of the bold

---

[1] " Yn kerdet ar traws maes argygroee ae ohen ae vryt a debygei y
not parth a ryt y groes ar hafren. . Ac yna y kerdassant ar traws
maes mawr argygroee hyt yn ryt y groes ar hafren. A milltir y wrth
y ryt o pob tu yr fford y gwelynt y lluesteu ar pebyllou a dygyfor o
lu mawr " (*Mabinogion*, ed. Rhys and Evans, pp. 146, 148). The townships of Gungrog Fawr and Gungrog Fechan occupy some two miles
of the western bank of the Severn, opposite Buttington.

[2] Gwallter Mechain, in the note on Argyngroeg in Lady Charlotte
Guest's *Mabinogion* (p. 322 of the one volume edition), and Mr.
Robert Owen, of Welshpool, to whom I am indebted for a full reply
to enquiries addressed to him on this subject.

[3] See the year 1052 : " Hac pugna facta est eodem die quo ante
xiii annos fratrem comitis Leofrici Eadwinum Walenses *per insidias*
interfecerunt" (*Mon. Hist. Brit.*, p. 605). The " ignominiosa morte "
of Heming's *Cartulary* (see note 1 on p. 129) points in the same
direction.

tactics which the new chieftain would employ, it was a comparatively easy matter.

The decisive character of the victory of Rhyd y Groes appears from the fact that no reprisals were attempted. Gruffydd found himself at liberty to take up other enterprises, and henceforth the English seem content to rest on the defensive. The writer who, after Edward's death, penned for his widow an account of the reign, tells how the Welsh, untamed in their snowy fastnesses, have of late dared even to cross the Severn and rain blows on the English realm; they are too strong, he says, while Gruffydd is their King.[1] This appears to have been the attitude of the nation; the rise of Gruffydd was a stroke of ill-luck, to be endured as best might be until some happy chance put an end to his power.

The main task of Gruffydd during the next few years was the conquest of Deheubarth, ruled over at his accession by Hywel ab Edwin. Of the struggle which this involved the Welsh chronicles give us a few details, but such as it is not easy to piece together in a consistent narrative. Immediately after Rhyd y Groes, the Northerners poured into Ceredigion, where they treated with scant respect the property of the "clas", or monastic community of Llanbadarn Fawr.[2] It is not likely that the expulsion of Hywel, of which the records then speak, was more than a temporary affair, for two years later (1041) he was in a

---

[1] *Lives of Edward the Confessor*, ed. Luard (1858), p. 425 ("fortemque nimis regnante Griphino").

[2] The "dibobles" of *Brut y Tywysogion* no doubt represents "populavit", *i.e.*, "ravaged". The reference to Llan Badarn occurs only in *Brut y Tywysogion* and *Brenhinoedd y Saeson*—one of the many evidences that the Latin chronicle of which they furnish two independent versions was, though closely akin to MSS. B and C of *Annales Cambriæ*, distinguished from them in being, at least in part, a Llan Badarn record.

position to meet Gruffydd as far north in his realm as Pen
Cader: there Gruffydd defeated him, and, among the spoils
of victory, took possession of his wife. This is not at all
hard to reconcile with the presentment of the Northern
prince in the pages of Map, but the *Brut of Aber Pergwm*,
in the clearer moral atmosphere of the sixteenth century,
deems an apology to be necessary, and informs us that
this was "the only deed, of all the deeds ever done by
Gruffydd, which did not meet with the approval of the
sages".[1] Hywel was, however, not yet disposed of, for in
1042 he still held the region round Carmarthen, defeating
at Pwll Dyfach, near Bwlch Newydd, a Danish host who
were ravaging Dyfed.[2] The struggle did not end until
1044, when the Southern prince, who was leading a fleet
of twenty Danish vessels up the estuary of the Towy, in
order to enforce his claims, was at last overwhelmed by
Gruffydd.

Gruffydd had now achieved his object, and added
Deheubarth to his original possessions. But provincial
feeling was strong in the south, and soon enabled a new
rival to show himself in the person of Gruffydd, son of
Rhydderch ab Iestyn. Two years of conflict followed, in
the course of which Gruffydd appears to have formed an
alliance with Swegen, son of Godwin, whose earldom included Herefordshire, and to have brought Swegen into
South Wales in order to prop up his shaken authority.
But the slaughter in 1047 of his household troops, his

---

[1] "A thyna'r unig weithred, o'r holl weithredoedd a wnaeth
Ruffydd, a beris anfoddlondeb i'r Doethion" (*Myr. Arch.*, Denbigh
edit., p. 695).

[2] A family of some consequence were settled at Pwll Dyfach in the
fifteenth and sixteenth centuries (*Greaith L. G. Cothi*. pp. 293, 298 ;
Dwnn, i. 95, 143). The local pronunciation is now Pwll Dyfarch, and
in the old one-inch ordnance map this has been further distorted into
Pwll-dwy-fraich !

"familia" or "teulu ",[1] to the number of 140, by the great men of Ystrad Tywi, turned the scale in favour of his opponent, and in 1049 it is Gruffydd ap Rhydderch who joins hands with a Danish hosting from Ireland, ravages the coast of Gwent and the manor of Tidenham,[2] and, by striking unexpectedly in the dawn of a July morning, scatters in dismay the shire forces of Hereford and Gloucester, assembled for the defence of the district by Bishop Ealdred of Worcester.

It was not until 1055 that the northern Gruffydd rid himself of his rival and became once more, what he continued to be for the rest of his career, supreme ruler of all the Welsh race. Meanwhile, a new menace to his power was involved in the establishment in 1051 of Ralph of Mantes, nephew of king Edward, as earl of Hereford, with a considerable Norman following. We are entitled, I think, to assume that it was the new position of affairs in the shire which led Gruffydd to adopt once more an aggressive policy towards England; in 1052 he led a plundering expedition in the direction of Leominster, which was with difficulty driven back by the combined

---

[1] The "teulu" of old Welsh literature is not the family of modern life, nor yet the household of mediæval times. but the "house-host" (Stokes, *Urceltischer Sprachschatz*, p. 321), the "comitatus" or armed escort of the prince. Its members were divorced from family life and the "penteulu" was their leader, the captain of the guard. See Aneurin Owen's edition of *The Welsh Laws*, i, 12-16, 358-60. 636 ; ii, 755-6, 819, 898 ; Triads on p. 305 of Oxford edit. of *Mabinogion* : introduction to *Breuddwyd Rhonabwy* (p. 144); *Brut y Tywysogion*, ed. Rhys and Evans, p. 291, l. 26.

[2] So I interpret the "Dymedham" of Florence. This thirty-hide manor of the abbey of Bath is styled "Dyddenhame" in king Edwy's grant (*Codex Diplomaticus*, Kemble. iii. 444), though the *Domesday* form is Tedeneham. The coast about the mouth of the "Wylisce Axa" (Usk) was probably held by Meurig ap Hywel of Morgannwg, who was, we may suppose, an ally of Gruffydd ap Llywelyn. See p. 145.

English and Norman forces. But it was in 1055, after the death of Gruffydd ap Rhydderch, that his great opportunity came, with the banishment of Ælfgar, son of the Earl of Mercia, and the return of the exile at the head of a Danish fleet. Ælfgar and he entered into an alliance, sealed now or later by the marriage of Gruffydd and Ælfgar's daughter, the beautiful Ealdgyth, who, after his death, became the wife of Harold. Together the two leaders invaded Herefordshire, defeated the forces of earl Ralph in a pitched battle, and took and sacked Hereford. I will not dwell on the details of a well-known story, except to say that the attack seems to me to have been made from the south, and to have been the occasion of that devastation of Archenfield, the Welsh Erging, by Gruffydd, which is mentioned in *Domesday*.[1] I base this opinion partly upon the fact that Earl Harold, when he had brought to the spot an army gathered from all parts of England to avenge the onslaught, made his way across the Golden Valley into Ewias,[2] and partly upon the fact that the peace which restored Ælfgar to his forfeited lands and dignities—a peace negociated between Gruffydd, Ælfgar, and Harold—was arranged at Billingsley, which, I take it, was the place so styled near Boulston, in Archenfield, and not, as has generally been supposed, Billingsley near Bridgnorth—far away in the heart of Mercia.

In the following year, Gruffydd and the men of Here-

---

[1] "Rex Grifin et Blein vastauerunt hanc terram tempore regis Edwardi et ideo nescitur qualis eo tempore fuerit." Bleddyn's share was no doubt done after 1063.

[2] "Ultra Straddele", says Florence of Worcester. The Herefordshire section of *Domesday Book* includes many references to "Stradel", "valle Stradelie", "valle Stradelei", and "valle Stratelie", which is clearly the "Strat Dour", "Estratour", and "Istratour" of the *Liber Landavensis* (ed. Evans and Rhys, pp. 76, 42, 32), viz., Valley Dore.

fordshire were again at war, but I am inclined to believe
that on this occasion the peace was broken by the English.
Bishop Æthelstan had been succeeded at Hereford by the
born fighter Leofgar, the priest whose moustachios, as
Mr. Plummer has explained,[1] caused so much scandal among
his brother clerics, and who now sought to prove his devotion to his patron Harold by an attempt to crush the
prince who had given so much trouble in the previous year.
It turned out unhappily; Leofgar and the sheriff and
many others were defeated and slain in a battle which was
fought near Glasbury.[2] The chronological tract called
O Oes Gwrtheyrn Gwrtheneu speaks of this encounter as
Gwaith Machawy; there is, in point of fact, a stream
called the Machawy, now known as the Bachwy, which
falls into the Wye some miles above Glasbury, and I am
disposed to think we must look here for the exact spot
which was the scene of the engagement.[3]

[1] *Two Saxon Chronicles parallel*, vol. ii (1899), p. 246. He was
" Haroldes corles mæsse preost," and clearly a soldier, with no love of
the clerical life.

[2] " Clasthirig " is the reading of the MSS. of Florence of Worcester,
according to *Mon. Hist. Brit.*, p. 608. An English " burh" seems at
some time or other to have been raised on the spot, but in all pro-
bability the district was in 1056 well within Gruffydd's border.

[3] " O gnut vrenhin hyt vachawy yny orun ruffud vab llywelyn ac y llas
esgob y saesson, dwy vlyned a deugeint. O weith machawy yny las
gruffud, naw mlyned " (" Bruts ", etc., from *Red Book of Hergest*, ed.
Rhys and Evans, p. 405). An old form of the name appears in the
" d[r]iffrin machagui " of *Lib. Land.*, 255. Speed, too, has Machaway
in his map of Radnorshire, but later writers appear to prefer Bachwy
and Bachawy.

Mr. Gwenogvryn Evans, in the preface to his edition of the *Bruts*
(p. xxiv), speaks of " O Oes Gwrtheyrn " as a "worthless compilation".
In the form in which it has reached us, the tract is no doubt full of
copyists' blunders, and for exact chronology is of very little service.
But an examination of Mr. Evans's text has convinced me that the
student of Welsh history cannot afford entirely to disregard it. Let
me give an instance of what I mean. It is said (p. 406) that in the

I pass over the second exile of Ælfgar, followed by a
second restoration with the aid of Gruffydd and Magnus,
son of Harold Hardrada of Norway,[1] and come to the
fatal year 1063, which saw the end of Gruffydd's
triumphant career. It has been supposed that the Welsh
chronicles assign this event to the year 1061, but, though
they appear to do so, it is clear that we have only to do
with a mistake of the copyists, and that 1063 is the year
really intended.[2] The campaign commenced with the
vain attempt of Harold to capture Gruffydd in his royal
vill of Rhuddlan; the story is interesting as incidentally

year after that of the proclamation of the interdict, and before that
of John's visit to Ireland, *i.e.*, in 1209, Llywelyn ab Iorwerth and
Hywel ap Gruffydd went with the king to "ruuein" to subdue the
ruler of that country. As it stands, this is nonsense, but, remembering that 1209 was the year of John's Scotch expedition, we read
"pridein" for "ruuein", and at once get something intelligible.
What is more, the statement (found nowhere else, I believe) is confirmed by independent evidence, for in the Misæ Roll of the 11th
year of John, entries appear to the following effect—

"Thursday, July 30th—(at Newcastle) 3½ marks given by the
    king to the seven 'busynatoribus' (=trumpeters, from
    O. Fr. busine?) of Llywelyn the Welshman to buy
    clothes."

"Tuesday, Aug. 4th—£19 2s. 5d. given by the king at Norham
    in quittance of Llywelyn's wages; paid to his clerk
    'Osturco'."

A day or two later—"20 marks, Llywelyn's expenses for one
    day, paid by order of the king to 'Weno' his seneschal,
    and 'Osturc' his clerk."

See the edition of the Roll issued by T. D. Hardy in 1844.

[1] Plummer's *Chronicles*, ii, 246. I do not hesitate to connect the
expedition of Magnus spoken of by the Welsh authorities with the
Norwegian fleet referred to by the English annalists under the year
1058.

[2] Both *Brenhinoedd y Saeson* and MS. C. of *Brut y Tywysogion* (Ab
Ithel's edition, p. 44) prefix to the year of Gruffydd's death the figure
1061, but both say of the succeeding year that it was the first of the
nineteen years' cycle, *i.e.*, it was 1064.

revealing to us the existence in the estuary of the Clwyd of a little fleet.[1] No doubt it was wise and almost necessary that Gruffydd should secure his hold upon Wales in this way, but sea power is a weapon Welsh princes have very rarely sought to wield, and in most cases, when they needed the help of ships, it was their custom to look to Ireland, to the Ostmen of Dublin, Waterford, and Wexford, whose skill in sea-craft is matter of common knowledge. The course of the more elaborate operations which occupied the summer is not altogether clear, but it would seem that Harold gathered at Oxford[2] light armed troops, such as might easily penetrate into the dense Welsh forests, and, sailing with these from Bristol, met, perhaps in the neighbourhood of Anglesey,[3] his brother Tostig, who had come along the northern coast from his Northumbrian earldom with a body of horsemen. The united forces began systematically to ravage North Wales in a way not hitherto deemed possible; their mobility introduced an entirely new factor into the struggle between Welsh and English. Gruffydd was now reduced to great straits; his ally Ælfgar, earl of Mercia since 1057, was in all likelihood dead, for we hear nothing of him after 1062, and it is most probable that the English government took the opportunity of his removal to embark on an enterprise which stood little chance of success in his lifetime. Ac-

[1] "His scipa and alle tha gewæda the thær to gebyrede "—MS. D. of the *English Chronicle;* "naves ejus cum armamentis "—Flor. Wig. (*Mon. Hist. Brit.*, p. 611). Vessels of seven tons' burthen have always been able to reach Rhuddlan bridge (Lewis, *Topographical Dictionary,* s. v. Rhuddlan).

[2] " Harold del suth de Oxenford " (*Gaimar,* v. 5076—Rolls ed. i, 215).

[3] John of Salisbury says (*Polycraticus,* vi, 6) that Harold reached Snowdon—" nivium itaque collem ingressus, vastavit omnia". " Nivicollini Britones " is a name he affects for the men of Gwynedd.

cording to the Norman poet, Geoffrey Gaimar, the
defection of the South was also added to Gruffydd's mis-
fortunes—" the South Welsh ", he says, " fought against
Gruffydd and overcame his people".[1] Remembering the
early history of the reign, we may regard this as most
probable, and it may not be amiss to lend an ear for once
to that most treacherous of guides, the *Brut of Aber
Pergwm*, when it tells us that the men of Morgannwg
and Gwent sided with Harold against Gruffydd in this
contest.[2] On the 5th of August, 1063, he was slain by his
own men, whose conduct in sending their chieftain's head
to Harold suggests that this was the stipulated price of
peace. Welsh tradition avers that one Madog Min pro-
cured the doing of the deed, and tells with glee how
Harold refused him the promised reward of his treachery
—the value of three hundred head of cattle—and how
soon after he was drowned on his way to Dublin.[3] Thus
fell, in the language of *Brut y Tywysogion*, " the head
and shield and protector of the Britons "; thus ended a
career as remarkable as any recorded in Welsh history,
and, I venture to think, as fruitful in results.

When, at the end of the reign of William I, a com-
prehensive survey was taken by the government of the
state of England, regarded as a taxable area, the jurors
were required to state how in each holding matters stood
" tempore regis Edwardi ", *i.e.*, at the beginning of the
year 1066. An examination of the entries which deal
with the manors on the Welsh border will show that in
that year a belt of waste country, almost certainly de-

---

[1] " Li Suthwaleis se combatirent
         Contre Griffin, sa gent venquirent "
                                    (Vv. 5079-80).
[2] *Myvyrian Archaiology*, Denbigh edit., p. 696.
[3] *Iolo MSS.*, p. 198.

populated by Gruffydd ap Llywelyn, still separated England and Wales. Manor after manor is entered as "waste", an expression which in the Survey denotes not so much the absence of population or any actual devastation as the absence of capital with which to work the land—the want of the oxen of the plough-team, without which the acre strips are valueless. The waste vills for the most part bear English names, and were no doubt at one time inhabited by English settlers, formed part of English shires and hundreds, and yielded an income to English kings, earls, and thegns. Gruffydd had, however, made them uninhabitable, or had seized them for himself; in some of them the land has been tilled by Welshmen ever since. Beginning with the Cheshire border, I may remark that the twenty hides which formed the original hundred of Atiscros[1] were in 1066, and long afterwards, an integral part of the shire, and that only a few of them are entered as "waste". They lay along the estuary of the Dee from Bagillt to the gates of Chester, backed by a great forest, fifteen miles long and four and a half broad,[2] of which the memory is still preserved in such names as Cefn y Coed, Coed y Cra, Ty'nycoed, and Coed Ewlo. The freeman Edwin who held Cownsillt and Kelsterton is believed by some[3] to be the father of Owain and Uchtryd ab Edwin, the man whom the heralds call "king of Tegeingl", but,

[1] The Survey speaks of them as twenty (harum xxti hidarum omnes siluas), but I can only make up 19½, even reckoning in the ⅔ of Wepre mentioned elsewhere. Readers of Mr. Round's *Feudal England* will, however, not forget the significance of the round number (see especially pp. 44-69). A fragment of the cross of Ati, which marked, no doubt, the meeting-place of the hundred, was still to be seen in the days of Pennant (*Tours*, 1810, i, 71).

[2] The *Domesday* league was of twelve furlongs (Maitland, *Domesday and Beyond*, p. 371).

[3] *E.g.*, Mr. H. Taylor in his *Historic Notices of Flint* (1883), p. 10.

apart from this, there is nothing to suggest that the
district was not as English as Kent itself. To the north,
however, in the hundred of Englefeld, matters were on a
different footing. Offa's Dyke ran through the district,
and east of the Dyke the vill-names are purely English—
Preston, Moston, Picton, Westbury (now Gwesbyr), Whit-
ford, Fulbrook (our Greenfield), Merton, and Caldicot.[1]
But "Earl Hugh", says the Survey, "holds Rhuddlan of
the king. There in king Edward's time lay Englefeld—it
was altogether waste—Earl Edwin held it. When Earl
Hugh received it, it was likewise waste". Rhuddlan, only
a few miles distant from the ancient frontier, had been
held by Gruffydd with so firm a grip as to be a naval base
and a principal residence of his; though the Welsh no
doubt lost their hold of the district in 1063, it was still
yielding nothing when Earl Hugh set on foot the process
of re-settlement. In the valley of the Alun, the same tale
is told; Bishopstree (Biscopestreu), our Bistre, once an
English settlement, as its name shows, was a manor of
King Gruffydd's, where his men brought him a fixed
render of provisions; in 1066 it was held by Earl Edwin,
but was waste, and so when it came into the hands of
Earl Hugh.

From Hope to Erbistock stretched the hundred of
Exestan, another twenty-hide district,[2] roughly represented in later times by Maelor Gymraeg. It lay east of
Offa's Dyke, and every vill mentioned in *Domesday* as belonging to it bore an English name. That it was settled
by the English long before Gruffydd's day, is shown by the

---

[1] In the Survey, Prestetone, Mostone, Pichetone, Wesb(er)ie, Wid-
ford, Folebroc, Meretone, Caldecote. For the situation of Fulbrook,
see Mr. Edward Owen's *Catalogue of Welsh MSS. in the British
Museum*, p. 77.

[2] The hides were distributed as follows—Hope, 1; Odeslei, ½;
Eitune, 1; Sudtone, 1; Erpestoch, ½; Alontune, 3; Gretford, 13.

grant of Hodeshlith (now Hoseley, near Gresford) to the church of St. Werburgh in Chester in 958.[1] But here also Gruffydd had been at work, so that at King Edward's death the whole hundred was waste, save a few hides on the west bank of the Dee. We are, in fact, told that the king gave Gruffydd all the land which lay across the water called Dee—a recognition, no doubt, as Mr. Palmer and others[2] have pointed out, of conquests made by the Welsh prince in this quarter—and, though the notice goes on to say that, when Gruffydd rebelled, the grant was withdrawn, this, I suspect, did not happen until 1063, for the country was still for the most part untenanted three years later.

We pass to Shropshire. The region around Oswestry (which is not mentioned, at least under that name, in the Survey) formed the hundred of the Mersete, of which Meresbury, now Maesbury, was the head. It was bounded on the west by Offa's Dyke, and was purely English. Yet nearly all of it is entered as waste under king Edward; this was the plight of Maesbury itself, of the large royal manor of Whittington, of Halston, West Felton, Osbaston, Kynaston, Maesbrook, and Melverley.[3] South of the last named place stretched the border hundreds of "Ruesset" and Whittingtree;[4] their vills were for the most part to the east of the Breiddin and Cefn Digoll, and appear to have suffered little; but those which lay along the course

[1] Birch, *Cartularium Saxonicum*, iii, 245-6.

[2] *Ancient Tenures of Land* (1885), p. 86.

[3] Meresberie, Wititone (18 hides), Halstune, Feltone, Sbernestune, Chimerestun, Meresbroc, Melourlei. "Hæc duo maneria wasta fuerunt", says the scribe at one point in the list, "ut multa alia". Mr. Palmer had drawn the moral for the Oswestry district in vol. x of *Y Cymmrodor*, p. 39.

[4] The "Witentreu" of *Domesday* survives in the name of Whittre Bdrige, near Chirbury.

of Offa's Dyke, from Edderton, near Forden, to Edenhope, near Bishop's Castle, are all said to have been waste under king Edward. The spot soon to be known as Montgomery stood in a great wilderness, which yielded no revenue to the king, and had been granted by him to three thegns for hunting purposes. It is surely not fanciful to see here an abiding result of Gruffydd's victory at Rhyd y Groes.

In the hundred of "Rinlau", which lay east of Clun, there is little evidence of disturbance; the dyke was here, as elsewhere, the ancient boundary, and appears not to have been crossed. But in the hundred of Leintwardine, which took in both sides of the Teme Valley, the phenomena familiar to us from our survey of the North Welsh border show themselves once more. Waterdine, Knighton, Ack Hill, Stanage, Norton, Brampton Bryan, Pedwardine, Bucknall,[1] were all reckoned members of this hundred, and all were waste in Edward's day, remaining so in many cases down to the time of the Survey itself.

And now we come to Herefordshire, the scene of Gruffydd's most triumphant excursions into English territory.[2] We shall expect to find here conclusive evidence of his activity, and the record does not disappoint us. For here the belt of waste manors is many miles broad, embracing many vills which are now in Radnorshire, but were included in those days in the Herefordshire hundreds of Hezetre and Elsdon. I will only mention some of the

---

[1] Watredene, Chenistetone, Achel, Stanege, Nortune, Brantune, Pedewrde, Buchehalle. Ack Hill is about a mile S.W. of Norton. The inclusion in this hundred and in Shropshire of the half-hide held by Osbern fitz Richard at Cascop is probably a mistake : see the Herefordshire Survey.

[2] For the early history of the Herefordshire border, see an article by R. W. Banks in *Archæologia Cambrensis*, fourth series, vol. xiii (1882).

more notable—Radnor, Whitney, Eardisley, Huntington, Kington, Pilleth, Cascob, Discoed, Titley, Knill, Willersley, Winforton.[1] Radnor was a large manor of fifteen hides, capable of giving employment to thirty ploughteams ; it had in all likelihood been English soil for many generations when Gruffydd laid his hand upon it. Even in 1086, at the date of the Survey, the mischief hereabouts had not been repaired, and, though the deserted manors were in many cases the property of King William, all he got from them was £15 a year paid by William fitz Norman for the profits of the great forest in which they lay.[2]

Crossing into the portion of Herefordshire which lies south of the Wye, we come to the sphere of operations in 1055 and 1056. It would seem as if hardly any part of this district had escaped the hand of the spoiler. Two of the manors belonging to the bishop of Hereford on the south bank of the Wye, viz., Preston and Tiberton, appear as waste in 1066 ; such is the entry also opposite almost every manor in the Golden Valley, more correctly called the Valley of the Dore,[3] while of Archenfield, which was enclosed by the Wye, the Monnow, and the Worm, it is said in express terms that " king Gruffydd and Bleddyn [his immediate successor] ravaged this land in the time of King Edward, and therefore its value at that time is unknown".[4] Archenfield differed from the districts through which we have hitherto been travelling

---

[1] In the hundred of "Hezetre", Raddrenove, Pelelei, Cascope, Discote; in the hundred of "Elsedune", Witenie, Herdeslege, Hantinetune, Chingtune, Titelege, Chenille, Willaveslege, Widferdestune.

[2] " Rex habet in Herefordscire ix maneria wasta de xix hidis. De forestis quas tenet Willelmus filius Normanni reddit xv libras regi."

[3] See note 2, p. 134.

[4] See note 1, p. 134.

in being a thoroughly Welsh district which had at some
time or other been annexed bodily to Herefordshire without thereby losing its Welsh characteristics. The story
of the three churches which the king had there, and
of the employment of their priests as the king's envoys
into Wales, is well known : Mr. Seebohm has drawn attention, too, to the specially Welsh character of the renders
of these Archenfield tenants—the sextars of honey, with
small money payments.[1] Let me add that this view of the
position of Archenfield is entirely borne out by the *Book
of Llandaff*, where a list is given of the churches of the
region at this period, each bearing a Welsh name, and of
the Welsh clergy who served them, and the Welsh proprietors who paid the tithes.[2] We even find the
"Cadiand", who in *Domesday* is said to have been the
holder of Kilpeck in the time of king Edward, entered as
a proprietor of that parish in the *Book of Llandaff* in the
more intelligible form of "Catgen du".[3]

South of Monmouth, the sinuous course of the Wye was
the ancient boundary between Welsh and English, and it
does not appear to have been crossed by Gruffydd.
Domesday bears witness, nevertheless, to his presence and
power in Gwent. Six Welshmen (the record runs) hold
nine vills in this district without paying any dues, for Earl
William of Hereford granted them, with the king's con-
currence, on the same easy terms as had been imposed by
king Gruffydd : among these tenants are Berddig, styled

---

[1] *English Village Community*, 1883, p. 207.

[2] *Liber Landavensis* (ed. Evans and Rhys), pp. 275-8. According to
Mr. Evans, the portion of the book containing this matter was
written about 1170.

[3] The ancient name of Kilpeck is Cilpedec, a form which, if it had
survived into modern Welsh, would probably now be Cil Peddeg.
Hence the *Domesday* Chipeete, the t being a mistake for c and ch
(as usual) representing a hard c.

the king's minstrel, and Abraham, archdeacon of Gwent,
both of whom appear in connection with the district in the
Book of Llandaff.[1] Gwent and Morgannwg were probably
the last of the regions of Wales to acknowledge the power
of the North Welsh prince, retaining their ancient line of
princes until a few years before Gruffydd's death. Hywel
ab Owain, king of Morgannwg, died at a great age in
1043; his place was taken by his son, Meurig ap Hywel,
who had already, owing to his father's infirmities, for
some time been actual ruler. Meurig annexed Gwent
Iscoed or Nether Went to his kingdom of Glamorgan, and
apparently made his son Cadwgan under king of the new

[1] "Berdic ioculator regis habet iii villas et ibi v carucas ; nil reddit.
Morinus i uillam, Chenesis i, filius Wasuuic i, Sessisbert i, Abraham
presbiter ii uillas. Ii habent vi carucas et nichil reddunt. Hos
misit Willelmus comes ad consuetudinem Grifin regis licentia regis
Willelmi" (Gloucestershire Survey, under the heading "Castellum
de Estrighoiel"). "Berdic guent" (one word in the MS.) attests, as
a layman, three grants entered in the *Book of Llandaff*. The first
(pp. 269-70) is a "privilegium" or general confirmation granted to
bishop Herwald at "ystum guy" by "Grifudi regis britannie et ut
sic dicam totius gualie de fine ad finem"—a description which ob-
viously fits no one but Gruffydd ap Llywelyn. The second (pp. 272-3)
is a grant to the same bishop of a vill near Llan Degfedd (between
Usk and Caerleon) made by "Caratocvs rex morcannue", the Caradog
ap Gruffydd who fell at Mynydd Carn in 1081. Great have been the
pretensions put forth on behalf of the house of Iestyn ap Gwrgant ;
the bubble is pricked in a moment when we find "iestin filius
gurcant" attesting this grant as the thirteenth and last but one of
the lay witnesses. The third grant witnessed by Berddig is the gift
(pp. 274-5) to Llan Daf of land near Llangwm, Monmouthshire,
which one Caradog ap Rhiwallon bestowed "uerbo comitis herfordie
et domini guenti Rogerii filii Willelmi filii Osberni", *i.e.*, between
1071 and 1075. In the Latin versions of the Welsh laws "cerddorion"
is regularly translated "ioculatores", the foreigner having no proper
sense of the dignified position of the bardic order, and "ioculator
regis" probably stands for "bardd teulu". Of the grants above referred to, "Abraham archidiaconus guenti" attests the first and the
third.

province. He died about 1060, and it was then, apparently, that Gruffydd seized the whole realm, to the exclusion of Cadwgan.[1]

I must now deal briefly with one or two aspects of the Norman attack on Wales which are of special interest. Harold's campaign against Gruffydd, while not at all deserving to be styled a conquest of Wales, had nevertheless the effect of disposing of the Welsh peril : as Gaimar says, men took no further heed of Wales.[2] It was divided once more among a number of chieftains ; Bleddyn and Rhiwallon, half brothers of the fallen prince, ruled in the north; Maredudd and Rhys ab Owain, nephews of Hywel ab Edwin, appeared at the head of the men of Deheubarth; while Cadwgan ap Meurig established himself in his

[1] For the death of Hywel ab Owain, see MS. B of *Annales Cambr.æ, Brenhinoedd y Saeson* and *Brut y Tywysogion* ("brenhin gwlat vorgan yny heneint "). That his son Meurig had assumed some kind of authority before his father's death appears from *Lib. Land.*, p. 257 : " de laicis : mouricus rex et hingel pater suus ". The document thus attested records how Meurig, after entering into a solemn treaty with Edwin ap Gwriad, king of "Gueniscoit", seized and blinded him so that he died. Due amends was made to the church for the violated oath, but Gwent ceased to be an independent kingdom. True it is that we find (on p. 261) a " catgueaun regis guenti" giving his consent to a grant of land at Llanbedr, near Kemeys Inferior, but I infer from the fact that the donor, Caradog ap Rhiwallon, was "unus de comitibus mourici regis morcanhuc," that this was none other than Meurig's son, who appears as king of Morgannwg after the Norman Conquest. Meurig joined in the election of Herwald, which took place not later than 1059 (*Lib. Land.*, p. 266), but does not appear in connection with any grant made in the time of that prelate.

[2] "Vnc puis de Waleis nout reguard" (v. 5084—Rolls edit., i, 215). The work of Harold, while able enough from a military point of view, and remembered with a certain pride by Englishmen for many generations, only restored what had been the state of things before the rise of Gruffydd. This is shown by Caradog ap Gruffydd's raid of 1065 upon Portskewot, no less than by the condition of the border in 1066 as revealed in *Domesday*.

father's realm of Morgannwg.[1] Such was the position of
affairs when William took possession of the English crown.
I need not remind you that the victory of Hastings and
the coronation at Westminster were but the prelude to an
obstinate struggle which extended over several years, and
that it was not until early in 1070 that the conquest of
England was in any proper sense complete. This is the
year, accordingly, in which the conquest of Wales may
be deemed to begin. A few words may well be said,
however, ere we enter upon this part of the subject, as to
the short-lived schemes of William fitz Osbern.

No one would hesitate to say that, in the long run,
South Wales became much more Normanized than the
North. Yet the salient feature of the quarter of a century
which follows the accession of William is the rapid progress made by the Normans in North Wales compared
with their sluggish rate of movement in the South. The

[1] Cadwgan first appears in the *Book of Llandaff* in connection with
a grant made by his father Meurig to bishop Joseph, who died at
Aosta (Agustan), "in uia sancti petri apostoli", in 1045 (*Lib. Land.*,
p. 252, *Annales Cambriæ* and *Bruts*). The king enjoins his sons
"catguocaun et ris" to respect his donation, when he is no more
(*Lib. Land.*, p. 260). Next comes (p. 261) the grant made to the same
prelate by Caradog ap Rhiwallon, and already referred to in note 1,
p. 144, a grant in which Cadwgan concurs as king of Gwent. On pp.
267-268 is an account of an attack made upon a relative of bishop
Herwald's ("berthutis nomine . . et medicum totius patric") by
the drunken "teulu" of "catgucauni regis morcannuc filii mourici",
who gave to the church of Llan Daf in atonement some land not very
far from the cathedral. This, I am inclined to think, happened after
the fall of Gruffydd ap Llywelyn, for we are expressly told on pp.
278-9 that Cadwgan ruled over "glat morcant usque ad nadum trunci
super tyuui" under William I, in whose reign he died. He was probably the "Caducan" whom Ordericus Vitalis mentions among the
Welsh kings overcome by William fitz Osbern (iv, 7—see ii, 219 of
edit. of Le Prevost), and with his death (about 1075 ?) the old line of
Morgannwg, descendants of the Hywel ap Rhys of Asser, in all
likelihood came to an end.

contrast is brought out vividly when we remember that at
the time of the *Domesday* Survey the most advanced
Norman post on the northern coast was at Degannwy,
while on the shores of the Bristol Channel it was no
farther than Caerleon.   Later history shows that this was
a reversal of the natural order, due to accidental causes,
and, chief among these, to the death of William fitz
Osbern and the ruin of his son Roger.   William became
earl of Hereford at the beginning of 1067;[1] he left England, never to return, at the end of 1070; yet, short as
was his four years' tenure of the earldom, and frequent as
were his absences from the county upon errands of
moment entrusted to him by the king, he contrived to
leave his mark upon the Welsh border.   Ordericus Vitalis
speaks of him as an active opponent of the Welsh, whose
kings, by name Rhys, Cadwgan and Maredudd, he over-
threw.   Among others, he waged war with the "Brach-
aniaunos", the men of Brycheiniog, who probably acknowledged the authority of Maredudd and Rhys ab Owain.[2]
These assertions find full confirmation in *Domesday*.   From
the Herefordshire Survey we learn that William built
"Wigemore" castle in a waste tenement called "Mere-
stun"; it is to him, also, we are, no doubt, to attribute
the "burgum" established there—a border settlement of
traders.   Earl William, again, built the castle at Clifford,

---

[1] *Florence of Worcester.*

[2] *Ordericus Vitalis*, iv, 7.   Ab Ithel's edition of *Brut y Tywysogion*,
following in its chronology *Brenhinoedd y Saeson* (see preface), gives
1070 as the year of the fall of Maredudd ab Owain in battle with
Caradog ap Gruffydd and the "French".   It was, therefore, natural
for Mr. Freeman to see in the incident the hand of Earl William.
But the year must, I think, be 1072, and I am inclined to believe
that, after one or two encounters, Maredudd and the earl had some
years ere this come to that understanding of which the outward
symbol was the grant of Ley.

where there was also a "burgum", with sixteen burgesses. Of "Castellum Ewias" (Ewias Harold) it is only said that the earl re-built it; this fits in well with Mr. Round's conjecture[1] that we have in it the "Pentecost's castle" of the days of Godwin. The Survey says nothing of the foundation of Monmouth Castle, but this omission is made good by the *Book of Llandaff*, which tells us it was raised in the time of Earl William, who gave half of it to three of his barons.[2] Lastly, the Gloucestershire Survey informs us that it was earl William who built the castle of "Estrighoiel", at the spot now best known by its old English name of Chepstow, the place of traffic. The building of this line of border fortresses reveals a set policy of conquest; we may connect it with what William of Malmesbury tells us of the earl, how his liberality to his retainers drew a great multitude of knights around him, which made him a power in his district, but did not altogether please the thrifty king.[3] It was no doubt a part of the same policy of aggression that in some cases he appears to have taken pains to conciliate the Welsh. Vills in Gwent that had been let rent free by King Gruffydd he granted to the holders on the same terms;[4] from the Herefordshire Survey we find that he granted to King Maredudd ab Owain the vill of Ley (near Lingen), and, moreover, obtained from king William the entire remission of the geld—a privilege afterwards extended to Maredudd's son, Gruffydd.[5] These measures point to a far-

---

[1] *Feudal England*, p. 324.

[2] *Lib. Land.*, pp. 277-8 ("Castellum de mingui").

[3] *Gesta Regum*, bk. iii, § 256.

[4] See p. 144, above.

[5] See Terra Grifin filii Mariadoc. Gruffydd was killed at Llan Dudoch, near Cardigan, in 1091, in an attempt to deprive Rhys ap Tewdwr of the crown of Deheubarth (*Annales* and *Bruts*). "Inuitauerunt" implies that he was an exile.

reaching scheme for the conquest of South Wales, but all came to nothing when William, in February 1071, was killed in a skirmish in Flanders. His second son Roger inherited his earldom and English estates, but these were staked and lost in a few years in a desperate struggle against the Conqueror's iron rule, and no other baron was allowed to step into the position which had been thus abused. The *Book of Llandaff* gives us to understand that many lesser figures were involved in the fall of Roger;[1] it is easy to see that the sudden change of *personnel* along the South Welsh border must have had a paralyzing effect upon the Norman advance, which is not resumed for some ten or twelve years. The one Welsh achievement of the house of Breteuil was the conquest of Gwent, over which no Welsh prince ever again bore rule.

Let me now briefly trace the progress of the Normans along the coast of North Wales. I think it has not been generally realised how rapid and effective this movement was during the reigns of the first two Williams, how narrowly Gwynedd escaped entire subjection to Norman rule. The base of operations was Chester, where in 1071 Hugh of Avranches was established as earl, with an authority little short of regal over the whole county. He probably had no difficulty in securing possession of the manors of Coleshill, Hawarden, and Bistre, where we find him in possession some years later;[2] the extension of his borders to the Clwyd was a more difficult task, which he entrusted to his cousin Robert, one of the Confessor's favourites. Robert

---

[1] " Illi tres cum multis aliis exhereditati sunt " (p. 278).

[2] In 1093 Hugh assigned to the abbey of St. Werburgh at Chester the tithes of his manors of "Haurdina", "Coleshul ", and "Bissopestred" (*Monasticon Angl.*, ed. 1819, ii, p. 386). "Coleselt" and "Biscopestreu " were in 1086 in the hands of sub-tenants, but "Hugo comes tenet in dominio Haordine . . in dominio sunt ii carucæ et iiii serui ".

entered about 1073 upon his long struggle with the Welsh,
and had in a year or two made himself master of the
place from which he was henceforth known as Robert of
Rhuddlan.[1] His epitaph recounts how at this stage of the
conflict, by a well-planned ambuscade, he surprised King
Bleddyn, seized very valuable booty, and almost obtained
possession of the person of the king himself.[2] This must
have been shortly before 1075, the year of Bleddyn's
death. His antagonist during the next six years was
Trahaearn ap Caradog, hereditary prince of the cantref of
Arwystli—the region round Llan Idloes and Llan Dinam—
who had contrived to make himself ruler of Gwynedd, by
what methods and in virtue of what claims it is not very
easy to say. Against him the contest was waged with
much success.[3] Robert's forces crept steadily along the
coast, possessed themselves of the cantref of Rhos, which
lay between the Elwy, the Conway, and the sea, and about
1080 raised, on a hillock which commands the estuary of
the latter river and was the site of a royal stronghold in
the time of Maelgwn Gwynedd, the first Norman castle of
Degannwy.[4] The process of dislodging Trahaearn was
rendered easier by the appearance of a rival claimant of
the crown; in 1075 Gruffydd ap Cynan ap Iago, grandson

[1] "Per xv annos [1073-1088] intolerabiliter Britones protrivit"
(*Ordericus Vitalis*, viii, 3—ed. Le Prevost, vol. iii, p. 284).

[2] "Præcipuam, pulchro Blideno rege fugato,
    Prædam cum paucis cepit in insidiis." (*Ibid.*, p. 288.)
The notes of Le Prevost hereabouts must not be taken too seriously.

[3] "Vicitque Trehellum" (*Ibid.*).

[4] Degannwy is the "arcem detantorum" (read "decantorum") of
the oldest MS. of *Annales Cambriæ* (*Y Cymmrodor*, ix, 164). It is not
mentioned in *Domesday*, being covered by the reference to "Ros",
for Creuddyn was a cymwd of Rhos (so all the lists) and was not
separated from the rest of the cantref until the time of Edward I.

of the Iago whom Gruffydd ap Llywelyn succeeded in 1039, came over from Ireland with the intention of recovering the lost patrimony of his house. We have for the career of Gruffydd ap Cynan evidence of a kind which is unusual in Welsh history, namely, a life which, though not strictly contemporary, was certainly written in the days of Gruffydd's son Owain Gwynedd, and appears to me to be of considerable historical value.[1] There are, no doubt, a number of minor errors, and many of the statements in the narrative of Gruffydd's early achievements are not to be implicitly trusted. Yet the *Life* seems to me for the most part a fairly trustworthy document, supplying many details which are not to be found in any other source; for instance, the name of the daughter of Brian Boru (given as "Alam") who married Sitric of Dublin. It is known to all that Gruffydd ap Cynan was born in Ireland of an Irish mother, and spent his youth in that country, until the time came for him to claim his due in Gwynedd. What has not been understood, I think, is that it was not

---

[1] "Historia hen gruffud vab kenan vab yago" was printed by the Rev. Robert Williams of Rhyd y Croesau in *Archæologia Cambrensis* for 1866 (3rd ser., vol. xii) from Hengwrt MS. 406 (now Peniarth MS. 17) of the middle of the thirteenth century, what was wanting at the end of this MS. being supplied from a later copy. It had previously been printed from another MS., under the name of "Buchedd Gruffydd ap Cynan", in the Myvyrian collection. A doubt may arise whether the life was not originally written in Latin, but that substantially what we have was put together before 1170 I feel certain. See, especially, the reference to the reigning kings of Waterford— "Ac un oe vroder a ossodes yn un or dinassoed a adeilassei er hon a elwit yn eu hyeith hwy porthlarg (the 'Port Lairge' of the Irish annalists) ae etived enteu a vuant vrenhined y dinas hwnw er henne hyt hediw" (p. 32). Mr. Gwenogvryn Evans gives in his *Report* upon the Peniarth MSS. (p. 339) the opening sentences of the *Historia:* his text suggests that absolute fidelity to the original must not be counted upon in that of the Rev. Robert Williams.

with the native Irish of Celtic blood, but with the Ostmen
of Dublin, the Scandinavian settlers around the mouth of
the Liffey, that he was connected. According to the *Life*,
his mother was " Ragnell " (or Radnall), daughter of
Anlaf, a son of Sitric of the Silken Beard, the king of
Dublin, who abdicated in 1035, and died in 1042.[1] He was
born in Dublin, in or about the year 1055, when Gruffydd
ap Llywelyn was at the height of his power in Wales, and
Cynan ab Iago, hopeless of making any headway against
him, had probably settled down as an Irish proprietor.[2]
He was brought up at Swords, some ten miles from the

---

[1] I have not been able to identify all the names in Gruffydd's
maternal pedigree, but within certain limits there is no difficulty in
fitting them in with what we know of Irish history. " Ragnell " (it is
also spelt " Raonell ") would seem to bear the name which occurs as
" Radnall " among the Waterford Danes (Todd's *War of the Gaedhil
with the Gaill*, p. 290). Her mother was " [m]ayl corcre " (for this as
an Irish female name see *Ibid.*, p. 265), daughter of " dimlug m. tethel ",
king of Leinster, *i.e.*, Dunlaing son of Tuathal, who died in 1014
(*Chron. Scotorum*). Her father was probably the Anlaf son of Sitric,
who was killed in 1012 (*Annals of Ulster*), and she would seem to
have had as first husband a Mathghamhain of Ulster. The account
of Sitric of the Silken Beard and of Anlaf Cuaran (to whom should
be assigned the position and achievements here set down to the
credit of his obscure grandson) appears to be in the main correct ;
" urien " is Brian Boru, " gurmlach " is Gormlaith, and " dimchath "
her son Donnchadh. For " hwnnw " in line 5 of page 33 read
" honno ", and for " vab " in line 8, " vraut ". Beyond the elder
Sitric we get into the region of genealogical romance.

[2] " Dwy flynedd a phetwar ugeint oedd Ruffudd ", says the *Historia*
(p. 128), when he died in 1137. It follows from this that Cynan
survived his father at least fifteen years, and may well have been
concerned in some of the attacks upon the power of Gruffydd ap
Llywelyn. But I know of no good authority for the statements of
Powel (ed. 1811, pp. 70, 71) associating him specifically with the
events of 1042 and 1052. The *Historia* implies that he died when
his son was of tender age—(" managei y vam idaw beunyd pwy a pha
ryw wr oed y dat a pha dref tat oed idaw ", p. 34), and, had he
survived his rival's fall in 1063, I think we should have heard of him.

place of his birth, the seat of an ancient monastery which
was included within the bounds of the Danish kingdom
of Dublin.[1] In any enquiry, therefore, into the effect of
Gruffydd's upbringing upon his later rule of Gwynedd, it
is to be remembered that the early influences which
moulded his character were not purely Celtic, but to a
large extent Scandinavian. Despite the help which was
given to him by Robert of Rhuddlan, Gruffydd did not
succeed in establishing his claim to the crown of Gwynedd
until 1081.[2] This was the year of the famous battle of
Mynydd Carn, fought (there can be little doubt) in South
Cardiganshire,[3] where the two representatives of the
ancient dynasties of North and South, Gruffydd ap Cynan
and Rhys ap Tewdwr, overcame and slew the upstart
princes, Trahaearn ap Caradog and Caradog ap Gruffydd,
who had kept them out of their own. The *Life* gives a
vivid description of the fight and the varied equipment of

---

[1] "Y lle aelwir yg gwydelec swrth colomcell" (p. 30). "Sord
Coluim Cille" is spoken of by the *Annals of Loch Cé* (s. a. 1035) in
such a way as to show it was within the realm of Sitric of the
Silken Beard. Cf. Haliday, *Scandinavian Kingdom of Dublin*, p. 142.

[2] MS. C of *Annales Cambriæ* speaks of Gruffydd on his first appearance as "Grifud nepos iacob", and thus, I think, clearly shows
its character as derived from a contemporary record. A few years
later, no one would have dreamt of calling him anything but Gruffydd
ap Cynan; in 1075, however, nothing was known in Wales of Cynan,
and it was as Iago's grandson this young man of twenty claimed
the Venedotian crown. This entry well illustrates the relations between the Latin chronicle represented by the *Annales Cambriæ* and
the two independent Welsh versions of it known as *Brut y Tywysogion*
and *Brenhinoedd y Saeson*. MS. C (Dom. i, fo. 143a) has "Grifud
autem nepos iacob non obsedit", non being a blunder of this copy
for Mon. *Brut y Tywysogion* translates this notice intelligently—"Ac
yna ydymladawd grufud uab kynan wyr Iago a mon" (*Bruts*, ed.
Rhys and Evans, p. 269). *Brenhinoedd y Saeson* (Cleop. B. v, fo.
132a) has "Grufud hagen nei James a oed yn gwarchadw manaw"!

[3] Note by Mr. Egerton Phillimore in *Y Cymmrodor*, xi, 167.

the forces engaged; the Danes wielded two-edged axes, the Irish flourished darts and spiked balls of iron, the men of Gwynedd fought with shield and glaive.[1] Gruffydd's victory was complete, but he did not long enjoy the fruits of it, for shortly afterwards he was taken prisoner at Rug in Edeyrnion, and handed over to Earl Hugh, in whose dungeons he languished for many years.[2] It is only in the *Life* we get any account of this imprisonment, but the story is confirmed by the epitaph of Robert of Rhuddlan, as given by Ordericus, and, in harmony with it, *Domesday* shows that in 1086 Edeyrnion was in the hands of the Normans.[3]

The great Survey shows clearly the posture of affairs in this part of the country at the time it was undertaken. Not only the hundred of Atiscros, referred to above,[1] but also Rhuddlan and what is now North Flintshire were in the hands of Earl Hugh of Chester, though Robert of Rhuddlan held a considerable portion as sub-tenant. Hugh and Robert divided between them the custody of the castle of Rhuddlan, the patronage of the church, and

---

[1] "Gwyr denmare ac eu bwyeill deuvinyauc ar guydyl gaflachauc ac eu peleu haearnaul kyllellauc ar gwyndyt gleivyauc tarcanauc" (p. 44). The great axe was a specially Danish weapon (*Social England*, i, 183). For the Irish suist or war flail, from which hung iron balls attached to chains, see O'Curry's *Manners and Customs of the Irish*, ed. Sullivan, i, p. 462-3.

[2] The *Historia* says "deudeng blyned" in one place and "un vlyned ar bemthec" in another, two figures which as xii and xvi would be easily confused. The difficulty as to the mention of Gruffydd in connection with the death of Robert of Rhuddlan in 1088 still remains.

[3] "Cepit Grithfridum regem," says the epitaph. According to the Shropshire Survey, Rainald the sheriff had "in Walis duos fines Chenlei et Derniou" (*i.e.*, Cynllaith and Edeyrnion). Earl Hugh held the neighbouring district of "Gal" (Yale).

[4] See p. 139, above.

the profits of mills, mines, fisheries, and markets—a list which shows that the region was no longer a desert march. Beyond the Clwyd, Robert was independent lord : he held Rhos and Rhufoniog, the two Welsh cantrefs which lay between the Clwyd and the Conway, in fee of the king. Only a strip along the coast, some six miles wide, was under tillage; the rest, Robert averred, was but marsh and forest, and could not be brought under the plough ; and, in view of the disturbed condition of the border, it is probable that the Survey commissioners accepted the statement without demur. Across the Conway, Robert was again in a new position : he held at a rent of £40 " Nortwales ", *i.e.*, the principality of Gwynedd, save only such portions (viz., Rhos and Rhufoniog) as he already held in fee and the lands of the bishopric of Bangor.[1] Gruffydd ap Cynan was probably at the moment in the hands of Earl Hugh, and the Conqueror had apparently given the temporary charge of his dominions to Robert, until he could make a satisfactory permanent arrangement. From his fortress of Degannwy, Robert could exercise some control over the opposite coast, but he does not appear to have penetrated far into the wilds of Eryri, for his epitaph claims no more for him than that

"Montem Svandunum, fluviumque citum Colvenum
Pluribus armatis transiliit vicibus."[2]

---

[1] " Terras episcopatus " must refer to Bangor, where we find a bishop shortly afterwards. No bishop of St. Asaph occurs until 1143, and the Survey mentions " Ianuuile " without reference even to a church. St. Asaph had, undoubtedly, been in earlier times (perhaps under Gruffydd ap Llywelyn) the seat of a bishop, but it was " pro vastitate et barbarie episcopo vacantem", to use the language of a writer of 1127 (*Historians of the Church of York*, ed. Raine, ii, 211).

[2] *Ord. Vit.*, viii, 3 ; in Le Prevost's edition, vol. iii, p. 288. "Colvenum " is, of course, the Conway.

One part of his grant of "Nortwales" was, he pointed out, in the hands of a brother baron: the hundred of "Arvester", *i.e.*, Arwystli, was on the showing of the Welsh an integral part of the principality, but had been seized by Earl Roger of Shrewsbury, who was apparently acting as grantee of the principality of Powys. This side-light on the history of Arwystli clearly shows how early the notion was (whatever its exact origin) that the cantref was no part of Powys, but an outlying member of Gwynedd, a notion which is reflected in its ecclesiastical relations. For until the rearrangement of 1859, the deanery of Arwystli was not only in the diocese of Bangor, but was separated from the rest of the diocese by an arm of the diocese of St. Asaph, which in fact completely hemmed it in on the northern side.[1]

Two years after the taking of the Survey, Robert of Rhuddlan was slain by the Welsh in a daring attack which they made upon his possessions in the Creuddyn peninsula. The dramatic story told by Ordericus Vitalis has been made familiar for us by the historian of the reign of William Rufus, and here I would only add that I do not think Mr. Freeman was right in believing that Ordericus confused the Great Orme ("montis Hormahevæ") with the hill of Degannwy itself.[2] The latter, as those who know the locality can bear witness, is by no means the kind of sheer cliff ("ardui montis præcipitium") likely to bring Norman warriors to a stand, nor would the Welsh have

[1] Arwystli acknowledged the authority of the bishop of Bangor in the middle of the twelfth century, for "Mauricius", bishop of Bangor from 1140 to 1161, confirms a grant made by Hywel ab Ieuaf (died 1185) of Arwystli, a great grandson of Trahacarn ap Caradog, to the church of Tref Eglwys, then held by the canons of Haughmond (*Archæologia Cambrensis*, third ser., vol. vi, p. 331).

[2] Freeman's *William Rufus*, vol. i, p. 125, note.

been so foolish as to ground their skiffs in a receding tide
beneath the very walls of Robert's stronghold.   I suggest
that the landing was stealthily made in a cove on the
north side of the Great Orme, beyond the ken of the
watchers of Degannwy; that the cattle and captives seized
were from the settlements on the tableland above, two of
them known in later ages as Cyngreadur and Yr Wyddfid ;[1]
that Robert, rushing to the spot with a few poorly armed
followers, was too late to save his property, because he had
to cover a distance of three miles from Degannwy; and
that the " difficult descent" which daunted all his followers
save one, so that he met his death almost alone, was the
line of beetling crags which towers above the sea near the
ancient church of St. Tudno.

We owe the story of Robert's death to the accident that
his brother was a monk of St. Evroul and interested
Ordericus in the affair, getting him to compose a set of
Latin verses to serve as an epitaph.   It was, in fact, but
an incident in the progress of the Normans—a momentary
check which did not seriously delay their advance along
the North Welsh coast.   Forthwith, the place of the fallen
leader was taken by Earl Hugh, who is said by Gaimar to
have received from Rufus a grant of " Nort Wales ",[2] in
succession, we may suppose, to Robert, and who in any

---

[1] " Athutno ynghyngreadur" occurs in the Hafod MS. of "Bonedd
y Saint" (*Myvyrian Archaiology*, Denbigh ed., p. 416).   Gwalchmai
refers to "gyngreawdyr fynyd" and its "gwenyg gwyn" in close
connection with "Morfa Rianed" (*Ibid.*, p. 144).   Dr. Owen Pughe,
in ignorance of its character as a place-name, treated the word as
a common noun, and sagely explained it as meaning "one who
aggregates or collects together".   Gwyddfid, or Yr Wyddfid, stood
in the neighbourhood of the "Happy Valley"; both it and Cyngreadur appear in the *Record of Carnarvon* among the possessions
of the bishop of Bangor (pp. 109-111, 235).

[2] l. 6043.

case acted for the next ten years as though Gwynedd had
been delivered entirely into his hands. After the seizure
of Gruffydd, the *Historia* tells us, the earl entered that
prince's territories with a great host and built castles
therein, one in Anglesey (at Aber Lleiniog), one in Arfon
" in the old stronghold of the Emperor Constantine, son
of Constans the Great " (*i.e.*, Carnarvon), one at Bangor,
and one in Meirionydd.[1]   There is other and better
evidence of the extent of his power. In 1092 a Breton
named Hervé was consecrated bishop of Bangor ; he was
a favourite of Rufus, and his subsequent history sufficiently
shows that it was only with the help of Earl Hugh he had
any prospect of being able to enjoy the revenues of the
see. Pope Paschal II at a later date speaks of the circumstances under which he had seized the bishopric ;
" barbarously and stupidly promoted to a barbarous see "
no doubt glances at the informalities of an election in
which the cathedral clergy were either altogether ignored
or coerced into a distasteful choice.[2] Again, in the year
after this election, the earl re-modelled the abbey of St.
Werburgh in his city of Chester, and added largely to its
endowments. It is significant, not only of his expecta-
tions, but also of his actual achievements, that he should
promise the monks two manors in Anglesey, one in Rhos,
the tithe of the fisheries of Anglesey, and the right to
have one ship, carrying ten nets, in the Anglesey fishing
fleet.[3] As it chanced, this year marked the climax of
Hugh's power in Wales, for in 1094 a revolt broke out
among the Welsh which was the beginning of a reaction
strong enough in a few years to drive the stranger back

[1] P. 114 of the *Archæologia Cambrensis* text.
[2] Haddan and Stubbs, *Councils*, etc., i, 299, 303-6.
[3] *Monasticon Anglicanum*, ii, 386.

across the Conway. The turn of the tide had come, and
henceforward the Normans were no longer an aggressive
power in North Wales.

In Powys, the period which is closed by the revolt of
1094 was, as in Gwynedd, marked by the progress of the
Norman arms. The waste vills in the border hundreds
were replenished with stock, and again furnished a revenue
to royal and baronial holders. Many Welsh districts,
among them Ial, Edeyrnion, Cynllaith, Maelor Saesneg,
Cydewain, Ceri, and Arwystli, came under Norman authority and paid renders of money or kine in token of subjection.[1] Earl Roger of Shrewsbury claimed the same
authority over Powys as was wielded by Earl Hugh in
Gwynedd, and the theory that the princes of this region
were subject to the lords of Salop survived the fall of the
house of Montgomery, and had still some force when
bishop Richard of London ruled the county as the representative of Henry I.[2]

In South Wales, on the other hand, little progress was
made after the death of William fitz Osbern in 1071.

---

[1] "Terram de Gal" (Shropshire Survey) was no doubt claimed by
Earl Roger as a part of Powys, but it adjoined the Cheshire hundred of Exestan, and Earl Hugh therefore found it convenient to
hold it as sub-tenant. "Chenlei et Derniou" were held by Rainald
the sheriff, as appendages to his great Oswestry holding. Both
Eyton (*Shropshire*, xi, 31) and Palmer (*Y Cymmrodor*, x, 44) believe
that the "Tuder quidam Walensis" who held of the Earl (Roger)
a "finem terræ Walensis" was Tudur ap Rhys Sais, and that the
land lay along the south bank of the Dee. Eyton also suggests
(xi, 172) that the "fine de Walis" belonging to the castelry of
Montgomery, from which Earl Roger got £6 a year, covered Cydewain
and Ceri, districts which must certainly have been in the earl's
hands, if, as alleged in the Cheshire Survey, he was in possession
of Arwystli.

[2] See the references to Richard in *Brut y Tywysogion* (ed. Rhys
and Evans, pp. 282, 284, 291).

The vills around Radnor were, it has been shown, still waste in 1086; the house of Breos had not yet set up its banner in the district.[1] On the Wye, Clifford, one of William's outposts, was still at the time of the Survey the limit of Norman authority, though very soon afterwards Bernard of Neufmarché began that process of conquest which made him in a few years lord of Brycheiniog. The records of St. Peter's abbey at Gloucester give 1088 as the year in which Bernard bestowed on the abbey the church and vill of Glasbury;[2] the place was probably one of his earliest acquisitions, and its dedication to religious uses had perhaps the character of an offering of first fruits. Further south, Walter de Lacy, mentioned by Ordericus[3] as William fitz Osbern's right hand man in the task of keeping down the Welsh, had made some impression upon Ewias, where in 1086 there was, besides William's renovated fortress at Ewias Harold and the castelry attached thereto, a separate Ewias, in which Welshmen rendering swine and honey dwelt, and which was held by Walter's son Roger. Gwent, we have seen, was won for the Normans before Earl William's death: whether it was in his day or later that the Usk was crossed, and a Norman castle set up at Caerleon is uncertain, but at the time of the Survey the settlement was a small one,[4] and I see no

---

[1] According to P. Marchegay (*Chartes du Prieuré de Monmouth*, 1879), Philip de Breos was at "Raddenoam" when he made a grant, not later than 1096, to the monks of St. Florent near Saumur (p. 14, note). The family thus acquired Radnor within the ten years following the date of *Domesday*.

[2] *Cartulary of St. Peter's*, Rolls edit., i, 80.

[3] iv, 7 ; ii, 218 of Le Prevost's edition.

[4] "Willelmus de Scolnes tenet octo carucatas terræ in castellaria de CARLION et Turstinus tenet de illo. Ibi habet in dominio unam carucam et tres Walenses lege Walensi uiuentes cum tribus carucis et duos bordarios cum dimidia caruca et reddunt quatuor sextarios

M

evidence that the conquest of Glamorgan had begun. True, there is some authority for the statement that in 1081 a beginning was made of the building of Cardiff,[1] but, as Iestyn ap Gwrgant did not in all likelihood become supreme in Morgannwg until the death of Caradog ap Gruffydd at Mynydd Carn in that year,[2] we require to allow a little more time for the consolidation of his power than this date, if understood to refer to a Norman settlement, would give us. On the whole, it is to the reign of Rufus we must look for the decisive advance here, as in Brycheiniog.

It is difficult to avoid the conclusion that the Conqueror, after the fall of Earl Roger of Hereford, gave no great encouragement to raids upon South Wales. He had no wish, perhaps, to see the barons of the Southern march grow powerful, seated as they were within striking distance of London. In 1081 he himself led an army into Dyfed, with what purpose is not very clear, for the artless suggestion of the St. David's chronicler, that he was solely moved

---

mollis. Ibi duo servi et una ancilla " (Herefordshire). It is not clear whether the six carucates held by Turstin "ultra huscham" (Gloucestershire) are the same.

[1] *Annals of Margam.* The notice is copied into the chronicle printed in *Archæologia Cambrensis*, third ser., vol. viii, p. 273, and, in a slightly altered form, into *Brenhinoedd y Saeson.*

[2] Iestyn, it has been already shown, is a subordinate witness to a grant made by "Caratocvs rex morcannuc ", *i.e.*, Caradog ap Gruffydd, about 1080 (*Lib. Land.*, p. 273). Another, and no doubt later document shows us " Gistinus filius gurcant " as surrounded by a "familia" or " teulu " of the usual princely pattern, which is strong enough to do violence to the sanctity of the church of Llandaff, and for the misdeeds of which Iestyn has to make amends in the traditional manner, by the gift of an estate (*Lib. Land.*, 271-2). This is, in order of time, the last grant in the book ; the Norman invaders bestowed no gifts on Llandaff, but, on the contrary, so despoiled the see that its twenty-four canons were reduced to two (*Ibid.*, 88).

by the desire to pay his respects to the relics of the great saint,[1] will not impose upon any one who remembers how practical a person William was. It may, however, be conjectured that an agreement was then arrived at with Rhys ap Tewdwr which secured the Southern prince from Norman attacks as long as the Conqueror lived, and had some force even during the early years of the reign of Rufus. In the Herefordshire Survey we find a certain "Riset de Wales" paying a render of £40 to the king. Remembering that this was just the sum paid by Robert of Rhuddlan for "Nortwales" or Gwynedd, one is very ready to believe that we have here the ferm paid by Rhys ap Tewdwr for his kingdom of Deheubarth. In addition, forty shillings were due from him, beyond the ferm, for the district of "Calcebuef", a name which, whatever its precise meaning, has as one element, I believe, that of the cantref of Buallt (styled Buell in the *Liber Landavensis*). Buallt, be it remembered, was no part of the realm of Deheubarth, but had its own line of princes, descended from Elstan Glodrydd, the ruler of " Rhwng Gwy a Hafren".[2] These entries may explain why Rhys ap Tewdwr had to contend with none but domestic foes until 1093, when he met his death at the hands of the Norman settlers of Brycheiniog. Bernard and his followers had, indeed, about 1088 attacked the region of Talgarth, but this probably meant, not that the agreement came to an end in 1087, but that Rufus was less strict in enforcing it upon the marcher lords of the South, now busily preparing for the great forward movement of the latter part of the reign. It is the year 1093 which marks the definite beginning of that movement. Rhys was slain about the 20th of April ; " about July 1st",

---

[1] " Orationis causa."
[2] See note to year 1077 in Appendix.

we read, "the French for the first time held Dyfed and
Ceredigion and set castles therein, and thereafter they
took possession of the whole of the land of the Britons."
When the great chieftain fell, there fell with him, so
ran the original of the *Bruts*, "regnum Britonum" (or
"Britanniæ "),[1] or, as Florence of Worcester puts it in the
same connection—"from that day kings (reges) ceased to
rule in Wales". The remark is meaningless, if we take a
wide survey of the history of Wales, for the title of king
was frequently given in later ages to Welsh princes; but
made by contemporaries, with no knowledge of the future
course of affairs among the Welsh, it meant that the last
of the great chiefs whose position was formally recognized
by the English crown had disappeared, and that henceforth
no regal rights were deemed to exist in Wales. The field
was open for the knightly adventurer.

---

[1] "Teyrnas y brytanyeit", *Brut y Tywysogion*, ed. Rhys and
Evans, p. 270; "brenhiniaeth Kymre", *Brenhinoedd y Saeson.*
"Britones " and " Britanni", translated "brytanyeit " in the Welsh
texts, are the regular words for "Welsh" in our chronicles until
about 1135.

APPENDIX.

The Text of MSS. B and C of "Annales Cambriæ"
for the period 1035—1093, in parallel columns.

The primary authority for the internal history of Wales during this period is the Latin chronicle, originally written up from year to year at St. David's, which is now represented by the sets of Welsh Annals in Cottonian MS. Domitian i and the Record Office MS. entitled the *Breviate of Domesday*.[1] The former is MS. C, the latter MS. B of *Annales Cambriæ*, as edited for the Rolls Series in 1860. It has been pointed out by Mr. Phillimore (whose text of MS. A[2] in vol. ix of *Y Cymmrodor* gives the student all he can desire) that the plan of the Rolls edition is one which makes it very difficult to form a proper conception of the evidence furnished by the various MSS., and that there are many errors in the printed text.[3] I have thought it might be useful, therefore, to print here in parallel columns, as a supplement to the foregoing paper, the portions of the two MSS. which cover the period under discussion. Italic letters represent expanded contractions; in other respects the MSS. are followed line for line and letter for letter. In the notes, *Brenhinoedd y Saeson* is, for convenience of reference, included in the term "Bruts."

---

[1] The official description is "Q.R. Miscellaneous Books, vol. i."

[2] MS. A records nothing after 954 and therefore does not here concern us.

[3] *Y Cymmrodor*, vol. xi, pp. 142-8.

Breviate of Domesday (fly leaves)=MS. B.
Page 11, column 3 (line 6).

Annus Maredut *filius* edwiní a fi
líís conaní occis*us* e*st*.   Caradauc
fili*us* Rederch ab anglís occis*us* e*st*
Cnut fili*us* Swein rex anglor*um* ob*iit*
Ann*us*
Ann*us*
Ann*us*
Ann*us* Grifín*us* fílí*us* lewelın i*n* no*z*
wallıa regnare ínchoau*it*. quí
dum¹ regnau*it* anglos *et* gentıles
pe*r*secut*us* e*st*. bellu*m* ín uado crucís
sup*er* sabrinam *cum* eís co*m*misít eos
q*ue* deuıcít.   E*odem* anno dext*ra*les
rexít br*ı*tones *et* hoelu*m* filiu*m* edwínı
ab ea expulít
Ann*us* Erwýn ep*ıscopus* meneu*ıe* ob*iit*
Ann*us* bellu*m* pencadeír ín q*uo* gr*ı*finus
sup*er*auít hoelu*m*.
Ann*us* bellu*m* pulldýwach ín quo
hoelus victo*ı* fuít Grifin*us* capt*us*
capt*us*² e*st* a gentılıb*us* dulín
Ann*us* hoelus fili*us* owein ob*iit*
Ann*us* hoelus fili*us* etwıní accepta
claſſe gentilium íntrat hostium tewý
que*m* Grifin*us* fili*us* lewelín bello
suſcepit eu*mque* uersu*m* clade suor*um* occid*it*

¹ Patched.   ² *Sic* in MS.

Cottonian MS. Domitian i=MS. C.
Fo. 141b, column 2 (line 23).

Ann*us*. Maredut *filius* eduẏn a fi-
liis kena*n* occ*u*dit*ur*.   Cradauc f*i*li*us* rederch ab anglicif occ*i*ditur.   Cnut f*i*li*us*
fveẏn rex anglo*rum* mo*ritur*.

Ann*us*. Ann*us*. Ann*us*. Ann*us*.   Gen-
tilef tenuer*unt* meuric *filius* ho-
wel.   Iacob rex uenedoc*i*e occ*u*ditur.   p*ro*
q*uo* Gr*i*futableuuelin regn*a*uit.
et houuel f*i*li*us* eduẏn expulit.

Ann*us*.   Her6ín ep*iscopus* menev*i*e mo*i*tur
Ann*us*.   Bell*um* pencadeir. *i*n q*u*o G*i*i
fud uícto*i* fu*i*t.   Eode*m* anno gr*i*fud
capt*us* fuít a gentilib*us* dulẏn.[1]

Ann*us*. Ann*us* Houuel f*i*li*us* eduẏn
        [accepta íngent*i* claffe][2]
acceptíf. xx. nauib*us* ge*n*tilium co-
ronat*us* *est*. *et* cepit defolare cambr*i*am.
cuí obuiauit gr*i*fud *filius* lewelín

[End of column and page.]

---

[1] The Cottonian MS. has here, through " like ending", run two
years into one.

[2] These three words are an interlineation.

Brev. Domesd. (B).
Page 11, column 3 continued.

Annus Ioseph episcopus landauensis rome obiit
Annus

Annus familia grifini ad modum. c̄ .

xl dolo optimatum ſtratewi cecidit
in cuius vindicta rex Grifinus deme
ciam et ſtratewi deuaſtauit. Nix cecidit
et durauit a kalendis ianuarii usque
ad feſtum sancti patricii quam apellauerunt
Annus   magnam niuem
Annus tota dextralis patria deserta est

Annus
Annus
Annus claſſis hibernie in dextrali parte periit
Annus
Annus
Annus
Annus Grifinus filius Riderch occidit

Dom. i (C).

Fo. 143a, column 1.[1]

et commiſſo bello in oſtio teÿuí *cum* magna *parte* exercitus ſui howel cecidit.

Grifud autem uictoꝛ fuit.

Annus. Sedicio magna oꝛta fuít
inter grıfud fılius lewelín *et* grıfud fılius rederc.

Annus. Annus. ſimilía grıfud admo-
dum. cxl. dolo optímatum. ſtratewẏ
et dẏuet.[2] Annuſ.

Annus. Hoc anno tota dextralis patria
deſerta *est* metu gentilium

Annus. Annus. Annus. Claſſis ẏ-
bernıe perit *in* dextralı *parte* cambrıe.[3]

Annus. Annus. Annus. Annus. Gri

---

[1] Folio 142 is one of the interposed leaves—see preface to Rolls
edit. of *Annales Cambriæ*, p. xxviii.

[2] Here again the scribe's eye has misled him, so that two sentences
have been telescoped into one meaningless mass.

[3] I cannot account for the "prædavit" of the Rolls editor (page 25)
and of *Monumenta Hist. Br.*, page 840. For the "pergilaud" of the
Myvyrian text of *Brenhinoedd y Saeson* (Denbigh edit., p. 663) read
"peryglaud" (Cleopatra B. v, fo. 128b).

Brev. Domesd. (B).
Page 11, column 3 continued.

et herefoidiam uaftauit [1]

[*End of column and page.*]

Page 12, column 1.

Ann*us* Magn*us* filius haraldi
vaftauit regionem anglo*rum*. aux
iliante. grifíno rege Biítonu*m*.
Ann*us* owínu*s* filius Grifíní ob*iit*
Ann*us*
Ann*us*
Ann*us*
Ann*us* Grifinu*s* *filius* lewelíni rex brito
num nobiliffimu*s* dolo suo*rum* occisu*s* e*st*.
Ann*us*[3] Ioseph Meneu*ie* ep*iscopus* ob*iit*
Ann*us*
Ann*us*
Ann*us*
Ann*us* Haraldu*s* gotho*rum* rex anglos
conatur si*bi* subiugare que*m* aliu*s* haral
du*s* filius Gotwíní repentíno bello
excep*it* *et* occidít ip*s*um autem p*ro* habita
víctoiía gloriantem Willel*mus* baftard noi

---

[1] There is at this point a good deal amiss in both MSS. In the
first place, the writer of MS. B has jumbled together the names of
the two Gruffydds, and run two annals into one. In the second place,
the death of Gruffydd ap Rhydderch and the sack of Hereford are
assigned by MS. C and presumably by the original of MS. B to two
different years (1056 and 1057), whereas, if we accept the evidence of
the various *Bruts*, both belong to the year 1056. That B and C had
a common source different from and (at least in places) inferior in
authority to the Latin original of the *Bruts*, appears from the fact
that the two MSS. have in exactly the same place (events of

Dom. i (C).
Fo. 143a, column 1 continued.

fut f*ilius* leuuelín interfecit gr*ı*fud
f*ilius* rederch.'
Ann*us*. deſtructio hereford a gr*ı*fud.

Ann*us*. fil*ius*² harold uastauit regioneſ anglie auxiliante ei gr*ı*-
fud b*r*itonu*m* rege.
Ann*us*. Oweín f*ilius* gr*ı*fud mor*itur*.

Ann*us*. Ann*us*. Ann*us*. Ann*us*. Gri-
fut f*ilius* leuuelín br*itonum* rex cecid*it*.
Ioſeph ep*iscopus* menevie mo*r*itu*r*.

Ann*us*. Ann*us*. Ann*us*. Ann*us*. Haroldu*s* rex gothoru*m* cu*m* magno exer-
citu inuaſit regioneſ anglie.
cuí obuíauít aliu*s* haroldu*s* f*ilius* Got-
wín *et* eu*m* interfecit. S*ed* iter*um* ſuperue-

1151-3) a hiatus of which the *Bruts* show no trace. Lastly, the *Bruts*
themselves are in error in ascribing the sack of Hereford to the year
1056, for the evidence of their common original, however good in the
main, can hardly stand against the consensus of three of the Saxon
Chronicles, placing the event in 1055.

² The writer of C no doubt took "Magnus" to be an otiose
adjective !

³ This "annus" is a mistake. The *Bruts* support MS. C in the
matter.

Brev. Domesd. (B).

Page 12, column 1 continued.

mannorum dux anglíe regno prruauit[1]
Annus
Annus
Annus bellum Mecheín inter filios ken
wín. scilicet. bledín et Ruallo et filios
grifíní. scilicet. Maredut et Idwal ín quo
filíí Grifíní ceciderunt.   Idwal bello
Maredut frigore.   Ruallo etiam filius
kenwín occisus est. bledín ın regnum suc
Annus   ceffit
Annus Maredut filíus owíní a fran-
cıs occisus est

Annus Meneuıa vaftata est a gentí
libus et bangor sımılıter. bleıduth epıscopus
meneuíe obıt.   Sulgenl° epıscopatui successıt

Annus. de Mungumerı hugo. vaftat
Annus[2]   karedigıaun.
Annus bledínt filius kenwín dolo
ducum[3]. ftratewẏ a reso fílío owíní occiditur.

---

[1] Not only in MSS. B and C, but also in the Latin original of the
Bruts (see MS. C of *Brut y Tywysogion* as cited in the Rolls edition,
p. 44), the events of 1066 are assigned to 1067.

[2] Again a mistake; cf. Rolls edition of *Brut y Tywrysogion.*

[3] *Brut y Tywysogion* shows that the original chronicle had both
descriptions—"drwy dwyll dryc ysprytolyon pennaethou ac uchelwyr
ystrat tywi," (*Red Book of Hergest*, ed. Rhŷs and Evans, vol. ii, p. 268).

Dom. i (C).
Fo. 143a, column 1 continued.

nít Will*el*m*us* q*uidam* no*r*mannorum dux.
et harold*um* anglor*um* regem uit*a et*
regno p*r*íuauit.
Ann*us*. Ann*us*. Ann*us*. methe*r*n int*or*
filiof cín6ín. i*d* *est*. bledȳn *et* ruallaun *et* filiof g*r*ifut. i*d est* maredut
et ídwal í*n* bello.¹ Maredut fr*r*go-
re. í*n* quo *etram* bello ruallaun occidít*ur*. bledín aut*em* regnauít.

Ann*us*. Ann*us*. Maredut f*ilius* o-
weín a cradauc f*ilius* gr*r*ffud *et* a

[*Column ends.*]
Fo. 143a, column 2.

francíf occ*iditur* fup*er* ripam remnẏ. Di-
ermíd fcotor*um* rex í*n* bello occ*r*dít*ur*.²
Ann*us*. francí uaftauer*unt* keredí-
gíaun. Meneuía uaftat*ur* a gentí-
lib*us*. *et* bango*r* fímíliter. Bledud
epíscop*us* meneuíe mo*r*ít*ur*. Sulgeni*us* epíscopa-
tum accepit.
Ann*us*. francí íter*um* uaftauer*unt* keredígíau*n*

Ann*us*. Bledín f*ilius* kenuín dolo
malígnor*um*³ homí*n*um de eftratewẏ

---

¹ Another confused entry, explained without difficulty when we have the text of MS. B before us.

² Dermot, son of Mael-na-mbo, King of Leinster, was, according to the contemporary chronicle of Tigernach, slain in battle in 1072 (*Revue Celtique*, vol. xvii, 4).

Brev. Domesd. (B).
Page 12, column 1 continued.

Annus Riderch filius caradauc *occiditur*.

Annus bellum Guínnítul inter filios cad
dugon. Goronuí et lewelín et resum
filium owíní et ab eo victi sunt.[1]
Annus bellum pullgudíc ín quo tra
hern rex Norwallíe víctor fuít
Resus et hoelus frater eius a trahaírn
filio caraduc occisus est

Annus filíus teudur. resus.
regnare inchoauit   [ta est
Annus Meneuia a gentilibus vasta-

---

[1] Goronwy and Llywelyn were not, as has been sometimes assumed
(*e.g.* by Powel, by the compiler of *Brut Aberpergwm*, and by Meyrick
in his *History of Cardiganshire*), sons of Cadwgan ap Bleddyn, but of
Cadwgan ab Elstan Glodrydd. See the pedigrees from Jesus Coll.
MS. 20, printed in Y Cymmrodor, vol. viii, where both Goronwy
and Llywelyn appear (p. 88) and the latter is said to be " o vnellt ".
Both battles (see 1075 above) were no doubt fought on the confines
of Buallt and Ceredigion, where the Camddwr is, in fact, still
known as a tributary of the Towy.

Dom. i (C).
Fo. 143a, column 2 continued.

a ref *filius* owein *occiditur.* cuí fuccel-
fit traharín *filius* cradauc eius confobri-
nus regnum uenedocie tantum tenens
Sed ref et rederch *filius* cradauc dextra
lem britanniam habuerunt. Grifud autem
nepof iacob *non* obsedit bellum[1]
camdubr *inter* filiof Kadugaun *et*
inter ref *et* rederch qui uictoref fuerunt
Annus. Rederch *filius* cradauc dolo
occiditur a confobrino fuo meirchaun.
Annus. Bellum *inter* filiof kadugaun
id est lewelín *et* gronoui. *et* inter ref *filium*
owein qui iterum uicti funt.
Annus. Bellum pullgudic in quo traharn rex venedocie uictor fuit.
et tota familia ref cecidit.   In
fíne uero *huius* anni ref *et* howel eius
frater a cradauc *filius* grifud occiduntur.
Sulgenus episcopatum deferit.   Et abra
ham accepit.   [nare
Annus. Ref. *filius* teudur incepit reg-

Annus. Meneuia a gentilibus uaf-
tatur. Et abraham a gentilibus occi
ditur. Sulgenus iterum episcopatum accepit.

---

[1] See note on page 154.

Brev. Domesd. (B).
Page 12, column 1 continued.

An*n*us. bellu*m* montís carn ín quo

[*Column ends.*]

Page 12, column 2.

traharn filíus carad[auc][1] *et* cara
dauc filíus G[rıfin]i *et* Meıler filı*us*
Ruallan a reso filıo [teu]dur *et*
a grıfino filıo conaní *occisi sunt*. Gur

geneu filíus Seısıl *occisus est*. Will*elmus*
rex anglíe *causa* oratıonıs *sanctum dauıd* ad
Ann*us*   iuit
Ann*us*
Ann*us*
Ann*us* Sulgenı*us* ep*ıscopatum* relıquı*t* cuí
Ann*us*   fre[2] *successit*
An*n*us Will*elmus* baſtard obíít cuí suc
ceſtís filıus suu*s* W. Rufus.
An*n*us res*us* filı*us* teudur a regno
suo expuls*us* es*t* a filíís bledínt. *scilicet.*
Madauc. cadugan. *et* Rırít. Res*us*
ve*ro* ex hibernıa claſſem dux*ıt et* reue*r*
títur. bellu*m* cu*m* ill*is* geſſít ín pen
llecheru ín qu*o* madouc *et* rırít cecid*erunt*

---

[1] A stain on the upper part of page 12 makes it difficult to read
some of the words at the top of this column and column 3. The
readings in square brackets must therefore be regarded as conjectural.

[2] The copyist was probably unable to read the first part of the
name of Wilfre.

Dom. i (C).

Fo. 143a, column 2 continued.

Annu*s* Bell*um* montif carn i*n* quo

tr*a*harn *filius* cradauc *et* cradauc *filius* gri
fud *et* meilír *filius* ruallaun *et*
ref *filius* teudur. *et* grifud *filius* eẏ
naun *filius* iacob occidu*ntur*. Wille*lm*us

[*End of column and page.*][1]

Fo. 143b, column 1.

rex angl*i*e ad f*a*nctum dau*i*d o*r*atio*ni*f causa
perrexit. Annu*s*. Annu*s*. Annuf.[2]

Annu*s*　　　　　　rex[3] fcotor*um* mo*r*it*ur*.
Annu*s*. Wille*lm*us rex obíít cuí fuc-
ceffit ed*u*ch fr*ater* et *i*pfe Wille*lm*us.[4]
Annu*s*. Ref *filius* teudur de regno
fuo expell*i*t*ur* a filíís bled*i*t. *i*d *est*. madauc. cadugaun. et rẏrid. Ip*s*e
ue*r*o ẏberni*a*m adíít. et claffe accepta reue*r*t*i*t*ur* i*n* britann*i*am. Bellu*m* pen-
lethereu gerit*ur* i*n* q*u*o duo filíj ble-

[1] At the bottom of this column, in a hand quite different from that
of the main text, is the following note :—
Annu*s* dom*i*n*i*. M.lxxxij. q*u*o anno Ref *filius*
teudur ded*i*t terram *de* penb*i*d*i*auc ecclef*i*e
f*a*nct*i* dau*i*d

[2] One "annus" has dropped out here.

[3] A blank has been left for the name of the king, who, it appears
from *Brenhinoedd y Saeson*, was Torlogh O'Brien. The date (1086)
is right.

[4] The margin has (in the same hand as the text) eirif, so that what
the scribe had before him was possibly " eiuf *filius*".

N

Brev. Domesd. (B).
Page 12, column 2 continued.

Annus archa sancti dauid ab ecclesia fura
ta est et auro argento que quibus tege-
Annus   batur spoliata est.

Annus Meneuia fracta est a gentilibus in
sularum. kediuoꝛ filius gollwin[1] obiit
Cuius filii inuitauerunt Grifinum filium
Maredut. quem resus filius teudur
expugnauit et occidit iuxta llandedoc.
Annus
Annus Resus filius teudur rectoꝛ dex
tralis partis a francis brechinauc. occisus est.
post cuius obitum Cadugaun filius bledint
predatus est demeciam pridie kalendas may.
Circiter kalendas Iulii franci primitus deme
ciam et keredigean tenuerunt et
caftella in eis locauerunt et abinde
totam terram britonum occupauerunt
Mailcholum scottorum rex occisus eft.

[1] The contraction for or placed over the w of this word is clearly
due to some slip of the pen.

Dom. i (C).
Fo. 143b, column 1 continued.

dit. *id est.* madauc et ririd ceciderunt.
et Ref uíctoɿ fuít.   Ingentem cenſum
captíuorum gentilibus *et* ſcotiſ Reſ
filius teudur tradidit.
Annus. Scrinium sancti dauid de ecclesia ſua
furatur et íuxta ciuítatem ex toto
ſpoliatur.   Terremotus ingenſ per totam bɿitanniam fuít.   Annus.

Annus. ſulgenus episcopus. lxxv̊̊. eta-
tíf ſue anno moɿitur. Meneuía
frangitur et deſtruitur a gentilibus.

Annus. Annus. Reſ filius teudur a
francíſ qui ın bɿecheníauc habita-
bant occiditur. *post cuius* obitum dẏuet uaſ-
tatur a cadugaun filius bledín.
postea circa kalendas iulíj francı keredi-
gaun *et* dẏuet inuaſerunt *et* caſ-
tella ın eiſ firmauerunt. Malcolum
rex ſcotorum occiditur a francíſ.